THE

Kimono

INSPIRATION

ART AND ART-TO-WEAR IN AMERICA

Edited by Rebecca A. T. Stevens
and Yoshiko Iwamoto Wada

The Textile Museum, Washington, D.C.
Pomegranate Artbooks ▪ San Francisco

Published by Pomegranate Artbooks
Box 6099, Rohnert Park, California 94927

Library of Congress Cataloging-in-Publication Data

The kimono inspiration: art and art-to-wear in America / edited by
    Rebecca A. T. Stevens and Yoshiko Iwamoto Wada.
        p.   cm.
    Includes bibliographical references and index.
    ISBN 0-87654-897-4 (hc.) — ISBN 0-87654-598-3 (pbk.)
    1. Wearable art — United States.   2. Kimonos — Influence.
    I. Stevens, Rebecca A. T.   II. Wada, Yoshiko Iwamoto.
    NK4860.5.U6K56   1996
    746.9'2 — dc20   95-52940
                                                                        CIP

Pomegranate Catalog No. A836

Designed by Riba Taylor, Sebastopol, California

Printed in Korea
07 06 05 04 03 02 01   9 8 7 6 5 4 3

First Edition

Contents

Foreword

The Kimono Inspiration: Art and Art-to-Wear in America explores the influence of the Japanese kimono on American artists, focusing on the contemporary appropriation of the kimono form by creators of art-to-wear. Although many American museums have presented exhibitions on the traditional Japanese kimono or on the impact of the Japanese aesthetic on Western art (i.e., *Japonisme*), this is the first exhibit to examine the relationship between the two subjects and document the emergence of the kimono as an American art form and symbol. It is with great pleasure that The Textile Museum presents this exhibition, which places the American use of the kimono in its historical and cross-cultural context.

The kimono, worn by aristocratic and wealthy Japanese women for hundreds of years, exudes a sense of beauty, grace, sensuality, and mystery to the Western world. It has intrigued the Europeans and Americans since the mid-nineteenth century, when Japan opened its borders. Artists of every discipline have become aware of the kimono's timeless beauty and, in various ways over the years, have made it a part of their repertoire.

The kimono's roots reach back to the days when Japan was a closed and self-contained society. Even today in Japan, while Western garments are worn in the working world, the kimono is still worn at weddings and on other special occasions. Some have been handed down from one generation to the next; others are new, but no less beautiful. With its classic shape and simple lines, the kimono lends itself to embellishment and ornamentation. It still attracts and inspires artists, from both the East and the West, who devise new and innovative ways to use the kimono's form.

The works in this exhibition show how an ancient Japanese shape has been explored and reinvented by American artists. Inspiration has led each artist to develop a unique approach to and meaning of this classic form. And in the future, we will undoubtedly see other ideas evolve. Japan has enriched the world by sharing its treasure—the kimono.

—Eleanor T. Rosenfeld,
Trustee, The Textile Museum

Preface

THE KIMONO INSPIRATION

The Japanese have a talent for incorporating beauty into daily life. Modern, industrial Japan, like industrial countries everywhere, must cope with the look of industrialization and its emphasis on mass production and expedience, which often overwhelm aesthetics, including consideration of balance and form. Yet every day, one encounters evidence of Japan's traditional concern for having beautiful things at hand: wonderfully crafted little *hashi-oki* on which to rest one's chopsticks, invitations printed on densely textured handmade paper in a seasonal hue, shapely roof tiles, translucent tea bowls. This historic concern—that what we lay our eyes and hands on should look and feel right—is a consideration I share from my work with clay. Since I arrived in Japan, it has been a daily pleasure to see that much of the traditional care taken in crafting useful objects still remains.

In the United States, I had the good fortune to be an advocate for American art and artists. And the more I get to know Japan through its art and crafts, the more I am convinced of the importance for nations to communicate in and discuss this artistic realm of life.

For almost fifty years, relations between Japan and the United States have been good, strong, and increasingly important to both countries. Perhaps our mutual respect and cooperation will make a difference in how peaceful and how prosperous the world will be in the future. Yet even now, while our ties are close, complex, and varied, our histories, geographies, languages, and much else about our two societies differ greatly. Because of this, it is easy to misunderstand one another, and finding means of communication that go beyond cultural differences is critical. I have always believed that the strength of the arts lies in their ability to pierce cultural blinders and reveal doorways in unexpected places. So I am pleased to contribute to a book that points to the influence of Japanese design on Western art. We hear and see a great deal about how Japanese culture has been transformed by its contact with the West, but we tend to forget that both sides have received something.

Of all the beautiful things one can see in use in Japan, the kimono is probably the boldest and most visually appealing. As clothing, it is considered too difficult and impractical to wear much anymore, and so the rare pleasure of seeing a group of kimono-clad women on the New Year or some other holiday offers a hint of how the emperor's court must have looked. In the recent Royal Wedding of Crown Prince Naruhito, one could see the beginnings of the contemporary kimono dating from the Heian period (794–1185), when the elite accomplished the art of being graceful in twelve-layer kimonos that could weigh more than thirty-five pounds.

The first Europeans to land in Japan were amazed by the local dress. There is little wonder that, when the fabrics were brought home, European artists were absolutely taken with designs and patterns that were new to them but so pleasing at first sight. I have only recently learned that the Japanese kimono industry was, in turn, revolutionized by the Europeans who brought with them to Japan new weaving methods—another lesson in the compound benefits of international contact and cross-cultural exchange.

Japan and the United States are two dynamic nations with much to give to the world, and much to learn from each other. The journey of kimono design from traditional Japanese dress to inspiration for American art traces one path in our growing mutual appreciation and understanding.

—Joan Mondale

THE WORLD IS GETTING SMALLER

After a fifteen-year absence, I returned to the United States in 1992. That was enough time to observe that the world is indeed getting smaller. Before, when we reflected upon this fact, we usually meant the convenience of traveling to another country by airplane. Today, when we express this sentiment, we are not only referring to our advanced means of transportation and communication, but to a way of life and thinking and to the cultural influences of the arts that affect the closeness of our interpersonal relationships.

Since my return to Washington, D.C., I have frequently visited the "Torpedo Factory" in nearby Alexandria, Virginia. The Factory is a beautifully designed art gallery, in which artists each have a small studio or room to display and sell their work. In this gallery, I see the influence of Japan and Japanese traditional arts. The shape and color of the pottery are very close to those of Japanese pottery. Teapots and coffee cups are very similar to Japanese tea sets with their simple, delicate, and pastel-colored patterns.

During a recent visit to the White House, I saw many contemporary American crafts exhibited there. And, to my amazement, I discovered that some of the pottery was decorated in exquisite colors of gold, red, dark green, and pale black—color schemes that very much remind me of kimono fabrics from almost ten centuries ago.

I remember that in the postwar years, Japan exported to the United States a large volume of silk materials as well as sold them as souvenirs to foreign visitors, most of them Americans. To attract American customers in those days, we thought that we had to make colorful materials with large patterns, which seemed too gaudy for most Japanese to wear. In retrospect, that may have been our misunderstanding. Now I know that Americans also love traditional Japanese materials with simple patterns and colors such as blue and white.

At parties in Washington, I often meet American women wearing pretty dresses made out of kimono or *obi* sash material. By observing these dresses, I am learning new ideas for ways to use our traditional fabrics. I also had the occasion to meet a well-known American dress designer, who showed me one of her originally designed kimono dresses. When she told me she had never been to Japan, I was speechless. I could not believe that somebody who had not experienced living in Japan could design such a very Japanese dress. So, it seems, the beauty of a tradition can transcend the time and culture from which it originated and become contemporary and international.

A tradition can also have a powerful effect on the state of mind as well as the behavior of individuals exposed to it. One of my daughters, who married recently in Washington, D.C., wore a kimono during the latter half of her wedding reception. Our guests seemed surprised to see her behave in such a traditional Japanese manner, after seeing her behave like any young American girl when she wore a white wedding gown earlier in the ceremony. Maybe as a young woman of Japanese origin—even though she has lived in this country long enough to be acquainted with the American lifestyle—she still unconsciously remembers the Japanese traditions that the kimono has carried for centuries. For special occasions, I also wear a kimono—the national dress—which makes me, too, feel a part of our cultural tradition. The kimono elicits from me certain gestures and behaviors that make me feel very Japanese.

Cultural interaction is a two-way process. Japan's increased exposure to Western culture has influenced kimono patterns and their colors in various ways. First, the patterns are no longer only of natural beauty, like trees and birds, but are often abstract designs. Second, the colors of the fabrics are no longer necessarily related to the age of the person who wears them. During my mother's generation, once a woman reached the age of thirty she did not wear red or bright colors. But today there is no special connection between the color and a person's age. And third, our way of wearing the kimono has changed and become more contemporary. We have two-piece kimonos that are as easy to wear as blouses and skirts. Even "ready to wear" tied *obi* are available to put on like sash belts.

The true culture and art of any heritage is not separated by national boundaries. Culture goes beyond physical borders and makes people more open to, and familiar with, different values that can enrich their lives. When cultures meet one another,

they can expand or even create new traditions. In old Japanese history, much was learned from neighboring countries such as Korea and China. It is very easy to observe many similarities in our traditions whose origins can be traced to our Asian neighbors. The black ships of Commodore Perry opened the door of Japan in 1854 not only to international commerce, but also to Western culture, which profoundly changed the traditional Japanese way of life. The postwar impact of American culture on Japan has been even greater and wider, from the political values of freedom and democracy to the social value of privacy and a more convenient way of living. But this cultural impact has been two-way. From architecture to food to fashion, the influence of Japanese culture can now be seen everywhere in America.

Last year was the fiftieth anniversary of the end of World War II. We shall not forget that tragic page in the history of our relations. But we also commemorate the last half-century of our friendly and productive relationship, and I cannot but hope that the ties between our two countries will become even closer and further strengthened by mutual understanding, which is best promoted through cultural interchanges. The Textile Museum's exhibition "The Kimono Inspiration: Art and Art-to-Wear in America" certainly contributes to that end.

The world continues to grow even smaller through cultural communications between all peoples.

—Masako "Mimi" Kuriyama

Acknowledgments

The Kimono Inspiration: Art and Art-to-Wear in America is the cooperative effort of many individuals. Co-curators Nancy A. Corwin, Julie Schafler Dale, Rebecca A. T. Stevens, and Yoshiko I. Wada have worked since 1991 to select the objects for inclusion in the exhibition and prepare the essays in this book. Stevens and Wada have also served as editors for the book.

Nancy Corwin especially acknowledges Andrea Norris, director of the Spencer Museum of Art, Lawrence, Kansas, and Corwin's graduate student curatorial interns at the museum—Gary Baura, who helped with the initial bibliography and found interesting information, and Michele Robinson, who helped check information on the completed manuscript. Corwin's seminar students, Margaret Kileen, Scott Shields, Beverly Joyce, Jean Zevnik, Kinon Durham, Tamyra Heim, and Sabre Whitt, all contributed enthusiasm and ideas to her essay. Margaret Klinkow, formerly director, and Elaine Harrington, formerly curator, of the Frank Lloyd Wright Home and Studio Foundation, were of great help, as was Phillip Dennis Cate, director of the Jane Voorhees Zimmerli Art Museum at Rutgers, The State University of New Jersey. Gabriel Weisberg, Dennita Sewell of the Costume Institute of The Metropolitan Museum of Art, Emily Potter Morse, Margot Riley, and Luke Jordan have also been very helpful with suggestions, information, and encouragement.

Julie Schafler Dale wishes to thank the many artists who generously agreed to be interviewed for this project. Their thoughts on the frequent use of the kimono form within their work and within the development of the Art-to-Wear Movement are the backbone of the Dale essay. In addition, Jason Pollen, current president of the Surface Design Association; Elsa Sreenivasam, first president of the Surface Design Association; and Barbara Garvey of Folkwear Patterns were exceedingly helpful. Dale also wishes to thank her friends Toni Greenbaum and Harrie Schloss for their unwavering support, humor, and editorial assistance throughout the project.

Rebecca Stevens would like to thank the staff of The Textile Museum for all of their assistance in this project: Crystal Sammons and George Rogers for their tireless efforts to secure the funding for the book and exhibition; Sara Wolf, Anne Ennes, and Cynthia Hughes for their advice on and assistance in mounting and traveling the exhibition; Richard Timpson, Tony LaGreca, and Frank Petty for their flexibility and craftsmanship in installing the exhibition; librarian Mary Samms, shop manager Sandy Borchetta, and information specialist Maury Sullivan for their encouragement and advice along the way. At The Textile Museum, the assistance of Mariko Iida, a museum intern from Tokyo, has been invaluable for her translations of Japanese texts, help in securing research materials, and unfailing good humor. Stevens would also like to single out the support of The Collections Management Department staff members, especially Madelyn Shaw, who plunged into the complicated logistical arrangements in midstream and made things go smoothly; Rebecca Eddins; and Amy Ward, who assisted our excellent photographer, Franko Khoury.

The preparation of the book benefited from the guidance of editor Mark Chambers and designer Riba Taylor, whose careful work has produced this beautiful book. Thanks also to Alex Castro, who designed the initial cover and graphic concept; Lynda DeWitt, who assisted with copyediting; Shelley Gollust; Jessica Morgan, who served as technical editor; Lloyd E. Herman, founding director of the Smithsonian Institution's Renwick Gallery of The National Museum of American Art, who shared his knowledge of catalogue publication; and Thomas Burke at Pomegranate Artbooks, who endorsed our ideas.

Yoshiko I. Wada would like to thank her mother, Sonoko Tsuchiya, for providing information on their family history and for confirming technical information about kimonos. Wada also would like to acknowledge her niece's valuable efforts in Japan. Mihoko Kajikawa secured important illustrations from relatives and took necessary photographs as well as researched historical materials. Wada is also indebted to Susanna Kuo for her beautiful and careful drawings of historical dress, and to John Friedman for his painstaking work in restoring crucial old and faded family photographs, and for taking new photographs of old family textiles. Finally, Wada wishes to thank Carole Greene for her editorial assistance early in the project, and Carolyn Duffy for her professional editorial work, her thoughtful input, and her persistence in helping to complete the project.

Exhibition planning and implementation at the end of the twentieth century is expensive, and no project could go forward without the support of generous museum patrons and foundations. We are particularly grateful for the generosity of The E. Rhodes and Leona B. Carpenter Foundation and to Neiman-Marcus for support in mounting the exhibition; the T. Backer Fund, Inc.; the Rau Foundation; Friends of Fiber Art International; Hecht's; Nancy and Carl Gewirz; and Eleanor and Samuel Rosenfeld. The Textile Museum is grateful to The Spencer Museum of Art for its donation of Corwin's time and the co-sponsorship of this book and exhibition, and to the Franklin Murphy Travel Fund of the University of Kansas Department of Art History for funding Corwin's research travel. The early financial support of an anonymous benefactor for the catalogue photography kept the project on track and is especially appreciated.

In addition, the authors would like to thank their family members and close friends for their encouragement and for sticking by them through the project, including Jim Dale, Gary Stevens, and Herc Morphopoulos.

Special and heartfelt thanks go to the director of The Textile Museum, Ursula E. McCracken, who offered her encouragement, enthusiasm, and support for this project from its inception.

—Nancy A. Corwin, Julie Schafler Dale,
Rebecca A. T. Stevens,
and Yoshiko I. Wada

Introduction

Rebecca A. T. Stevens

For more than one hundred years, the kimono has been a motif in American art and popular culture. It appears in paintings, drawings, prints, and photographs, and on the bodies of entertainers, artists, and fashion-conscious American women. Americans see the kimono as an art object and an exotic garment with multiple and sometimes contradictory meanings. It has symbolized both the submissive woman and the ardent feminist; seduction and sensual pleasure as well as refined taste and aesthetic sensitivity. Now, in the ultimate merger of art and dress, the kimono has been appropriated by the creators of a new American art, art-to-wear, which realizes the potential of clothing as a means of artistic expression.

The Kimono Inspiration: Art and Art-to-Wear in America explores the use and meaning of the kimono in America and traces the transformation of this quintessential Japanese garment from its ethnic origins, through its many appearances in fine art, costume, and high fashion, to its role in the contemporary Art-to-Wear Movement. Previous discussions and studies of the kimono, influenced by the aesthetics of modernism, have revolved mainly around the garment's beauty and formal qualities, ignoring its sociological context and meanings. This book and its related exhibition explore the American use of the kimono as a garment, as a symbol, and as an art form, and in doing so expand the dialogue on the diversity of styles and intentions of art making in our global world.

Understanding the Tradition of the Kimono in Japan and America

The kimono, or *kosode*, as it was originally called, evolved over a millennium from a Chinese robe into a uniquely Japanese garment. To the Japanese the kimono signifies and reaffirms fundamental Japanese cultural values. Through subtle variations in style and materials it communicates personal and social messages of gender, status, and aesthetics.

This use of clothing as a cultural marker was well established by the tenth century (Heian period) as illustrated in the Japanese classic *The Pillow Book of Shōnagon Sei*, the personal journal of a lady-in-waiting at the court of the Japanese empress. Here numerous references to dress underscore its importance to rank, status, and personal aesthetics. For example, with respect to the empress, Shōnagon Sei observes:

> The Empress . . . had not changed her clothes since I saw her before and was still wearing the same . . . jacket; but she was dazzlingly beautiful. Where else would one see a red . . . robe [*karaginu*] like this? Beneath it she wore a willow-green robe of Chinese damask, five layers of unlined robes of grape-coloured silk, a robe of Chinese gauze with blue prints over a plain white background, and a ceremonial skirt of elephant-eye silk. I felt that nothing in the world could compare with the beauty of these colours.
>
> "How do I look today?" Her Majesty asked me.

"Magnificent," I replied, realizing at once how inadequate a response this was.[1]

This brief passage reveals three concepts that are basic to understanding the cultural importance of clothing in Japan and, in turn, the appeal of the kimono to American artists. First, the empress was "dazzlingly beautiful" not because of her physical features but because she was wearing an extraordinary garment. Second, only a person of the empress's status could wear such a fine robe, which unequivocally marked her as a uniquely powerful person of the highest status. Finally, the manner in which the empress arranged the many layers of her costume was an aesthetic tour de force; even the word "magnificent" was an insufficient expression to describe the empress as she was dressed. The kimono, which evolved from these early robes, continues to be used by the Japanese to make multiple statements of personal and social content, as Yoshiko Wada explains in "The History of the Kimono—Japan's National Dress" and "Changing Attitudes Toward the Kimono: A Personal Reflection."

As the essays in this book demonstrate, these complex uses of the kimono resonated strongly with the views of nineteenth- and twentieth-century American artists, especially those involved in the Art-to-Wear Movement.

The Kimono's Journey to the West

Tales of Japan became part of Western lore long before Europeans visited the island country. The travel writings of Marco Polo (1254–1324) contributed to the mystique even though the explorer never visited the land he called *Cipangu*. Polo described it as a place of great wealth, rich with goods that Europeans desired. Later explorer Christopher Columbus was certain that he had discovered *Cipangu* when he landed in the New World. Japan, however, was not actually visited by Europeans until Portuguese sailors landed on one of its small southern islands in 1543.[2]

Beginning in the mid-sixteenth century, Europeans—particularly the Portuguese, Spanish, and Dutch—actively traded with Japan, importing silk textiles among other Japanese goods. Along with these traders came Catholic missionaries, who successfully converted thousands of Japanese to Christianity. Alarmed by the intrusion of Western religion and culture into traditional Japanese life, ruler Tokugawa Iemitsu declared it illegal for the Japanese to travel to other countries. By 1640, Japan's borders were virtually closed to the outside world. Only the Dutch East India Company was allowed to conduct business in Japan, and its contact was limited to the man-made island of Deshima near Nagasaki.[3] Such isolation only expanded Japan's exotic aura for Westerners. The allure of Japanese art and culture intensified, and the few Japanese objects that came to the West via the Dutch were highly prized.

The Dutch began importing kimonos into Holland as early as 1615. Much sought after, these garments (with the sleeves resewn into a Western jacket style) were worn as at-home coats by wealthy men and given as gifts on special occasions. The Dutch East India Company regarded these kimonos, or *Japonsche Rocken*, as such treasures that eight Japanese chests filled with them were given to Charles II of England in celebration of his coronation. Eventually demand exceeded supply,[4] and by the beginning of the eighteenth century the Dutch were importing Westernized imitation kimonos, called "banyans," which were made in India. Some banyans were sold in America to affluent Southern planters who wore them as informal jackets.[5] Although most Americans and Europeans were not aware of the Japanese nuances—for example, the age appropriateness of certain colors or the literary allusions represented in the surface decoration—they did value the garment's beauty and rarity. Hence, the imported kimonos became associated with wealth, high social status, and sophisticated taste in the Western mind.

In the second half of the nineteenth century, when Japan was forced to establish trading agreements with major Western powers, a new aesthetic philosophy was sweeping England and subsequently America. The writings of John Ruskin (1819–1900) followed by those of William Morris (1834–1896) revolutionized the way people thought about art and its importance to society.[6] Proponents of this philosophy decried the distinction between fine arts and crafts. Under this new aesthetic, mass-produced, machine-made objects were said to merely mimic elaborate decorative styles of the past with no understanding of the original maker's intentions. Handmade objects of straightforward design were seen as the honest expression of the artisan and the preferred form of artistic endeavor. Supporters of this new aesthetic embraced the imported objects from Japan, where craftspeople still employed traditional, nonmechanized methods of production.[7] This new standard made beautifully handcrafted kimonos an instant success with the art cognoscenti in Europe and America.

When Commodore Perry successfully pressured Japan to open its borders in 1854, the Japanese kimono was a rarely seen object in America. However, it began arriving in America in significant numbers in the 1870s when artists and travelers began to collect kimonos as souvenirs and art objects. Japanese decorative woodcuts, depicting kimono-clad women, were also collected, encouraging this growing interest in the kimono. Beginning with the international exposition in London (1862) that featured exhibits of Japanese products and culture, world fairs and international expositions brought increased attention to handmade Japanese objects. The Japanese Pavilion at the 1876 Philadelphia Centennial Exhibition gave average Americans their first opportunity to see Japanese goods on a grand scale. This exposition launched a "Japan Craze" in America, an obsession with things Japanese or things made in a Japanese style. The kimono, viewed in America as the Japanese national dress, was a common motif of this popular movement. This fascination with all things Japanese continued unabated until the end of the nineteenth century.[8]

1   Japanese toy display at the 1876 Philadelphia Centennial Exhibition
     Stereoscopic card published by the Centennial Photographic
        Company, Philadelphia
     Library of Congress, Prints and Photographs Division

The Kimono Enters American Art and Popular Culture

The Japanese exhibit in Philadelphia included display cases of Japanese dolls wearing kimonos and other traditional garments (see fig. 1). To American women of the day, these kimonos appeared to be loose-fitting, comfortable garments that could be slipped on and easily held in place with a single sash or tie. What a contrast with the current American fashion — stiff, multiple layers of petticoats and confining corsets. The kimono seemed the ideal model for a new, more natural kind of American garment that allowed freedom of movement.[9] By the end of the nineteenth century, dress patterns of the kimono, or at least the American version of the kimono, were available to dressmakers. American haute couture and loungewear continued to be influenced by the kimono as late as the 1920s.

Nancy Corwin's essay "The Kimono Mind: *Japonisme* in American Culture" details these developments and explains how, in addition to the international expositions, dealers specializing in oriental objects made Japanese kimonos available to collectors and unconventional women wanting to make a daring fashion statement. Such American tastemakers as architect Frank Lloyd Wright and dancer Ruth St. Denis collected and, in the case of St. Denis, even wore genuine kimonos. Hence, the kimono became associated with the avant-garde art world, an association that still exists.

Even before the "Japan Craze" in America, the kimono became an important element in creative expression when American artists responded to its symbolic associations rather than to its form as a garment. These associations were varied and often contradictory. For some artists, the kimono symbolized the exotic allure of the Orient; for others, it was proof of artistic taste. James McNeill Whistler, for example, began painting kimono-clad women as early as 1863. Later, other notable painters, such as William Merritt Chase and Miriam Schapiro, also included kimonos or kimono-clad women in their paintings.

American popular interest in the kimono diminished in the tense years prior to and during World War II. However, souvenir kimonos collected in great numbers by returning GIs rekindled interest (see fig. 2).[10] Many of these kimonos became family heirlooms and may have served as an entrée into Japanese culture for a new generation of Americans who had no knowledge of the earlier "Japan Craze."

This postwar interest in Japan combined with a rekindled interest in the craft aesthetic created a new wave of kimono influence in America during the late 1960s and 1970s. Coinciding with this wave was

2   Cynthia R. Boyer
      East-West
      Felt jacket inspired by a kimono collected by the artist's husband, John A. Boyer, while he was serving as a Japanese language translator for the U.S. Army in 1946
      Photograph by Freddie Leiberman

an increased recognition of fiber arts as a legitimate form of creative expression. The serious investigation of textiles during these two decades provided innovative ways for artists to explore alternative art-making techniques and formats. For some of these artists, the kimono became a type of canvas on which they created their art, as Julie Dale explains in "The Kimono in the Art-to-Wear Movement." These fiber artists were inspired by the use of clothing in ancient cultures to communicate messages about power, magic, religion, myth, emotion, and beauty. As a result, garments such as the kimono, which had long been used in this way, were explored and revered for their formal elements of shape, line, surface decoration, and symbolic associations. This innovative use of clothing as an art form soon developed into an

aesthetic movement whose creations were called wearable art or art-to-wear. In the 1970s, museums and galleries began to present exhibitions of this new art form. Many of the works in the Art-to-Wear Movement, especially after 1977 according to Dale, are based on the kimono form as it is understood in America. In fact, the kimono and its multiplicity of meanings provided the Americans of the Art-to-Wear Movement with the perfect prototype of an expressive garment.

Note to the reader: In the following essays all Japanese names are written in the Japanese name order, with the family name preceding the individual's given name(s). Names for historical periods in Japan are general, and inclusive dates reflect primarily art, rather than political, periods.

NOTES

1. Sei Shōnagon, *The Pillow Book of Sei Shōnagon,* trans. and ed. Ivan Morris (London: Penguin Books, 1967), 231.

2. For a more complete discussion of this topic see Martin Collcutt, "Circa 1492 in Japan: Columbus and the Legend of Golden Cipangu," in Jay Levenson, ed., *Circa 1492: Art in the Age of Exploration* (Washington, D.C.: National Gallery of Art, and New Haven, Conn.: Yale University Press, 1992), 305–307.

3. George Sanson, *A Short Cultural History of Japan* (Palo Alto, Calif.: Stanford University Press, 1964), 365–367.

4. Bianca M. du Mortier, "'Japonsche Rocken' in Holland in the 17th and 18th Centuries" (translated for the author by Mariko Iida), *Dresstudy* 21 (spring 1992): 7–9.

5. Katherine B. Brett, "The Japanese Style in Indian Chintz Design," *Journal of Indian Textile History* V (1960): 44; and Mattiebelle Gittinger, *Master Dyers to the World* (Washington, D.C.: The Textile Museum, 1982), 181, 190.

6. George P. Landow, "Ruskin," in *Victorian Thinkers* (Oxford: Oxford University Press, 1993), 112.

7. William Hosley, *The Japan Idea: Art and Life in America* (Hartford, Conn.: Wadsworth Atheneum, 1990), 29.

8. Ibid., 42.

9. Sally Buchanan Kinsey, "A More Reasonable Way to Dress," in *"The Art That Is Life": The Arts and Crafts Movement in America, 1875–1920,* ed. Wendy Kaplan (Boston: Museum of Fine Arts, 1987), 359–360.

10. Harold S. Williams, *Foreigners in Mikadoland* (Rutland, Vermont, and Tokyo: Charles E. Tuttle Company, 1983), 193.

3   James Abbott McNeill Whistler
       (American, 1834–1903)
     Sketch for Rose and Silver:
       The Princess from the Land
       of Porcelain, 1863–1864
     Oil on fiberboard, 24½ x 13½ in.
     Worcester Art Museum
     Worcester, Massachusetts
     Theodore T. and Mary G. Ellis
       Collection

Part One

The Kimono in American Art and Fashion, 1853–1996

4   Claude Monet
      (French, 1840–1926)
      La Japonaise
        (*Camille Monet in
        Japanese
        Costume*), 1876
      Oil on canvas,
        91¼ x 56 in.
      Museum of Fine Arts
      Boston, 56.147
      1951 Purchase Fund

The Kimono Mind

JAPONISME IN AMERICAN CULTURE
Nancy A. Corwin

1. Collections and Collectors

Japanese style and beauty first struck me when I saw my mother's kimono, a padded winter one of black silk displaying at the knee a bold design of twisted pine branches covered with snow. She got it in Japan as a young woman, just after the turn of the century. She wore it with the slim grace of the Princess from the Land of Porcelain in Whistler's painting that hangs in the famous Peacock Room at the Freer Gallery of Art in Washington, D.C. Mother's taste in clothes was elegant, and the kimono attained its striking effect not through brilliant color or intricate pattern, but by its dramatic white-on-black design. I can remember putting it on and letting it trail behind me; I believe a future collector of Japanese art was born then.[1]

Mary Burke wrote this about her mother, Mary Livingston Griggs, who traveled to Japan and around the world with family members in 1902. Like many other travelers to Japan, Griggs returned to America with a kimono as a souvenir. Simple nostalgia for this family souvenir inspired the daughter to actively collect Japanese art and learn about Japanese culture — a pattern followed by many collectors.[2]

The kimono, with its long and rich tradition in Japan, captured the imagination of Western cultures as no other garment has done. There are many complex reasons for its popularity in the West, and for its evolution during the past one hundred and fifty years from an intriguing souvenir to a work of art considered worthy of collecting. In the Western mind the kimono remains today the most enduring symbol of Japan and Japanese style, but one that is also invested with many additional — often contradictory — meanings, including exoticism, eroticism, female virtue through domestic good taste, women's liberation, and high fashion.

Early Attitudes:
"Orientalism" and Sexuality

Even before the mid-nineteenth-century opening of Japan to the West, the European and American love affair with Japan derived, in part, from a longing for the exotic, for the "other" of distant shores and strange lands. While "exotic" meant "escapism" for some, it represented inspiration for others, and the two meanings have remained part of Western art and culture into the present. In both cases, the exotic Orient was part reality and part nostalgic fantasy.

It is important to remember that Orientalism was a strong component in the thinking of nineteenth-century Europe at the height of its colonial power in the non-Western world. Political colonialism is linked with nostalgic romanticism in Orientalism, and both ingredients contributed to the kimono's popularity in the West. Cultural historian Edward Said's discussion of the political and psychological aspects of nineteenth- and twentieth-century Western attitudes toward the Middle East in his book *Orientalism* sheds light on the appeal of Japan and the kimono in the United States and Europe. Said describes Orientalism as a search for missing or repressed elements — the subconscious longings and desires — of Western society. In order to govern subject peoples in countries such as Egypt and India, he explains, people in the West defined Orientals (an overarching term that included people from the Middle and Far East) with such terms as *instinctive, irrational, intuitive, childlike, lazy, cunning,* and *feminine*.[3] Westerners perceived these qualities as the opposite of themselves, yet they felt an underlying attraction to many of them. Some aspects of Orientalism, particularly the sensual and the feminine, became linked in Western minds to Japan and the kimono.

The writings of anthropologist and cultural historian James Clifford on the politics and psychology of collecting artifacts from other cultures can be applied to further explain the kimono's reception in the West. Clifford points out that when people collect, they are collecting acknowledged parts of themselves, but they are also collecting repressed or unacknowledged parts. In the process they try to incorporate all those parts. By collecting, they gather things that they not only wish to *have*, but that they wish to *be*.[4] Thus for people in the West, collecting kimonos seems to have been an act of incorporating the sensuous beauty and exoticism—even eroticism—they've felt their own culture has lacked.

In these ways, during the past one hundred and fifty years many complex and contradictory meanings have become attached to Japan and the kimono. Astonishingly, the kimono has been associated with the virtuousness of domestic simplicity and good taste, as well as with eroticism and sensuality. Because it has been perceived as a feminine garment from a country with radically different notions of women's status and sexuality, the kimono has become a vehicle for expressing controversial ideas about gender and sexuality.

When Commodore Perry brought the first Americans to Japan in 1853, the country was shrouded in mystery—the people and their customs were known only through rumor and hearsay. Soon, however, the rumors of vastly differing sexual customs and of the docile, submissive behavior of Japanese women were confirmed. The practices of the geisha and nude bathing of men and women together in public baths were interpreted in the West as evidence of lax sexual morality, and were seen as both horrifying and titillating. An ensign in Perry's first expedition judged the practice of the Japanese bath to be lewd.[5] The first British consul, Sir Rutherford Alcock, noted in his journals published in 1863 that "Japan is essentially a country of anomalies, where all—even familiar things—put on new faces, and are curiously reversed—finally, the utter confusion of sexes in the public bath houses, making that correct which we in the West deem so shocking and improper, I leave as I find it—a problem to solve."[6] The fact that Alcock and U.S. Ambassador Townsend Harris were "given" Japanese women to live with furthered the idea of moral license. These popular misconceptions became attached to the kimono in the late nineteenth century just as it was becoming fashionable as a dressing gown in the West.

The practice of the geisha also fascinated and disturbed Westerners. According to anthropologist Liza Dalby, "The idea of the exotic geisha, seductress skilled in the Kama Sutra arts of pleasing men, was part of the European-American cultural stereotype of the Orient even before Perry's ships. . . . This may be a fascinating topic, but it remains one that says more about Western obsessions than it does about the geisha themselves."[7]

The geisha was not a prostitute in the Western sense but an accomplished entertainer and conversationalist, trained in that role from girlhood. Only one of her many functions was sexual. Westerners were appalled that geisha were sold into the profession by their parents, were confined to the pleasure quarters of the cities such as the Yoshiwara district of Edo (Tokyo), and were often displayed in cagelike balconies at the fronts of their residences.

Early photographs taken by Westerners, such as Felice Beato and Baron von Stillfried, helped to perpetuate the idea of the erotic/exotic Japan through the image of the geisha. On a more popular level, a type of hand-tinted photographic postcard, published in Yokohama around 1905, shows a ten-yen bill and a young geisha pouring sake (fig. 5). Printed on the front of the card is the sexually suggestive message, "She has left me, nothing only, dreamy eyes, that haunt me still, but my memory fondly lingers, when we spent that 10 Yen bill."[8] Geisha owned particularly extravagant and beautiful kimonos, and this furthered the association of the kimono with eroticism in the Western mind.

In the last forty years of the nineteenth century, van Gogh, Tissot, Monet, Renoir, and many other artists living in France, including Whistler, painted Western women in kimonos. While the symbolism of the kimono in these paintings varies, the French were on the whole more open and emphatic about the kimono's eroticism. Van Gogh's painting *Japonaiserie: Oiran* (1887), for example, leaves no doubt about his interpretation of the geisha as a prostitute. He depicted a courtesan from a Japanese print and surrounded her with cranes and frogs—the French words for those animals (*grue* and *grenouille*) were popular names for prostitutes.[9] Tissot, in his collection of prints titled *The Parable of the Prodigal Son* (1881; see fig. 6), hinted at prostitution by depicting low-life entertainers in kimonos (see fig. 6a, *The Prodigal Son #2: In Foreign Climes*, 1881), and he emphasized the erotic with the suggestive drape of the open kimono over a nude body in his 1864 painting *Japonaise au bain* (1864). Monet, in his *La Japonaise* (1876; fig. 4, p. 22) painted his wife in a long red kimono, but posed her as a courtesan in a Japanese print. Renoir, on the other hand, painted portraits of several high-society women attired in kimonos, apparently to show their good taste and knowledge of the latest fashion trend. One French naval officer, referring to geisha said, "The Japanese, some say, honor vice. Why not rather admit that in the manner of the ancient Greeks they render homage to beauty?"[10] American painters, in contrast, downplayed heavily erotic overtones in their kimono paintings.

5   "She has left me," c. 1905
     Hand-tinted collotype print with undivided back,
        3½ x 5½ in.
     Postcard published by photographer Karl Lewis
     Yokohama, Japan
     Collection Luke and Mary Anne Jordan

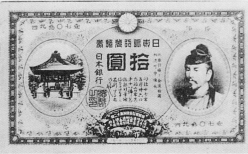

6   James Jacques
       Joseph Tissot
       (French, 1836–1902)
       The Parable of the
       Prodigal Son
       (frontispiece), 1881
       Etching printed in
       brown ink,
       14 x 17⅝ in.
       Sterling and Francine
       Clark Art Institute,
       Williamstown,
       Massachusetts

6a   James Jacques
       Joseph Tissot
       (French, 1836–1902)
       The Prodigal Son #2:
       In Foreign Climes,
       1881
       Etching and drypoint,
       12⁵⁄₃₂ x 14⅝ in.
       Sterling and Francine
       Clark Art Institute,
       Williamstown,
       Massachusetts

It is essential to note that America's relationship with Japan and with the kimono differed from Europe's. Mid-nineteenth-century America was still a fledgling country involved in consolidating its frontiers and resolving its civil war. To the Japanese, it was not an international power as was Europe. Still, the United States boldly initiated trade with Japan in 1854 when Perry arrived, and again in 1858 when Townsend Harris negotiated a trade treaty. While the Europeans pursued military colonialism, the Americans pursued trade. After the 1868 Meiji restoration of imperial rule, Japan increased its trading relationship with the West—consulting with the United States on agricultural matters and with Prussia and Britain on building their army and navy, respectively. In pursuit of trade, the United States invited Japan to participate in the Philadelphia Centennial Exhibition in 1876. It was this event that introduced Americans to Japanese art.

The First American Collectors

By the late 1870s, America began to forge its own particular relationship with Japan and with "things Japanese" as the first American travelers and collectors ventured there. One of the earliest was Edward Silvester Morse (1838–1925), a Boston zoologist, who traveled to Japan to pursue research. Later, this avid collector of Japanese art bequeathed his ceramics collection to the Museum of Fine Arts in Boston. Other pieces, including his folk textiles, went to the Peabody Museum in Salem, Massachusetts, where Morse was director from 1880 to 1916.

Ernest Francisco Fenollosa (1853–1908), another Harvard-educated Bostonian, went to Japan in 1878 to teach philosophy. He too became a collector, eventually obtaining many quality works of art. Fenollosa educated other important early collectors, such as the Havemeyers of New York, artist-designer Arthur Wesley Dow, and Fenollosa's own protégé Okakura Kakuzo, who collected for the Boston Museum of Fine Arts and succeeded him as curator of the Department of Chinese and Japanese Art in 1906.[11]

In 1882, William Sturgis Bigelow (1850–1926) arrived in Japan and traveled around the country with Morse and Fenollosa. Like Morse, Bigelow was trained in science, which made him excellent at classification—a quality of mind that tends to be strong in a collector. Bigelow's large personal fortune allowed him to collect widely, so he was able to take advantage of the excellent mentoring he received from Morse and Fenollosa. Bigelow deposited his collection at the Boston Museum of Fine Arts in 1889 and officially bequeathed it to the museum in 1911. The Bigelow collection of ninety-five *Nō* theater kimono-type robes is the largest in the United States.[12] As a result of this and other donations, the Museum of Fine Arts has one of the country's finest collections of Japanese garments.

In 1886, American artist John La Farge (1835–1910) also traveled to Japan, mainly to sketch, paint, and photograph the country. He had been introduced to Western art in a Japanese style—a style named *Japonisme* by French collector and critic Philippe Burty in 1872—during his art studies in France in 1856 (see fig. 7, p. 28). At that time, La Farge began to build the first of his several collections of Japanese art.[13] He married Margaret Perry, the granddaughter of Commodore Perry, so he had ample reason to be interested in Japan. His traveling companion on the 1886 trip was American scholar and writer Henry Adams. When they first arrived in Tokyo, La Farge and Adams were accompanied by Bigelow, who was a cousin of Adams's late wife, and by Fenollosa. This trip occurred between La Farge's 1870s Boston Trinity Church commission on murals and stained glass, and his similar work in New York City in 1885–1888. This was a time of heightened interest in the decorative arts in America, where Japanese art was an important influence on current aesthetics.

La Farge and Adams were fascinated by tales of oriental or "archaic" women who were "gloriously free of the sexual inhibitions of their American sisters" and also wonderfully submissive.[14] These qualities appealed to men in a Victorian society where morality was tight and women were becoming ever more vocal and independent. Neither Adams nor La Farge seemed to investigate these notions very aggressively, although they did enjoy observing the naturalness with which nude Japanese worked and slept outside in hot summer weather.

Japanese women, indeed all oriental women, were admired by Western men for their perceived childlike, obedient, delicate, and submissive natures. As cultural historian Bram Dijkstra has pointed out, these were thought to be ideal traits for Western women and were stressed in literature and art.[15] The kimono became a vehicle for these ideas about feminine behavior, despite the fact that the kimono was worn by both males and females in Japan at the time. That the kimono was considered a desirable and exotic, perhaps also erotic, souvenir was evidenced by the fact that Henry Adams wrote to his married ladylove, Lizzie Cameron, "Shall I bring you an embroidered 'kimono' for a dressing-gown, or would you rather have a piece of lacquer? or a sword?"[16]

Another important collector and art dealer in the 1880s was the German-born Frenchman Sigfried Bing (1838–1905), who later changed his name to Samuel Bing. Dismayed by his initial attempts to sell quality Japanese objects in the United States, Bing set out to educate Americans by publishing the journal *Le Japon artistique* from 1888 to 1891. In late 1895, he opened a shop in Paris called *La Maison de l'Art Nouveau* at 22, rue de Provence. Collectors such as Henry Osborne Havemeyer turned to Bing and others for guidance during the 1880s.

Havemeyer was introduced to Japanese art collecting by Samuel Coleman, whom he accompanied to the 1876 Philadelphia Centennial Exhibition. Coleman, an artist, designer, and collector, was a member of Louis Comfort Tiffany's design firm. He later designed Havemeyer's New York house and introduced him to Tiffany. Havemeyer and his wife, Louisine, never traveled to Japan, but assembled their extensive collections through dealers, auctions, and other travelers. Most of their collections were given to The Metropolitan Museum of Art in New York in 1929. Charles W. Freer, the founder of the Freer Gallery in Washington, D.C., also began collecting in the 1880s with advice from Bing, Fenollosa, and others. Freer traveled to Japan in 1895, but his initial inspiration came from Whistler's paintings. Neither the Havemeyers nor Freer formed collections of kimonos.

7   John La Farge (American, 1835–1910)
A Woman in Japanese Costume at an Easel, 1868
Ink wash and Chinese white on uncut woodblock,
5¾ x 4³⁄₁₆ in.
The Carnegie Museum of Art, Pittsburgh, 18.41.2
Andrew Carnegie Fund

One of the greatest nineteenth-century American authorities on Japan was an Irish-Greek immigrant, Lafcadio Hearn (1850–1904), who settled in Japan in 1890, where he wrote and taught English literature until his death. Hearn's great talent and contribution was as an interpreter of Japan to the West. His first book, *Glimpses of Unfamiliar Japan* (1894), was more artistic and insightful than the usual traveler's book. He never mastered the Japanese language, but by retelling many Japanese stories, especially children's fairy tales, "Hearn surpassed all other writers in conveying a vivid picture of Japan," according to historian Clay Lancaster.[17] Hearn's books caught the imagination of many individuals, including American printmaker Bertha Lum, who lived in Japan and illustrated his stories. Dancer Ruth St. Denis used Hearn's stories for her Japanese dance-dramas in 1913 and later.

World Fairs, Travel, and Early-Twentieth-Century Collectors

The 1890s also brought another important milestone for *Japonisme*—the 1893 World's Columbian Exposition in Chicago. This world's fair brought more Japanese art and architecture to American attention than ever before. Authentic Japanese buildings were constructed by specially trained Japanese workers and were furnished with art. Tea was served to the public by kimono-clad Japanese women and Americans saw and purchased many kinds of Japanese art objects.

By the turn of the century, many Americans traveled to Japan for adventure, for business, and, drawn by the country's exotic/erotic associations, even for honeymoons. These travelers brought back souvenirs, some of which eventually found their way into art or material culture collections. Frank Lloyd Wright was among the many travelers who returned with souvenir kimonos that are now part of museum collections.

As a result of the writings and activities of these early Japanophiles, the number of American collectors of Japanese art grew enormously in the early twentieth century, and many museums benefited from their generosity. Some museums received collections specifically focused on kimonos and other textiles. The Metropolitan Museum of Art in New York, for example, has the largest holdings of Japanese textiles, including *kosode*, Bing's textile samples, and 29 *Nō* robes from Havemeyer and other donors.[18] The Museum of Fine Arts in Boston has the largest collection of *Nō* robes in the country—95 collected by William Sturgis Bigelow in Japan in the 1880s—but they represent only three varieties of this type of robe. In 1935, the Museum of Art, Rhode Island School of Design, received the Lucy Truman Aldrich collection of 47 *Nō* robes, which represents all varieties of roles in the *Nō* drama, including ghosts and warriors. In addition, Aldrich donated 104 priest mantles, or *kesa*, which are rectangular fabric pieces that have been sewn and appliquéd together, as well as other Japanese, Chinese, and Indian textiles.[19] The two most knowledgeable and reputable dealers in Japan, the Yamanaka Company and Nomura Shojiro (1879–1943), guided Aldrich's purchases and superbly documented their origins.

Nomura was the primary preserver of Japan's textile heritage during the years it was underappreciated at home. He operated a shop in Kyoto from 1908 until the late 1930s and sold to many Americans. The Los Angeles County Museum has 60 robe fragments purchased from Nomura by Bella Mayberry in 1917. These are framed in a traditional manner under sleeve-shaped mats. Los Angeles also has complete *kosode* and *furisode* robes donated in 1939. The Metropolitan Museum of Art in New York, The Textile Museum in Washington, D.C., and Mills College in Oakland, California, all have pieces obtained from Nomura. Frank Lloyd Wright also bought from Nomura, and dancer Ruth St. Denis purchased a silk *happi* coat from him in 1925. Nomura played a formative role for Western collectors of kimonos, both public and private, who used them for dress or for public display. Nomura's own collection of 156 complete robes and many fragmentary robes remains safely preserved and appreciated in Japan.[20] Other notable American kimono and textile collections can be found at the Art Institute of Chicago, the Cleveland Museum of Art, the Denver Art Museum, the Indianapolis Museum of Art, and the Peabody Museum in Salem, Massachusetts.[21]

Other Attitudes: Medievalism and the Ideals of the Arts and Crafts Movement

Objects such as the kimono, in collections or as individual souvenirs, influenced other American ideas about Japan and its people besides those based on sexuality. One of the most popular Western myths of Japan was expressed by painter John La Farge in his 1897 book *Bric-a-Brac: An Artist's Letters from Japan.* In it, La Farge characterizes the Japanese as possessing a childlike sincerity considered lost in the postmedieval West. For La Farge, Japanese paintings were "pictures of the simplicity of attitude in which we were once children. For indeed the meaning of our struggle is to regain that time, through toil and the fullness of learning, and to live again in the oneness of mind and feeling which is to open to us the doors of the kingdom."[22] This notion was part of a romantic, primitivist fantasy of finding in nonindustrial societies a lost naturalness and regard for instincts. This idea was as common in America in the 1870s as it would be in the 1970s.

The writings of La Farge and others also reflect the ideals of excellence in the handcrafts espoused by artists of the Arts and Crafts Movement. Japanese craftswork was extolled for its "honesty," meaning its fine crafting and its truth to materials. Ironically, at that very time, Japan was modernizing and turning away from handcraft and toward industrialization. In promoting their goods to the West, however, the Japanese emphasized the handcraft tradition and equated themselves with medieval European artisans, knowing that these ideas would appeal to Westerners.

It is curious that Japan was regarded by the West as both immoral and virtuous at the same time—immoral because of the

public baths and the geisha, and virtuous because the Japanese conformed to the ideals of the Arts and Crafts Movement. John Ruskin and William Morris, whose ideas formed the basis for the English and subsequently the American Arts and Crafts movements, also stressed the importance of nature as the basis for art and artistic design. The Japanese were seen as being in tune with nature in their art and their everyday lives.[23] Ruskin and Morris also believed that the applied arts were as important as painting and sculpture, and that beautifully designed and crafted work ensured harmonious living, both physically and spiritually. Furthermore, they felt that people's lives must be in tune with their work, allowing them to take pride in the things they produced. The Japanese, like the medieval European artisans, were seen as hardworking craftspeople who produced their wares in small family workshops that "validated the dignity of the individual worker."[24] This view was part of a nostalgic Western longing for a happier and more beautiful existence, free of the disruptions and social dislocations of modern industrialized society. The Compte de Beauvoir, a French traveler who visited Japan in 1867, characterized Japan as having the "innocence of earthly paradise," and he added that "the costumes of our first parents have nothing which shocks the sentiments of these people who still live in a golden age."[25]

The Importance of James Abbott McNeill Whistler

American expatriate artist James Abbott McNeill Whistler (1834–1903) played a pivotal role in increasing the passion for Japanese art and style in the West, through his interpretation of Japanese style in his paintings and through his collecting. Whistler, who took up residence in Paris in 1855 and moved to London around 1859–1861, was one of the earliest artists to portray Western women in kimonos. His *Rose and Silver: The Princess from the Land of Porcelain* (1863–1864; frontispiece and fig. 3, p. 20) is probably the most widely known of such paintings by any artist. It was painted, as were all of his works showing women in kimonos, before trade was widely opened up between the West and Japan. Yet it shows a sophisticated knowledge of the design principles found in Japanese prints. His use of flat forms, cropped compositions, flowing lines, and subtle color harmonies as well as the pose and placement of the woman, and details of Chinese rugs and Japanese screens provided a way of "seeing" that profoundly influenced later artists.

Whistler's early knowledge of Japanese objects and style was acquired in the late 1850s in Paris.[26] He was exposed to and collected oriental objects from the first Paris shops to sell such wares. The historic La Porte Chinoise at 36, rue Vivienne, which had existed as a sort of salon and store since 1826, and Madame Desoye's shop, which opened at 220, rue de Rivoli, in 1862, could have been among his sources. It is known that these and other more ephemeral oriental shops were frequented by Whistler, Manet, and other artists and intellectuals, such as the collector and critic Philippe Burty.

In his many paintings, Whistler presents women as exotic objects, something to be owned, possessed, collected, and admired. At a time when wives were still considered to be their husband's property, these women were subjects for the male gaze. This was also a time when collecting — seen as a corollary to the importance of property ownership in Western industrialized countries — was popular with many people. Whistler himself collected blue-and-white porcelain and other oriental objects. He is one of the first of a number of American (and European) artists to include women as objects among other objects in such paintings, absorbing them into an exotic fantasy.

Whistler's *Japonisme* paintings were a major source of inspiration for those interested in Japan. His work influenced Charles Freer and the young Louisine Havemeyer, who visited Whistler's London studio in 1881 to collect Japanese art.[27] Whistler also influenced William Merritt Chase and others who continued painting intimate scenes of women robed in kimonos in the 1890s and into the twentieth century. Later, American Ethel Traphagen was inspired to design fashions based on the kimono and on the color tonalities of Whistler's paintings. Beyond their artistic importance, Whistler's paintings also served as an important early source of information on Japan and Japanese taste. Contributing to the "Japan Craze" was an interesting role, indeed, for an artist who never actually traveled to Japan.

8   Child's kimono collected by
     Frank Lloyd Wright, 1905
     Katazome resist dyeing
        on silk
     Collection Mrs. Robert
        Llewellen Wright

2. Souvenirs

As with collections of art and kimonos formed by knowledgeable travelers to Japan in the late nineteenth and early twentieth centuries, souvenirs were a frequent means of communicating both facts and myths about that exotic land. These souvenirs included photographs, books, fans, and ceramic or metal objects as well as kimonos and other textiles. They were not always objects of high aesthetic quality, but they were affordable and interesting to the average traveler, who had to be reasonably wealthy to make the trip in the first place. Souvenirs function as records of travelers' memories and often give a more accurate picture of the popular ideas about another country than do art collections.

The Function and Meaning of Souvenirs

Poet-folklorist Susan Stewart says that a souvenir is a memory, a substitute for a past experience, an object of nostalgia, and a harbinger of longing. It replaces memories of the body with memory of the object. A souvenir, she continues, is something that distinguishes each experience from other ones. It marks a unique event, for "we do not need or desire souvenirs of events that are repeatable."[1] Thus a single kimono or a photograph of oneself in a kimono would suffice for the traveler to remember a visit to Japan. A souvenir is made special once it is removed from its "natural" setting, but it retains meaning only by its relation to that original location, Stewart says. The souvenir implies or needs a narrative to make it function. To replace the authentic experience with remembered experience is something the object is able to do, as Stewart points out,

but only in an impoverished way. An exotic souvenir such as a kimono also implies separation, danger, and adventure; it is a sign that the possessor ventured to a distant land—Japan—and survived. "To have a souvenir of the exotic is to possess both a specimen and a trophy; on the one hand, the object must be marked as exterior and foreign, on the other it must be marked as arising directly out of an immediate experience of its possessor."[2]

If it were custom-made, as these kimonos often were, it assumed an added aura of adventure and authenticity. Unlike kimonos gathered for collections, souvenir kimonos reveal something about the personal lives and feelings of the individuals who acquired them. Many such garments eventually entered museum collections in the West.

Souvenir Photographs of Kimonos

Photographs were among the most common souvenirs of Japan in the nineteenth and early twentieth centuries. The first known camera arrived in Nagasaki in 1848, and various Japanese samurai clan members that supported Western studies were soon experimenting with the new medium. By the time Italian-born Felice Beato arrived in 1863 to set up a photography studio with his partner, sketch artist Charles Wirgman, there already were professional Japanese studios in Nagasaki, Yokohama, and Hakodate.[3] Beato, a former combat photographer, and Wirgman, a correspondent for the *Illustrated London News*, met in China and subsequently founded the first English-language Japanese magazine, *Japan Punch,* later called *Far East*. Until 1869, they managed a photographic studio in Yokohama. With Beato as photographer and the watercolorist Wirgman hand-tinting the photos, they produced popular views of Japan and its so-called native types—geisha, samurai, wrestlers, craftspeople, and average village people—for Western consumption.

9   Young man holding a parasol and a fan, c. 1900
     Silver-gelatin print, "cabinet card" format,
        5⁹⁄₁₆ x 3⅞ in.
     Portrait from the studio of K. Tamamura,
        Yokohama, Japan
     Collection Luke and Mary Anne Jordan

Their photographs were a good record of a vanishing Japan, but were skewed by Western notions and helped form and reinforce Western stereotypes of Japan. Their studio was purchased in 1877 by Baron Raimund von Stillfried (1839–1911), who also produced interpretive photographs of what was by then a more westernized Japan for Western tastes. Von Stillfried, who was admired as the best photographer in East Asia, bequeathed his material and the Beato-Wirgman material to his Japanese disciple, Kusakabe Kimbei, when he returned to Vienna in 1883.[4] The photographic works of Beato-Wirgman, von Stillfried, and their Japanese contemporaries, with its soft focus and nostalgic picturesque views, definitely influenced America's view of Japan and things Japanese such as the kimono.

In the 1880s, the innovations of gelatin dry plates and printing-out papers made it unnecessary for the photographer to have a darkroom nearby.[5] With easier processing, more amateurs became involved in photography; for example, Henry Adams and John La Farge took their own photographs on their trip to Japan in 1886. Also, as a result of the simpler processes, various types of professional photographs became available to the average person. By the 1860s, the carte-de-visite, a form of photographic personal calling card, was popular in the West and became common in Japan as well. These offered views of ordinary Japanese people wearing kimonos or Western dress. By the 1870s, photographs in other formats became widely available and replaced the carte-de-visite in popularity.

Americans visiting or living in Japan likewise had their photographs taken, often wearing kimonos, to send to friends as postcards or to exchange as calling cards or souvenirs. These types of popular photographs were produced commercially in great numbers in Japan and the West. They were frequently collected into albums that contained one's own friends and travels, along with photographs of famous people and places. It is hard to appreciate now how much pleasure these albums gave people in late Victorian times. Three photographs from the early 1900s showing kimono-clad Westerners posed against painted scenery in a Japanese photographer's studio serve as examples. The first, a type of mounted photograph called a cabinet card—made in Yokohama—is of a young man holding a parasol and a fan (fig. 9). The second, an unmounted photograph set in the studio's paper frame, shows a woman wearing a kimono and a black-lacquered Japanese wig (fig. 10). The third and slightly later type—a photographic postcard from about 1910—was taken at the Japanese home and garden of a Western couple, Mr. and Mrs. Post Wheeler, who posed wearing kimonos with their two servants (fig. 11). By posing for photographs in kimonos, Westerners obviously obtained an amusing and valued souvenir. These photographic cards in their many forms helped to popularize the kimono and make it an easily recognizable and desirable garment.

10   Western woman in Japanese attire, c. 1917
      Silver-gelatin print, 5⁵⁄₁₆ x 3⅝ in.
      Portrait from Mitsukoshi and Company
         (department store), Japan
      Collection Luke and Mary Anne Jordan

11   "The Wheeler Family
      at Home—Tokio,"
      c. 1910
      Silver-gelatin print,
      3½ x 5½ in.
      Inscription, reverse:
      "The Wheeler
      Bungalow at
      Tokio—Mr. and Mrs.
      Post Wheeler"
      Collection Luke and
      Mary Anne Jordan

The Kimono as Souvenir

Four kimonos, each acquired by a different traveler in the early 1900s, illustrate the various meanings of such souvenirs — meanings that contributed much to the American concept of the kimono. The first garment, a blue and orange, stencil-dyed, silk crepe kimono (fig. 12), belonged to Emily Tilinghast Potter, who visited Japan while traveling with her family in about 1917. This padded silk kimono was kept in a trunk as a family treasure and worn by Potter, and eventually by her two daughters, as a loose formal coat over evening dresses on special occasions. According to one of the daughters, Emily Potter Morse, it was never worn as a dressing gown. The kimono's unusual and bright color combinations must have made it a most exotic garment when worn in the United States in the 1940s and 1950s. Perhaps it was inspiration from this souvenir that led Morse to spend 1956–1957 in Japan teaching at an American School.[6] A repository for two generations of memories, this kimono was given by Morse to the Costume Institute of The Metropolitan Museum of Art in New York.

The second kimono (fig. 13), also in the Costume Institute, was not only a travel memory but a symbol of flamboyance and style. It was donated as part of the estate of Elsie Whelen Goelet Clews (1880–1959), the wealthy daughter of a Pittsburgh family and a former resident of New York City and France. The complete ensemble, which dates from 1906, includes a white silk under-kimono, a brocaded *obi*, and a pair of *tabi*. The kimono Clews brought back from the trip to Japan, China, and Korea is a delicate silk whose color graduates from deep violet at the top to pale violet and white near the hem. On the bottom portion where the color fades is a hand-painted landscape that includes mountains, a blue sea, trees, birds, and a pavilion. A few subtle gold embroidery stitches accent leaves on the trees and light on the water. The shoulders are marked on the front and back with traditional circular crests containing a swanlike bird encircled by the Latin words "Ex Candore Decus," meaning "out of dazzling radiance comes beauty."[7] The crest makes this kimono truly a work of two cultures — an *objet de Japonisme*.

Museum records state that this kimono was custom-made by the court dressmaker in Yokohama for Clews while she was the guest of H. E. Lloyd Griscom, the U.S. ambassador to Japan. According to Margot Riley of the Fashion Institute of Technology in New York, Clews, who was then Goelet, kept the kimono through her March 1913 divorce from Goelet and her December 1914 marriage to Henry Clews, a wealthy artist trained by Rodin. She took the kimono with her to Paris and to their home in the south of France, Château de la Napoule. The château survives today as the Fondation des arts Henri Clews, a residency for artists.

Elsie Clews was an active, six-foot-tall woman with a bold and confident sense of style — a fashion leader who patronized such well-known designers as Charles Frederick Worth,[8] Jeanne Lanvin, and Paul Poiret. These designers, particularly Poiret, were strongly influenced by the kimono in those years of tea gowns and soft boudoir clothing, so it is not surprising that a woman who wore kimonos had her second wedding gown designed by Poiret. Poiret is credited with banishing the corset by adopting a kimonolike silhouette, and with employing a colorful Orientalism in his designs.

12 Kimono formerly owned by Emily T. Potter,
       c. 1917
    Katazome resist dyeing on silk
    The Metropolitan Museum of Art, 1986.327.1a–k
    Gift of Emily Potter Morse in memory of Emily
       Tilinghast Potter, 1986

13 Kimono formerly owned by Elsie Clews, c. 1906
    Hand painting and embroidery on silk
    The Metropolitan Museum of Art, 61.2.a–e
    Gift of Mrs. David J. Colton, 1961

14　Kimono altered into a Western-style dress for
　　Mrs. Woodrow (Edith) Wilson, c. 1920
　　Yūzen dyeing and embroidery on silk
　　Collection Woodrow Wilson House, a property
　　　of the National Trust for Historic Preservation,
　　　Washington, D.C.
　　Gift to Mrs. Wilson from the Japanese Silk
　　　Growers Association

It is likely that the Clews kimono func-
tioned as a costume at theatricals and
masquerades that she hosted at the château.
Such events were favorite forms of entertainment for high society in the early
twentieth century. Clews had a masquerade
costume designed by Poiret, who was
himself known for hosting extravagant
masquerades. In this way, a kimono that
began as a souvenir became not merely an
exotic fashion statement but possibly an
amateur theatrical costume, following a
trend in professional theater of the day.[9]

The third souvenir kimono (figs. 14, 14a)
was owned by the second wife of Woodrow
Wilson, Edith, who frequently traveled to
Japan. It was a gift and, in a sense, a
souvenir of her time as first lady. The
kimono was given to Wilson in 1920, along
with rolls of silk and two samurai swords,
by representatives of the Raw Silk Growers
Association of Japan. There is no evidence
that she wore the kimono before she had it
altered by a Baltimore, Maryland, seam-
stress into a Western-style dress.[10] This
gray-blue, silk crepe garment retains the
vertical lines of the kimono, with *yūzen*
resist-dyed and painted green leaves and
violet wisteria flowers as well as embroidered ivory and green leaves. The kimono
was probably designed as a symbol of
cooperation between the two nations; at the
back of the neck and on the shoulders,
where one would typically find a family
crest, are the crossed flags of the United
States and Japan. One can only speculate
on the many interesting comments this
unique dress garnered at state occasions
and social gatherings. Edith Wilson,
however, apparently did not feel that
wearing an unaltered kimono was appropriate for a woman in her position. The
exotic, unconventional connotations attached to the kimono in the United States
were firmly established by that time, and
the first lady undoubtedly did not want to
be thought of as unconventional.

14a   Detail of fig. 14

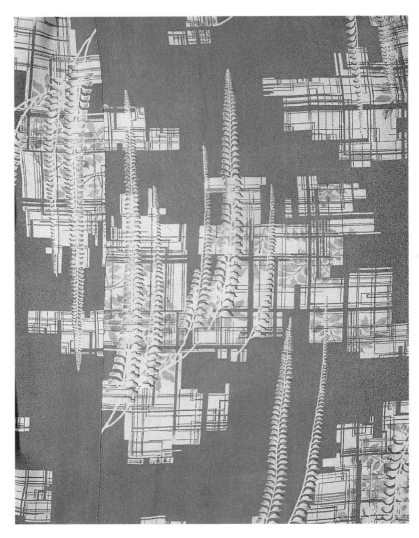

15   Detail of child's kimono
collected by Frank Lloyd
Wright, 1905
Katazome resist dyeing
on silk
Collection Mrs. Robert
Llewellen Wright

The fourth souvenir kimono (fig. 8, p. 32, and fig. 15) was brought back by Frank Lloyd Wright from his first trip to Japan in 1905. This kimono is child-sized and was given to two-year-old Robert Llewellen Wright, the youngest of Wright's six children with his first wife, Catherine.[11] Like the later Wilson kimono, it is made of gray-blue silk crepe, but the Wright kimono has a *katazome*-stenciled design of purple and white wisteria on what at first appears to be a trellis. On closer inspection, however, the trellis looks like a ground plan of a Wright house, rendered in his sketchy, straight-line style. It is not known whether Wright designed this child's kimono, or if he was attracted to it because of its similarity to his own work. It is known that Wright's own style of graphic design and composition exhibited influences of Japanese art after this 1905 trip.[12]

The Importance of Frank Lloyd Wright

Frank Lloyd Wright was an artistic trendsetter in the United States from the turn of the century until his death in 1959, and he was an active proponent of the aesthetic merits of Japanese objects and design. Wright had a number of opportunities to learn about Japanese art before his first trip to Japan in 1905. The architect Joseph Lyman Silsbee, who was his first employer in 1887, collected Japanese prints and was related by marriage to Ernest Fenollosa.[13] At the 1893 World's Columbian Exposition in Chicago, Wright visited the Ho-o-den, or Phoenix Hall, which had been constructed by Japanese craftsmen. After the fair, Wright purchased a nine-by-three-foot carving from that building of two phoenix birds eating in a kiri tree, a work that Takamura Koun of the Tokyo Fine Arts School carved for the exposition.[14] However, Wright's main area of collecting was woodblock prints (see fig. 16), which he sold to finance much of his early design work. Japanese prints and architecture were major influences on his architectural ideas, but textiles also had an impact on his design aesthetic. Not only did he use the Japanese textiles he collected to decorate his own home, their design also affected his architecture.

Wright purchased several priest's mantles, or *kesa*, on the 1905 trip (see fig. 17), four of which are preserved at his Oak Park Studio House. These *kesa* were never worn by Wright, but instead were displayed as

table runners. The rectangular *kesa*, with its pieced modular construction and its appliquéd squares in each corner—symbolizing the guardians of the four corners of the universe—is remarkably similar in design to the ground plans of many Wright buildings, such as Unity Temple in Oak Park. Two of his *kesa* have orange blocks in the corners, which were of obvious appeal to Wright because he had used a red-orange square containing a cross within a circle as his logo since the 1890s.[15]

16   Yanagawa Shigenobu (Japanese, 1787–1832)
       Young Woman with Painted Fan, late 1820s
       Colored Surimono woodblock print, 8 x 7¼ in.
       Spencer Museum of Art, The University of
          Kansas, 28.7589
       William Bridges Thayer Memorial

17 *Kesa* (Japanese priest's mantle), Edo period
Pieced and appliquéd silk
The Frank Lloyd Wright Home and Studio
   Foundation, Oak Park, Illinois, 1990.34.164
Photograph by Phil Mrozinski

In addition to buying his son's kimono on the 1905 trip, Wright most likely purchased others, though none were documented or survived in the Home and Studio Foundation collection.[16] He undoubtedly owned other kimonos, because his local Oak Park, Illinois, newspaper, *Oak Leaves*, printed this report on March 24, 1906:

> A Japanese social was held on Wednesday evening at the residence of Mr. and Mrs. Frank Wright on Forest Avenue under the auspices of the Unity club of Unity church; a very interesting trip through Japan, illustrated with lantern slides, the examination of the many beautiful prints and curios recently brought from Japan by Mrs. Wright, and several appropriate musical selections, combined to make a most enjoyable evening. Tea was served by the young ladies of the club, all being in typical Jap [*sic*] costume.[17]

Between 1913 and 1921 Wright made other trips to Japan to work on his Imperial Hotel commission. On these later trips, Wright purchased textiles from Nomura and the Yamanaka Company as well. Although no records of purchase exist, other kimonos survive in the Wright collection at Taliesen West.

To comprehend the importance for his art of Wright's interest in textiles, one must understand the concept of the "House Beautiful" and its centrality in his philosophy of design. As part of the arts and crafts ideal of the unity of the "applied" and "fine" arts, which he embraced wholeheartedly, the House Beautiful concept placed the home at the center of family life, and maintained that family life had an effect on how the home was designed and vice versa. According to Margaret Klinkow, director of the Wright Home and

Studio Archives in Oak Park, Wright's own family was his best experimental client, and the needs of his large family (six children born between 1890 and 1903) helped him formulate his ideas. His constant remodeling experiments in the Oak Park home and studio influenced the design of his Prairie Style houses and their contents. Wright designed and published William Gannett's 1896–1897 book *The House Beautiful*, and was profoundly influenced by his ideas. Gannett's book describes the importance of the careful decoration of the home in creating an atmosphere of family love, where beauty and good design are linked with morality and harmonious living. Wright's own home expressed these tenets of the House Beautiful by reflecting the couple's interests: in collecting beautiful things and good books, and in entertaining friends; in simple taste and natural decorations based on medieval and Japanese models, and in a total unified design scheme.[18] The Prairie Style homes he designed for clients, with their focused hearths and dining room furniture ensembles, their use of natural wood and brick, and their references to Japanese architecture, reflected these ideals.

18   Lucille (Lady Duff Gordon)
      Original sketch on paper, c. 1916–1924
      The Fashion Institute of Technology, New York

3. The Kimono in Art and Life

The kimono seemed like an exotic garment to Americans at the turn of the century, but it also conveyed ideals of practical comfort and linked women to intimacy and the home. It carried subtle connotations of the dilemma of women's changing place and status in the world. By 1900, this dilemma was politicized as the kimono became a symbol of economic and social status for upper-class women and of liberation for self-sufficient women of the theater who wore the garment publicly. At the same time, its many variations as dressing gowns and housework dresses indicated that the average woman's place was in the home. Internationally, the kimono stood for Japanese national identity, while in the United States it symbolized both the repression and liberation of women. That women belonged to the domain of interior space was a notion actively promoted in England and the United States by those involved in the Arts and Crafts Movement. Thus, the kimono-inspired dress and the many paintings of women in kimonos that were so popular in America during the late nineteenth and early twentieth centuries represented not only the physical reality of fashions and home life, but a set of conflicting and changing ideas about gender identity, women's role outside the home, women's struggle for equal rights and the vote, and women's relations with men. All of the elastic and contradictory messages of the kimono continue into the 1990s.

The Great Wave: The Painted Image of the Kimono

The picture of the Western woman in a kimono that became popular in Europe and the United States at the turn of the century owes its existence to works by Whistler from the 1860s and 1870s. Whistler's women in kimonos all appear in intimate, interior scenes. These settings are closed to the outside world and the looseness of the garments suggests a dressing gown worn at home in the privacy of a woman's boudoir.

In his painting *Rose and Silver: The Princess from the Land of Porcelain* (1863–1864; frontispiece), Whistler posed a woman in the manner of a courtesan from a Japanese print. Her kimono is tied loosely with a wide red sash, not in the tightly bound, constricted way it was usually worn in Japan.[1] Over this kimono is another kimono worn open as a coat or robe. Such layered, loose garments were reminiscent of Japan's Heian period in the tenth century, and of drapery in classical Greek sculpture. However, kimonos were still sometimes worn loosely in layers in nineteenth-century Japan.[2] In Whistler's painting, the princess holds a fan and stands on a Chinese rug before a folding Japanese screen. The woman is named Christine Spartali, but the viewer is not concerned with her identity. She is on display as part of a still life of precious and exotic oriental objects—even the title implies that she is part of a decorative porcelain collection.

The Balcony (1864/1870; fig. 19) depicts four women loosely clad in kimonos, lounging on an outdoor balcony. Again, the haremlike setting is restricted from the larger world by the railing and awning, and the presence of a Japanese *samisen*— a stringed instrument played by geisha— enhances the painting's erotic overtones. In *Caprice in Purple and Gold No. 2: The Golden Screen* (1864; fig. 20) a woman wearing a kimono is seated before a Japanese screen looking at Japanese prints. She seems much like an object among objects, and the viewer feels like an intruder on her privacy. In 1872, Whistler made pastel and oil sketches of women wearing a kimono and holding a parasol or fan. Here, too, the open garments flow loosely onto the floor in the manner of Japanese prints, not the way kimonos were worn on the streets of Japan.

In the nineteenth century, the naturalness in Japanese clothing was often equated with the costume of classical Greece. Whistler sketched women in loose Greek costume in the 1870s at the same time that he was interested in the kimono. In his *Ten o'Clock Lecture* of 1885, in which he stated his formalist aesthetic, Whistler linked the two: "the story of the beautiful is already complete—hewn in the marbles of the

19   James Abbott McNeill Whistler (American, 1834–1903)
Variations in Flesh Color and Green: The Balcony, 1864/1870
Oil on wood panel, 24½ x 19½ in.
Freer Gallery of Art, Smithsonian Institution, 92.23

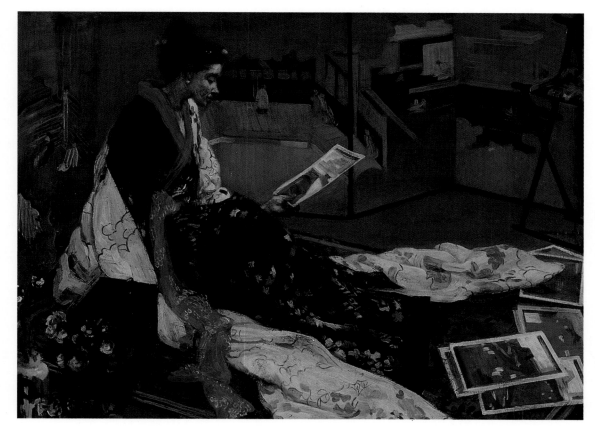

Parthenon and broidered with the birds upon the fan of Hokusai at the foot of Fusiyama."[3] John La Farge, on his 1886 trip to Japan with Henry Adams, echoed this idea in a letter in which he wrote that geisha were "a reminder of old, complete civilizations, like that of Greece."[4] Likewise in an article for *Scribner's Magazine*, Sir Edwin Arnold, a British scholar living in Japan, wrote that Japanese women in the teahouse possessed the "musical gait of [the] Greek maiden on the friezes of the Parthenon."[5]

Japonisme—the incorporation of Japanese elements into Western art—did not result in a single style. It was found in the idealized, formalist art of Whistler and other modernists, such as the French and American Impressionists as well as in the naturalistic, more representational art of the Pre-Raphaelites and those within the Arts and Crafts Movement, who had been inspired by Ruskin and Morris. Whistler stood firmly against John Ruskin's concept of art following nature, in favor of an "art for art's sake" based on formalist principles. Whistler was a modernist for whom

art was not a replica of nature, but an expression that spoke with its own formal language. Both types of artists represented important segments of nineteenth-century thinking and both were interested in the kimono for different reasons: the modernist formalists for its abstract beauty and lack of imitative reference to the human body, and the aesthetic movement for the meanings and historical associations attached to the garment.

Some of the artists in a group of American Impressionists calling themselves "The Ten" were known for their use of Japanese elements. Among them Robert Reid, Childe Hassam, Edmund C. Tarbell, and William Merritt Chase painted kimono pictures.[6] Chase used the kimono motif more often than the others, and it is his work that best typifies the kimono's message in American art. An eclectic and cosmopolitan painter who loved using costumes from foreign countries, Chase was influenced by the paintings of Alfred Stevens (1823–1906), a Belgian artist living in Paris who was an early enthusiast for Japanese art. Chase also knew and admired Whistler, and his

21   William Merritt Chase (American, 1849–1916)
     Girl in Blue Kimono (The Blue Kimono), c. 1888
     Oil on canvas, 57 x 44½ in.
     The Parrish Art Museum, Littlejohn Collection,
         61.5.21

22   William Merritt Chase (American, 1849–1916)
The Mirror, c. 1901
Oil on canvas, 36 x 29 in.
Cincinnati Art Museum, 1901.44
Museum Purchase

kimono paintings reflect Whistler's influence in figure pose and composition. Like Whistler, Chase depicted kimono women as decorative objects, reflecting the prevailing attitude toward women as part of men's home and property. These paintings, also like Whistler's, were created for the male gaze. Yet on close examination, Chase's women, though still enclosed in their domestic settings, seem less languid and passive and more robust. They seem less generalized in representation than Whistler's, and they often look directly at the viewer.

In *Girl in Blue Kimono* (1888; fig. 21), a woman seated on a Chinese couch faces the viewer directly from the center of the composition. She is posed in a setting that celebrates beauty and exoticism, surrounded by decorative objects—a Chinese rug, a Japanese screen, and a bronze or ceramic vessel. The strength of her relaxed,

self-assured, direct gaze makes her more than just one of the decorative objects—she becomes a recognizable person.

In other works, such as *The First Portrait* (1886), *The Kimono* (1895), and *The Japanese Print* (c. 1888 or c. 1903), the women are again decorative, but rather than existing as passive objects they are engaged in an activity. Chase's brushy style gives these works the freshness and spontaneity of a snapshot, and ensures a casual informality. A common motif of the period is a boudoir scene in which a woman is looking into a mirror. In Chase's *The Mirror* (c. 1901; fig. 22), a kimono-garbed woman actively looks back at the viewer from the mirror, but the room she inhabits seems small and close. Many interpretations have been associated with the mirror—vanity, lesbianism, the limited, enclosed world of a woman, or the ideal woman of the male gaze, defined as pas-

23   William Merritt Chase (American, 1849–1916)
Alice in the Shinnecock Studio, c. 1909
Oil on canvas, 33⅛ x 42¾ in.
The Parrish Art Museum, Littlejohn Collection,
     61.5.6

sive and reflective like the moon. Conversely, the mirror can also be seen as a symbol of woman's self-sufficiency and unwillingness to be only a reflection of her husband (see fig. 23).[7] These same interpretations have been associated with the kimono; thus both the mirror and the kimono reinforce the painter's message.

Robert Reid also painted a number of kimono pictures in the early twentieth century. In *The Violet Kimono* (1910–1911; fig. 24), a woman is seated in an open kimono at her dressing table arranging flowers in a vase. She is turned away from us, and her gaze, reflected in the mirror, is directed toward her task of arranging flowers. The mirror reflects a second, circular mirror in back of the viewer, creating a seemingly endless series of

mirrors. This could mean, as cultural historian Dijkstra suggests, that a woman's world reflects incessantly into itself.[8]

There was a marked contrast between the straightforward, wholesome women of these American paintings and the decadent Symbolist women of British and Continental art, with their heavy overtones of eroticism and narcissism. The American images carry none of the connotations of the dangerous, deadly "femme fatale" popular among French and Belgian artists, and they do not express hostility toward women as do the sinister, snaky figures of English artist Aubrey Beardsley. Belgian James Tissot's awkwardly erotic painting *Japonaise au bain* (1864) seems sinister in comparison with these American works.

The kimono in American paintings seems to make a more positive statement about women than it does in European works.

The fin-de-siècle period was certainly a time of tension and hostility between the sexes. As women fought for and achieved more independence and rights, men felt threatened by the "nouvelle femme," who was regarded as a threat to the bourgeois family. In Europe, the dark Symbolist paintings were expressions of those fears; and in America, fear was behind the depictions of women in domestic interior scenes that conquered and contained them. Independence, a strong will, and self-love

were not admired traits in a woman, according to most of the male-authored literature of the turn of the century.[9]

Clever economic and political propaganda convinced many women that they should be domestic and submissive. In France, explains art historian Debora Silverman, a declining birth rate and a drop in the sales

24 Robert Reid
     The Violet Kimono, c. 1910–1911
     Oil on canvas, 29 x 26¾ in.
     National Museum of American Art,
        Smithsonian Institution, 1929.6.88
     Gift of John Gellatly

of mass-produced decorative arts brought about a national campaign that urged women to stay home and buy more of these products. With help from the Central Union of the Decorative Arts, this policy of female fecundity and decorative domesticity attempted to convince women that they were the natural rulers of a glorious domain of the decorative arts—the home—and should stay there.[10] Women had been stereotyped as decorative objects, and were further defined as makers of decorative crafts because crafts were believed to take great patience and little thought to produce. Now, ironically, women were being asked to help the economy by buying such objects. Similar ideas and policies affected America. Of course, staying home was only an option for the wealthy and the middle class because working-class women had no

choice but to work.[11] Thus the kimono, as a representation of the ideal woman of this time, also came to represent a privileged class.

The problem of assessing Victorian sexuality and repression arises in connection with kimono paintings and photographs. In addition to domestic virtue and good taste, do these pictures hint, even slightly, at a loosening of sexuality? Historian Peter Gay asserted that American, educated, upper-class Victorians were freer and more sexually uninhibited than is usually supposed, but his research is based on limited primary sources, and it is difficult to know what was true in actual practice.[12]

One interpretation is certain: the kimono and the intimate interior space, while declaring virtue and hinting at exoticism, represented the social confinement of women. Garment and house define her as belonging in a sensual, interior world and in clothing that could never extend into the space of the outside world.[13] In this sense, the kimono was but one more prop in the depiction of women as soft, intimate creatures, unable to express their own will, and confined inside the home for men's housekeeping needs and sexual pleasures. As fashion historian Valerie Steele explains, "It was conceivable that an actress like Ellen Terry might go hatless and corsetless, in Grecian attire, but it would be less than respectable for ordinary women to follow suit."[14] It was not until the 1970s in America that this situation would fully change and the kimono would become primarily a liberated garment.

25   Gertrude Käsebier (American, 1852–1934)
Untitled (Portrait of Mrs. Vitale), c. 1912–1920
Gum bichromate print, 7½ x 6 in.
Spencer Museum of Art, The University of
   Kansas, 73.18
Gift of Miss Mina Turner

A LESSON IN PATRIOTISM.

John Bull. "*YOUR ARMY SYSTEM SEEMS TO WORK SPLENDIDLY. HOW DO YOU MANAGE IT?*"
Japan. "*PERFECTLY SIMPLE. WITH US EVERY MAN IS READY TO SACRIFICE HIMSELF FOR HIS COUNTRY —AND DOES IT!*"
John Bull. "*REMARKABLE SYSTEM! I MUST TRY AND INTRODUCE THAT AT HOME!*"

26   Bernard Partridge
      A Lesson in Patriotism
      Cartoon from *Punch*,
          July 6, 1904
      Photograph courtesy
      Punch Library, London

The kimono paintings of Chase and other members of "The Ten" were not mere male fantasies or wishes—they depicted reality. In the early twentieth century, wealthy people wore kimonos as elegant leisure garments at home. Photographs taken by American photographer Gertrude Käsebier (1852–1934) offer evidence of this (see fig. 25).[15] Alice Roosevelt Longworth, who went to Japan with her congressman husband on their honeymoon, received gifts of kimonos from the emperor himself. Unfortunately, these garments no longer exist, and no one in the family remembers whether or not she wore them. James Magee, a descendant of President McKinley whose grandmother was a friend of Longworth, remembers that his own family often dressed in kimonos for dinner. He also recalls seeing photographs of Alice Longworth and his grandmother eating dinner at the White House in kimonos.[16]

An elegant kimono not only signified wealth and luxury, but was often a sign that the wearer had taken an exotic trip to Japan. And while buying Japanese things had been a craze in the late nineteenth century, travel to Japan became a craze in the first decades of the twentieth century. Japan's new military might impressed the West, and was probably another reason that countless travelers made the journey. In 1895 Japan defeated China in the Sino-Japanese War, and ten years later Japan won a war with Russia over territories in Korea and Manchuria. By 1902 Japan had allied itself with Britain. Immediately following that victory in 1905, Americans and Europeans swarmed to Japan, bringing back countless photographs and souvenir kimonos with them. A 1904 cartoon from *Punch* (fig. 26) illustrates Japan's new international status, with the Japanese nation personified by a kimono-clad woman.

Dress Reform and the Ideals of the Arts and Crafts Movement

Enthusiasm for the kimono in the late nineteenth and early twentieth centuries resulted from the confluence of the "Japan Craze" with two important social and artistic movements—women's dress reform and arts and crafts. The Women's Dress Reform Movement advocated loosely fitted garments that were healthful, functional, and allowed women's bodies natural movement unrestricted by tightly laced corsets and encumbrances, such as hooped skirts and bustles. Early political reformers of women's rights advocated dress reform—they equated restrictive clothing with women's unequal status in society. These ideals of simplicity, utility, and comfort also fit in well with the Arts and Crafts Movement.

From the 1850s onward, artists and wives of artists associated with the British Arts and Crafts Movement shunned elegant finery and stressed plain goods and simple design, which were consistent with their principles. Their actions were based on the movement's socialist ideals of class and sex equality, and the notion that satisfying work should produce simple but beautiful everyday objects affordable to all. William Morris designed comfortable clothing for women based on styles from the Elizabethan period in his native England. By the 1880s, his ideas spread to the United States.

Dress reform in the United States actually began in the 1840s, and continued into the 1850s with the Bloomerists, who advocated a style of garment designed by Amelia Bloomer that was a combination of long, loose trousers gathered at the ankles and a knee-length skirt. But reform was a long, slow process, feared and resisted by many women as well as men. At first, the reformers' clothes—called "science costumes" because their design was based on scientific studies that found constrictive clothing injurious to the human body— were worn only by children and people who were ill. Both physicians and suffragettes campaigned strongly against the tightly laced whalebone corsets and the resulting unhealthy hourglass figures. Such clothes not only imprisoned women as helpless, dependent creatures who could not move, they explained, but also deformed their bodies and caused illness. The corset was a form of social control, as Kathleen Marra Headlee and other modern scholars have suggested. Just as the Chinese bound the feet of women, the Victorians laced women into corsets.[17] Corsets were a form of enclosure as confining to women as the home and domestic sphere. This designation marked women as inferior to men, who had more space and more ease of movement, both physically and psychologically.

Dress reform attracted national attention when participants in the World Health Convention in New York endorsed it in 1864.[18] In the 1870s, reform garments, such as a set of underwear called the "Emancipation Suit," were available by mail order. The American Free Dress League was founded in 1874, and two world's fairs helped to publicize the movement. At the Philadelphia Centennial Exhibition of 1876, a number of reform garments were on display, and one from a company called the Alice Fletcher Depot won a medal for design. The 1893 World's Columbian Exposition in Chicago, with its famous Women's Building, brought wide publicity to reform dress. Some women wore reform garments to the fair, and talks were given on the subject at the Women's Building.[19]

Despite the publicity for dress reform, it was not until around 1900 that less constricting corseting and a straighter silhouette won general acceptance. By the 1870s a new dress silhouette had developed that was constructed of long modular panels of cloth reaching from shoulder to hem—a structure influenced by the Japanese kimono. It hung from the shoulders gently and did not constrict the waist. This new, unconventional clothing in the 1870s also featured wide, loose sleeves that daringly bared the arm to the elbow. Wives of artists and intellectuals wore this new, more functional and comfortable style, and by the turn of the century, Frank Lloyd Wright and others began designing other similar dresses. Wright's ideas were also inspired by the fact that his own mother was in sympathy with the Women's Dress Reform Movement, and according to him, "She never believed in corsets. Never wore them."[20]

Wright designed dresses for his wife in this new "princess" style, which swept in a continuous drape from the shoulder to the floor and appeared from the back to be unseamed. As he said, "Catherine herself wore so well the clothes I designed for her that it was always a temptation to get new dresses. Designing them was fun."[21] Wright also designed dresses for the wives of his architectural clients, Susan Lawrence Dana, Isabelle Martin, and Lora Hieronymus Robie. His dress from

around 1910 for Isabelle Martin (see fig. 27), whose house he had designed in 1904, reflected the long, kimonolike lines of the princess style. A photo of Martin in the dress shows her posed like the courtesan in the Japanese print on the wall beside her.

The principles of naturalness, simplicity, utility, and comfort were basic tenets of Wright's architecture that echoed the ideas of the Arts and Crafts and Women's Dress Reform movements. Speaking about his search for functional simplicity in architecture during those years, Wright noted that his houses were called "'Dress reform houses' . . . by the charitably disposed. What others called them will hardly bear repetition."[22]

27   Mrs. Darwin D. (Isabelle) Martin, 1912, arranging
       flowers in her 1904 Frank Lloyd Wright–designed
       residence in Buffalo, New York, wearing a dress
       probably also designed by Wright
       University Archives, State University of New York,
       Buffalo
       Photograph by Muller, 1912

Fashion and the Kimono

Between the Philadelphia Centennial Exhibition of 1876 and the 1920s, women's dress in the United States underwent many changes as dress reform influenced an ever-widening circle of people. Corseting loosened until it was eliminated altogether, and a more gently curved silhouette became the norm after the first decade of the twentieth century. Leading reformists in America and abroad favored a return to the classic Greek principle that clothes should drape softly and hang from the shoulder. Oscar Wilde, an outspoken supporter of arts and crafts and dress reform, traveled to more than ninety cities in North America promoting styles from the ancient Greeks, the early American colonists, and the Japanese. In a letter written in 1884, he noted that "the laws of Greek dress" were now being realized in dress that was suspended from the shoulders and relied on the drape and fall of the fabric for its beauty.[23] In clothing, just as in painting, enthusiasm for the ancient Greek style was related to the interest in the loose flowing lines of the Japanese kimono.

The home became the major site for enlightened dress as women began wearing more functional styles for housework and dressing their children for more active play. The arts and crafts home of around 1900 was a total and unified work of art, or *gesamtkunstwerk*, and that totality included clothing worn by the woman and the children of the house. These new styles reflected the new ideal woman, who, particularly in North America, was active and healthy. This ideal affected how women were depicted in paintings and on stage as well as what they wore and what they did in everyday life. Many women engaged in sports—tennis, archery, badminton, ice skating, bicycling, hiking, and even mountain climbing. Much of this new freedom was a result of continuous efforts by such organizations as the Society for the Promotion of Physical Culture and Correct Dress.

Art Historian Anne Hollander offers an additional reason for the popularity of looser, more planar construction of women's clothing. With the rise of abstract art and decorative design, according to Hollander, people began "to accustom their eyes to visions of themselves as shapes. . . . In many Eastern countries visual sensibility had been accustomed for centuries to the idea of human looks reduced and abstracted into patterns, as if they were vases or fans."[24] Robed figures in Japanese prints do not have their bodies clearly articulated. In its embellishment and with its asymmetrical pattern placement, the kimono takes no account of the construction of the human body. "The robe has its own complete artistic autonomy, as if it were a painted screen," Hollander continues.[25] Thus the popularity of kimono-type garments from around 1900 into the 1920s was aesthetically motivated. The wearer became a display hanger for a work of art, and the canvaslike qualities of the kimono inspired artists such as Frank Lloyd Wright, Wassily Kandinsky, Sonia Delaunay, and others to design clothes.

For the average woman, the new kimono garment was not exotic or erotic, but rather a plain, functional, "democratic" type of dress that she could sew for herself. Simplicity was the keynote of the kimono style, which was looser-waisted than the princess-style dress. However, both styles were popular because they offered freedom of movement as well as long, straight lines and broad surfaces that were well suited to structural bands of ornamentation. The result was a garment that subtly blended Pre-Raphaelite and oriental elements.[26] The new dress was made of natural linens and cottons and embroidered with patterns from nature. Sewing patterns were available in women's journals (see fig. 28) for kimono wrappers, kimono waists (blouses), utility kimonos or "bungalow aprons" to be worn for housework over other clothes, and kimono sacques for children. Local newspapers offered endless advice and instruction on how to sew and embellish clothing with embroidery. Gustav Stickley's arts and crafts publication *The Craftsman* actively promoted reform dress and the philosophy that sewing one's own garments led to a "better and more reasonable way of living."[27] The implication in all of this was clear: to be a good woman, one must sew. Since functionality was the key, all ornamentation was to be structural in design, a principle clearly related to the architectural ideas of Wright, Stickley, and others in the Arts and Crafts Movement.

The elegance, exoticism, and novelty once associated with the kimono were never quite lost, however, even with the new emphasis on plainness and domestic virtue. The famous European designers, including Charles Frederick Worth, Lucille (Lady Duff Gordon) (fig. 18, p. 44), Madame Joseph Paquin, and Paul Poiret, used the new, simpler, looser kimono styling to convey a sense of elegance. Worth designed a kimono-sleeve costume as early as the 1860s, and variations of it became popular in the United States.[28]

For upscale at-home wear, the tea gown, developed in the 1890s and popular until the 1920s, was the most common type of loose kimono styling. Evening wear was also influenced by the kimono. A notable example of this was an evening dress designed in 1913 by Ethel Traphagen (see fig. 29) that was said to have been inspired by Whistler's painting *Nocturne*, which itself was based on a Japanese woodblock print. The garment echoed the deep blues and blue-greens of the painting, and the sinuous draped lines, winged shoulder treatment, and wide, *obi*-type sash were clearly connected to the kimono. In 1913, the *New York Times* sponsored a contest to show—particularly to those who considered Paris the fashion center of the world— the talent of American designers. Traphagen's evening dress won a prize in the contest. At that time, she taught costume design at Cooper Union in New York, but later she opened her own fashion design school. Traphagen owned a large collection of kimonos that she acquired in 1936 on a visit to Japan.[29] Her longtime interest in the kimono reflects its enduring influence on American fashion design.

28   Page from *Le Costume Royal* pattern book, February 1903
Library of Congress

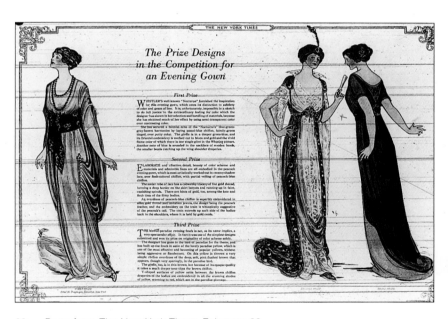

29   Page from *The New York Times*, February 23, 1913, illustrating Ethel Traphagen's design for an evening gown (left)
Courtesy The New York Times Company

The Kimono in Theater, Opera, and Dance

Throughout its history in the West, the kimono has appealed to theater people because of its flowing lines and dramatic draping qualities. As Bernard Rudofsky said in his 1965 book *The Kimono Mind*, "Costumes and costuming never fail to cast a spell on imaginative people. To some the touch of exotic robes is as intoxicating as drugs, to others, strange clothes provide a means of escape from that nearly escape-proof prison, one's self. Still others they help to find themselves."[30]

Theater personalities often wore dramatic clothing in their private lives as well as on the stage. The lives and costumes of these independent women were closely watched by the public and had a great influence on popular fashion. One such free spirit, British actress Dame Ellen Terry (1847–1928) did not wear corsets and sometimes

wore kimonos. She lived with architect and furniture designer E. W. Godwin (1833–1886), who created some of Terry's stage costumes and settings and also designed Japanese-style dresses for her.[31]

The most famous actress of the late nineteenth and early twentieth centuries in both Europe and America was the Dutch-born French actress Sarah Bernhardt (1844–1923). "The Divine Sarah" also disapproved of corseting and wore exotic, unusual costumes—on and off stage—that were often loose and flowing. With a keen instinct for drama, she played her private life as if she were on stage, deliberately cultivating an eccentric and erotic vampish image. Her stage personality was that of a "femme fatale," and she accentuated that persona by sleeping and being photographed in a coffin.

Bernhardt never performed on stage in a kimono, nor did she tour Japan. But many of her costumes, such as her "Elisabeth Reine d'Angleterre" gown, are kimonolike in their drape and flow. It is believed that she owned a Japanese kimono because her friend Reynaldo Hahn reported finding her sunning after a seaweed bath, wearing a Japanese robe, a panama hat, and a

30   Louise Abbema
Sarah Bernhardt in Her Japanese Garden, c. 1885
Pastel on paper, 14½ x 28 in.
The Jane Voorhees Zimmerli Art Museum, Rutgers,
   The State University of New Jersey, 1987.0742
Acquired in the name of Warner-Lambert Company
Photograph by Victor Pustai

green veil around her neck.[32] A charming and intimate fan-shaped pastel drawing by her close friend Louise Abbema shows Bernhardt in a Japanese garden wearing a Japanese kimono tied with an *obi* (fig. 30). Bernhardt scholar William Emboden sees this image as a poetic fantasy, or "Japonaiserie" as it was called at the time, because it used a fashionable exotic image rather than an actual scene.[33] Adventurous women were keen to imitate Bernhardt. That connection between the daring sophisticate and the kimono, so prevalent in Bernhardt's day, still persists.

The popular American actress Lotta Crabtree (1847–1924) was equally independent, breaking traditions of women's role in life as well as in the theater.[34] Crabtree wore a kimono in the play *Mam'zelle Nitouche* in 1885. Her costume, like the play, was an odd mixture of East and West. The play had nothing to do with Japan, but kimonos and Japan were so popular that they were used to sell bicycles, sewing thread—and even new plays.

Opera was also swept into the "Japan Craze." Gilbert and Sullivan's operetta *Mikado* was a satire on English people that used stock Japanese theater types—the jolly Ko-Ko, the cruel Pooh-Bah, the overrefined Yum-Yum, and other names never heard of in Japan.[35] Though it contained inaccuracies and caricatures of Japan, it became so popular that five productions crisscrossed the United States between August 1885 and May 1886. Like *Star Wars* film characters in the 1970s, the three little maids in *Mikado* were used to advertise all kinds of products, such as soap and sewing thread.[36] The appearance of these kimono-clad images attracted the public's attention and promoted the products.

Puccini's *Madame Butterfly*, which opened in Milan in 1904, was a more authentic portrayal of Japan (see fig. 31), but it perpetuated the Western myth that kimono-robed women were creatures of submissive self-sacrifice and uninhibited sexuality. The story originated in the novel *Madame Chrysanthème* by Pierre Loti (1850–1923), an important figure among the Paris Symbolist literati. Purportedly based on Loti's own experience, *Madame Chrysanthème* was widely read (Vincent van Gogh mentions it in letters to his brother Theo[37]), and it shaped an image of old Japan that lives on today. To this work, John Luther Long added a tragic ending in 1897, creating *Madame Butterfly*. David Belasco produced Long's book as a

31   *Madame Butterfly*, New York premiere,
February 11, 1907
Cast, left to right: Helen Mapleson,
Louise Homer, and Geraldine Farrar as
Butterfly
Metropolitan Opera Archives

play in New York in 1900, and then took the play to London, where Puccini saw it and formed the idea for his opera.[38] The constant retelling of this story attests to the allure of Japanese women and the kimono. The exotic, fragile, self-sacrificing Butterfly, who dies for love, was a powerful fantasy image in the West. Butterfly reinforced a male ideal of femininity that a woman's duty was to live loyally and die for her man, a subject frequently found in nineteenth-century literature, from novels to sermons. Long's book was illustrated by C. Yarnall Abbott with pictures of Western women wearing kimonos. It is one of many popular romance and fantasy novels of the time that placed Western women in Japanese stories—and in kimonos.

American dancer and choreographer Ruth St. Denis (1880–1968), probably the best known and most spectacular performer of the early twentieth century, used costumes and themes from Japan, India, Egypt, China, and other "exotic" countries (see fig. 32).[39] For St. Denis, "exotic" meant spiritual, and though there were tantalizing elements of eroticism in her costumes, she did not take on the deadly persona of the "femme fatale." Her dances usually presented stories of spiritually and morally courageous women. Her best known Japanese dance-drama, *O'Mika,* was based on a story from Lafcadio Hearn's book *Shadowings.* It featured St. Denis in a variety of roles, including a courtesan, a thirteenth-century Japanese poetess with long hair and open flowing robes, and a warrior in pants carrying a sword. In this and other works, St. Denis used both original and copies of Japanese costumes. *O'Mika* was first performed at the Fulton Theater in New York City on March 13, 1913, and while it was not a critical success, it became well known through adaptations and photographs (see fig. 33). In 1916, St. Denis and her partner/husband, Ted Shawn, performed a vaudeville version of the "Dance of the Flower Arrangement" from *O'Mika.*

St. Denis enjoyed wearing exotic costumes off stage as well. Arnold Genthe and Edward Weston photographed her wearing kimonos (see figs. 33 and 34), and snapshots of St. Denis from her personal album illustrate just how much the kimono influenced her choice of everyday fashion. In a 1918 photograph, she is wearing a dress with an *obi*-like waistband, an overlapped kimono bodice, and kimono sleeves. The album itself, now in the Dance Collection of the New York Public Library, is covered with embroidery from an antique Chinese robe.[40]

32   Ruth St. Denis as the courtesan in *O'Mika,* 1913
      Photograph by Clarence White Studio
      The Dance Collection, The New York Public
        Library for the Performing Arts
      Astor, Lenox, and Tilden Foundations

33   Ruth St. Denis as the thirteenth-century poet in
       O'Mika, c. 1913
     Photograph by Arnold Genthe
     The Dance Collection, The New York Public
       Library for the Performing Arts
     Astor, Lenox, and Tilden Foundations

34   Ruth St. Denis
     Photograph by Edward Weston
     The Dance Collection, The New York
       Public Library for the Performing Arts
     Astor, Lenox, and Tilden Foundations

35 Ruth St. Denis and Ted Shawn, Coronado Beach,
California, c. 1918
Photograph attributed to Harold Saylor
The Dance Collection, The New York Public
Library for the Performing Arts
Astor, Lenox, and Tilden Foundations

36 *Valeska Suratt, Vampire of the
Silent Movies,* 1919
Photograph by Orval Hixon
Silver print, 14 x 11 in.
Spencer Museum of Art,
The University of Kansas, 71.355
Gift of Orval Hixon

In addition to teaching at their Angeles school, St. Denis and Shawn toured the United States with their Denishawn Dance Company (see fig. 35), reaching small towns such as Lawrence, Kansas, as well as larger cities.[41] From 1925 to 1927, they studied and performed in Japan and many other Asian countries. Photographs taken from these trips show St. Denis wearing kimonos, both on and off stage.

Further evidence that the kimono was popular among actors, dancers, and movie stars is seen in Orval Hixon's 1920s photograph *Valeska Suratt, Vampire of the Silent Movies* (fig. 36), in which the actress wears a kimono-style jacket. Since that time, many performers have worn kimonos. Washington, D.C., artist B. J. Adams attests to the popularity of the kimono among theater people in the late 1970s and early 1980s. Working out of her gallery near the Kennedy Center for the Performing Arts, Adams sold kimonos to actress Colleen Dewhurst, opera singer Benita Vallenti, and many others who wore them as coats or robes when not performing.[42]

The Second Great Wave:
The Kimono after 1945

American interest in Japan and the kimono continued in the fashion and art worlds after the 1920s, but a burst of enthusiasm occurred after World War II.[43] As it had in the nineteenth century, this new wave of *Japonisme* coincided with an arts and crafts movement—the post–World War II crafts revival. This time Japan had a much more visible impact on Western crafts and design than it had on painting and sculpture. Although painters such as Mark Tobey and writers such as Jack Kerouac became devotees of Zen Buddhism in the 1950s, their lessons from Japan were not as literal or visible as those in the crafts.

Once again, the Orient offered a kind of liberation for Western culture through its tradition of closeness to nature and its identity as an exotic "other" with whom Westerners could fantasize their identities. The kimono continued to be a popular souvenir, and was often brought

back by soldiers from World War II and the Korean War. As a young soldier in 1946, for example, John Alton Boyer acquired discarded kimonos from Japanese citizens being repatriated from Korea to Japan (see fig. 37). For Boyer, now a lawyer in Washington, D.C., the kimono symbolized Japan and the positive aspects of Japanese culture.[44]

Collections of kimonos continued to flourish, but beginning in the 1950s, collecting interests moved beyond the elegant silk garments that first attracted American attention. The handcraft movement increased interest in folk art and primitivist styles, and this increased interest in indigo-dyed Japanese folk textiles.[45] The attraction to garments of common and working people, such as

37   Kimono, Showa period, mid-twentieth century
     Ikat-dyed silk
     Collection John A. Boyer

farmers and firemen, was also influenced by the work and writings of Yanagi Soetsu. His *mingei,* or folkcraft, renaissance in Japan, led to the establishment of *mingei* museums, which exhibited traditional handcrafted objects. It also helped spawn a government program that designates outstanding craftspeople as "Living National Treasures" as a way of honoring and preserving Japan's crafts heritage. Yanagi's writings were known in the United States by the early 1950s, so that when he and fellow folkcraft advocates English potter Bernard Leach and Japanese potter Hamada Shoji traveled to the United States in 1952–1953, American potters and other craftspeople were very receptive to their ideas.

Although Edward Silvester Morse had established a folk textile collection at the Peabody Museum in Salem, Massachusetts, in the late nineteenth century, most American collections of Japanese folk textiles are twentieth-century creations. A notable collection of folk garments and textiles was assembled by Fifi White of Kansas City, Missouri, and is now part of the extensive collection at the Seattle Art Museum.[46]

It was not until the mid-1970s that the kimono again achieved widespread popularity in American art and fashion. By this time, Japanese craft techniques and sensibilities were admired and emulated by many American textile artists. In painting as well as in art-to-wear, the kimono became a potent carrier of feminist and political messages. New York painter Miriam Schapiro, a founder of both the Feminist Art Movement and the Pattern and Decoration Painting Movement, began using the patterned kimono form to symbolize the new woman. No matter that this garment was worn by both sexes in Japan, it was reinterpreted by Schapiro and others in the West as symbolizing the feminine as it had been a century earlier.[47] In 1976, Schapiro created a fifty-two-foot-long painting titled *Anatomy of a Kimono* (fig. 38), which wrapped around a corner and encompassed two walls in Andre Emmerich's New York gallery, where it was first shown. This impressive piece was shown again at Beaver College in Glenside, Pennsylvania, and at Reed College in Portland, Oregon, and it had a great impact on textile artists and many art-to-wear artists.[48] Schapiro's inspiration for the piece was one of the many books on Japanese costume and textiles that was published for American audiences in increasing numbers in the 1970s.[49] *Anatomy of a Kimono* could be said to form a kimono collection all its own. It bears a remarkable resemblance to the "Hiinagata" screens that Nomura completed in 1934 to preserve the fragments of antique kimonos that he had recovered.[50] Schapiro also created a vestment series based on the kimono, and, in a commissioned work for the airport in Orlando, Florida, she again utilized the kimono form.

In the 1970s, Japan also began to assume a larger place in American popular consciousness because of its rise as a world economic power and its aggressive competition with the United States in the areas of electronics and automobile production. According to some historians, 1974 marked the end of the boom in which the United States dominated markets and prospered while the rest of the world recovered from World War II.[51] That Japanese influence permeated popular American culture was evidenced by James Clavell's novel *Shogun,* published in 1975. This story, about a stranded English sailor in Japan who joins the samurai class in the early seventeenth century, became a popular romantic television miniseries. In 1980, an American singing group called The Vapors recorded the song "I Think I'm Turning Japanese."[52] The lyrics consisted of repeating that phrase and other nonsensical lines in a catchy way. This nonsensical use of Japanese characterizations to attract attention to unrelated subjects was reminiscent of Gilbert and Sullivan's nineteenth-century operetta *Mikado.*

The new awareness of Japan was not all benign. Some Americans, used to the Americanization of other cultures, were offended by what they perceived as the Japanization of America. A wave of "Japan bashing" in Detroit and other industrial centers took place around 1980. As America's international balance of payments tipped in favor of Japan, racist

38   Miriam Schapiro
     Anatomy of a Kimono, 1976
     Textile and acrylic paint on canvas in ten panels,
        80 x 624 in.
     Photograph courtesy Miriam Schapiro

38a   Detail of fig. 38

remarks were heard about the new "Yellow Peril," a phrase from the turn of the century. On the whole, however, Americans adjusted reasonably well to their loss of assured dominance in the world. In some cases, the new situation even brought recognition of the chauvinism in earlier attitudes toward non-Western cultures. The 1980s and 1990s were marked by an increased national effort to create a multicultural society, which was aided by a new understanding among anthropologists and cultural historians of how the concept of "otherness," with which Westerners had interpreted Eastern cultures, had limited their vision.

A small number of Japanese American artists responded to these political events. Seattle-born painter and performance artist Roger Shimomura developed works from what he discovered in his grandmother's diary, which detailed her trip to the United States as a picture bride and the subsequent internment of her family, including Roger, during World War II. His subsequent paintings and performances dealt with the dilemma of living in two cultures and of coping with past and present anti-Asian racism. In Shimomura's work the kimono is a prominent Japanese symbol. Many figures wear this "cloak" of identity, some proudly and others against their will.

38b   Detail of fig. 38

Shimomura's paintings employ a combination of American comic book and Japanese *ukiyo-e* print styles, and their subjects range from action-packed, samurai-type tales to erotic stories. In *The Return of the Yellow Peril* series, he confronts the problem of Japan bashing and racism in 1990s America with wry humor and irony. He portrays his friends in Lawrence, Kansas (where Shimomura teaches at the University of Kansas), living out America's worst nightmare: the country has been taken over by the "Yellow Peril," symbolized by the people wearing kimonos over their Western clothes. Writer William Burroughs, one of Lawrence's most famous residents,

is pictured with a gun, hat, and kimono (see fig. 39), defending himself from a violent Japanese samurai ghost—an allusion, perhaps, to Burrough's own violent past and to his love for guns. Like a denied part of the self, the kimono here becomes an identity that is both foreign and familiar, a representation of national attitudes toward foreign influences displayed on the individual level.

Garments, like second skins, indicate racial and national identity in Shimomura's works.[53] He is concerned about a political climate in which issues of race and economics are not distinguished from one another, and where Americans of Japanese ancestry are not distinguished from Japanese nationals and others of Asian ancestry.[54]

39   Roger Shimomura
      The Writer William Burroughs in a Kimono, 1991
      Acrylic on canvas, 60 x 50 in.
      Collection Bill Trudeau

40   Masami Teraoka (American, b. Japan 1936)
      31 Flavors Invading Japan/Today's Special, 1982
      Color woodblock print, 11¹⁄₁₆ x 16⁹⁄₁₆ in.
      The Nelson-Atkins Museum of Art, Kansas City,
         Missouri, F84-13
      Gift of The Print Society

Another Japanese American artist who portrays the kimono-clad figure is printmaker and painter Masami Teraoka. Like Shimomura, Teraoka combines the action and eroticism of Japanese *ukiyo-e* prints with the energy and humor of American comic books. Using graphic styles from both of these genre, Teraoka, however, targets the reverse situation—the Americanization of Japan. Sometimes it is difficult to recognize whether his figures are Westerners or Japanese. In his woodcut *31 Flavors Invading Japan/Today's Special* (1982; fig. 40), a wild-eyed, lascivious Western woman with light brown hair and a kimono sliding off her shoulders licks a huge ice cream cone in a very erotic manner. The ice cream cone is as much an emblem of America's culture as the kimono

is of Japan's. Teraoka's work offers a humorous and ironic view of the cultural and economic borrowing that has gone on between Japan and America.

By the late 1970s and early 1980s, the kimono had become a popular garment to wear in public—at least by an adventurous segment of the population who wanted to make individualistic statements with their clothing. That spirit of independence resulted from the social revolution and the Women's Movement of the 1960s, and expressed itself in the "hippie" look of loose, unconstructed clothing. At this time, it was best to have authentic garments—handmade in exotic countries—which were available in ethnic clothing stores. Many copies of African dashikis,

Polynesian sarongs, and Japanese kimonos were produced by American textile manufacturers, but they invariably looked mass-produced. These loose, ethnic styles of modular construction required less tailoring and fitting than the constrained, fitted styles of women's clothing that had returned in the 1940s and 1950s. American popular culture created a new reform clothing movement, which promoted the individuality of the wearer and rejected the mass-produced look. People again turned to the kimono, wearing it open over pants or long dresses.[55] These kimonos became souvenirs, not of geographical travel but of a mental journey of changed consciousness and newfound freedom.

Authenticity, which is an important characteristic of souvenirs, became available to the average American in 1973 when Ruby Uehara of Honolulu founded the Orizaba Company and began importing used kimonos by the bale from Japan (see fig. 41).[56] Americans loved these discarded and wrinkled kimonos. Gallery owner B. J. Adams purchased a bale of kimonos and sold them to her Washington clientele. Groups of friends often ordered a bale, drew lots, and divided up the kimonos.[57] Most of the garments dated from the 1940s

41   Kimono, Meiji period
      Yūzen dyeing on silk
      Collected in 1982 from a 500-pound bale of
         imported kimonos
      Collection B. J. Adams

through the 1970s, but occasionally good quality older pieces, or funky newer ones, were found. One newer kimono owned by artists Nick and Lou Vaccaro of Lawrence, Kansas, has Japanese warplanes on it.

The Birth of Art-to-Wear

The Art-to-Wear Movement was a response to the 1960s desire for individualized, homemade, and comfortable ethnic clothing.[58] It also sprang from upheavals in the art world that occurred when artists rejected traditional forms of painting and sculpture associated with the elitist economic power structure. Artists such as Robert Smithson, Dennis Oppenheim, and Robert Rauschenberg, among others, rebelled against market and museum connections by creating site-specific land and body art that altered existing landscapes, and used the body as a canvas or an element in performance. Art-to-wear artists saw the body as a site for moveable creations. Numerous art-to-wear groups formed, including Friends of the Rag in Seattle. This group combined wearable art with performance art and often staged spontaneous street theater in unique costumes (see fig. 42). During the 1970s and early 1980s, some museums and galleries also mounted art-to-wear exhibitions. The various strands of the kimono's life came together in art-to-wear—the souvenir artifact; the individual statement; the ethnic, foreign, and exotic clothing; the handcrafted functional work of art; and the flashy theater costume—to create a new and unique art form.

The kimono still endures in the West as a frequently used symbol with political and sexual messages that are often intertwined. Politically, the kimono still symbolizes the Japanese nation. An example is a 1985 article in the economics journal *Datamation* that discussed the opening of Japan's market to American industry under the title "The Kimono Is Open."[59] And the connection between the kimono and the myth of the exotic, mysterious, and erotic oriental woman still endures, as evidenced by a play and film of the early 1990s titled *M. Butterfly*, a work that also carries political overtones.[60]

Over the years, discussions and studies of the kimono have largely ignored its complex layers of meanings, and instead, have revolved around its beauty and formal artistic qualities. This "art for art's sake" method of viewing the kimono must now be balanced with a contextual approach that examines the kimono's significant political and social meanings as well.

42   Susan Nininger
      Going Fishing, 1978
      Sewn and assembled mixed media
      Collection the artist
      Photograph by Roger Schreiber

NOTES

Collections and Collectors

1. Mary Burke, "History of the Collection," in *A Selection of Japanese Art from the Mary and Jackson Burke Collection,* catalogue of the exhibition at the Tokyo National Museum, May 21–June 30, 1985, organized by the Tokyo National Museum, the *Tokyo Shinbun,* and the *Chunichi Shinbun,* 1.
2. The Burke Collection does not include kimonos.
3. Edward Said, *Orientalism* (New York: Vintage Books, 1978), 38–42.
4. James Clifford, "On Collecting Art and Culture," in *The Predicament of Culture: Twentieth Century Ethnography, Literature, and Art* (Cambridge, Mass.: Harvard University Press, 1988), 216–218.
5. Bernard Rudofsky, *The Kimono Mind: An Informal Guide to Japan and the Japanese* (Garden City, N.Y.: Doubleday, 1965), 134; referring to *With Perry in Japan: The Diary of Edward Yorke McCauley,* n.p., n.d., 108.
6. Jean-Pierre Lehmann, *The Image of Japan: From Feudal Isolation to World Power, 1850–1905* (London: George Allen and Unwin, 1978), 43–44.
7. Liza Dalby, *Geisha* (New York: Random House, Vintage Press, 1985), xvii.
8. This postcard, from the Luke Jordan Collection, was published by Karl Lewis, photographer, in Yokohama. It is a hand-colored collotype with an undivided back that dates to approximately 1905. On the back is the number 025.
9. R. J. Baarsen et al., *Japanese Influence on Dutch Art: Imitation and Inspiration from 1650 to the Present* (Amsterdam: Rijksmuseum, 1991), 112.
10. Lehmann, *The Image of Japan,* 76, quoting G. Layrle, "Le Japon en 1867-I," *Revue des Deux Mondes* 73 (Feb. 1, 1868): 640.
11. See Elise Grilli, "Okakura Kakuzo, a Biographical Sketch," in *The Book of Tea,* ed. Okakura Kakuzo (Rutland, Vt.: Charles E. Tuttle, 1956), x, 129. This book by Okakura Kakuzo was first published in 1906, and was written to explain Japanese art and culture to Westerners.
12. See Yoshiko Wada, "The History of the Kimono," herein, for a description of these garments.
13. William Hosley, *The Japan Idea: Art and Life in Victorian America* (Hartford, Conn.: Wadsworth Atheneum, 1990), 88. A number of Japanese objects he owned are now in the collection of The Brooklyn Museum.
14. Patricia O'Toole, *The Five of Hearts: An Intimate Portrait of Henry Adams and His Friends, 1880–1918* (New York: Clarkson Potter, 1990), 174.
15. Bram Dijkstra, *Idols of Perversity: Fantasies of Feminine Evil in Fin-de-Siècle Culture* (New York: Oxford University Press, 1986); see esp. chaps. 1 and 7.
16. O'Toole, *The Five of Hearts,* 173.
17. Clay Lancaster, *The Japanese Influence in America* (New York: Walton H. Rawls, 1963), 258.
18. Julia Meech and Gabriel Weisberg, *Japonisme Comes to America* (New York: Peter Lang, 1991), 27.
19. Susan Anderson Hay, "Providence, Paris, Kyoto, Peking: Lucy Truman Aldrich and Her Collection," in *Patterns and Poetry: Nō Robes from the Lucy Truman Aldrich Collection at the Museum of Art, Rhode Island School of Design,* ed. Hay (Providence, R.I.: Rhode Island School of Design, 1992), 10.
20. Margot Paul, "A Creative Connoisseur: Nomura Shojiro," in *Kosode: 16th–19th Century Textiles from the Nomura Collection* (New York: Japan Society and Kodansha International, 1984), 15.
21. See also Dale Gluckman and Sharon Takeda, eds., *When Art Became Fashion: Kosode in Edo Period Japan* (Los Angeles: Los Angeles County Museum, 1992).
22. John La Farge, *Bric-a-Brac: An Artist's Letters from Japan* (1897), quoted in Jane Converse Brown, *The "Japanese Taste": Its Role in the Mission of the American Home and in the Family's Presentation of Itself to the Public as Expressed in Published Sources—1876–1916* (Ann Arbor: University of Michigan Press, 1987), 156.
23. Vincent van Gogh voices this commonly held opinion in a letter to Theo in 1888: "Come now, isn't it almost a true religion which these simple Japanese teach us, who live in nature as though they themselves were flowers?"; as quoted in *The Complete Letters of Vincent van Gogh,* vol. 3 (London: Thames and Hudson, 1958), 55.
24. Hosley, *The Japan Idea,* 48.
25. Lehmann, *The Image of Japan,* 90.
26. On October 7, 1858, Whistler met the painter Henri Fantin-Latour at the Louvre and spent time with him at the Café Molière that evening. Fantin-Latour was known to have owned Japanese prints that had belonged to writer and critic Charles Baudelaire, an early collector (according to Toshio Watanabe, *High Victorian Japonisme* [New York: Peter Lang, 1991], 214). Whistler also knew Delâtre, who was the engraver of Félix Bracquemond's Japanese studies after Hokusai's *Manga.* Bracquemond owned such a book and took it with him to cafés and studios Whistler and other artists frequented.
27. Julia Meech, "The Other Havemeyer Passion: Collecting Asian Art," in *The Splendid Legacy: The Havemeyer Collection* (New York: The Metropolitan Museum of Art, 1993), 130, 204.

Souvenirs

1. Susan Stewart, *On Longing: Narratives of the Miniature, the Gigantic, the Souvenir, and the Collection* (Baltimore, Md.: Johns Hopkins University Press, 1984), 135.
2. Ibid., 147.
3. Jeffrey Gilbert, *The Origins of Photography in Japan,* vol. 1 of *The Complete History of Japanese*

Photography (Tokyo: Shogakukan, 1985), 179.

4. Chantal Edel, *Once Upon a Time: Visions of Old Japan. Photographs by Felice Beato and Baron Raimund von Stillfried. And the Works of Pierre Loti*, trans. Linda Coverdale (New York: Friendly Press, 1986), 12–30. Originally published in France under the title *Mukashi, Mukashi, 1863–1883*.

5. Gilbert, *The Origins of Photography in Japan*, 178.

6. Information is from author's telephone interview, December 17, 1993, with the daughter Emily Potter Morse. The kimono was also accompanied by two *obi*, a pair of *tabi, geta*, an *obi* pad, and two hairpieces. Museum catalogue no. 1986.327.1a–k.

7. University of Kansas professor Keith Percival translated this crest and thinks the words may be a quotation from Erasmus's catalogue of popular Latin proverbs. The crest may not be her family motto, although the Metropolitan Museum's records note it as the Goelet crest.

8. Charles Frederick Worth was born in England in 1825 and died in Paris in 1895. He began his clothing design career in England but moved to Paris, where he and his sons ran the longest-running house of couture in history for four generations. The English House of Worth, run by nonfamily members, endured for over a century.

9. I am indebted to two sources for my information on the Clews kimono. Dennita Sewell of the Costume Institute of The Metropolitan Museum of Art in New York enabled me to see the garment and have access to the files of that department. Secondly, Ms. Margot Riley, who is completing her thesis for the Master's Degree in Museum Studies at Fashion Institute of Technology in New York on the wardrobe of Mrs. Clews, was very generous with information she gleaned from Mrs. Clews's clipping scrapbooks and from other archival material in France and the United States. Her spring 1994 master's thesis should be a valuable study on fashion history and the taste of an era.

10. Rebecca Stevens located this piece. The Woodrow Wilson House of Washington, D.C., allowed us to examine it and furnished information from their files. Mariko Iida, an intern at The Textile Museum, researched the piece and suggested how it had been altered.

11. Rebecca Stevens discovered this kimono in the collection of Robert Llewellen Wright's widow, Elizabeth Wright.

12. See examples of Wright's perspective drawings of the Warren Hickox and Thomas P. Hardy houses in the exhibition and gallery guide *Wright's Road to Japan, 1893–1905*, Aug. 21–Nov. 5, 1993, at the Frank Lloyd Wright Home and Studio Foundation, Oak Park, Ill., October 1993.

13. Elaine Harrington, "Frank Lloyd Wright and the Art of Japan," *Wright Angles: Newsletter of the Frank Lloyd Wright Home and Studio Foundation*, vol. IVL (Mar. 1992): 9.

14. The work is now in the collection of the University of Illinois at Chicago.

15. According to Elaine Harrington, former curator of the Frank Lloyd Wright Home and Studio Foundation, Wright's son David reported to her that he remembered his father bringing back two seals from Japan in 1905. Harrington says that Wright's personal red square logo was used on the stationery of his architectural studio when it opened in 1898. It appears on Wright's dated correspondence in the 1890s.

16. Mrs. David Wright, another of Frank Lloyd Wright's daughters-in-law, suggests that Robert Llewellen Wright's kimono was part of an estate that the Wrights bought in Japan in 1905, in a letter to Elizabeth Wright dated November 1993.

17. *Oak Leaves*, March 24, 1906, p. 12, courtesy of the Frank Lloyd Wright Archives at the Home and Studio Foundation in Oak Park, Ill.; also cited in Robert C. Twombly, *Frank Lloyd Wright: His Life and His Architecture* (New York: John Wiley and Sons, 1979), 115.

18. Margaret Klinkow, "The Wright Family in the House Beautiful," text of a slide lecture, Frank Lloyd Wright Home and Studio Foundation, Oak Park, Ill., 1991, 7.

The Kimono in Art and Life

1. The softer sash or *obi*, often in red *shibori*-dyed silk, was also used in Japan. An example is included with the Emily T. Morse kimono bequest in the Costume Institute of The Metropolitan Museum of Art in New York, discussed in section 2.

2. Whistler overlaps the "Princess's" kimono correctly from left to right, demonstrating his accurate knowledge of the kimono.

3. Toshio Watanabe, *High Victorian Japonisme* (New York: Peter Lang, 1991), 246.

4. Jane Converse Brown, *The Japanese Taste: Its Role in the Mission of the American Home and in the Family's Presentation of Itself to the Public as Expressed in Published Sources—1876–1916* (Ann Arbor: University of Michigan Press, 1987), 176.

5. Ibid., 179. This quote originates from *Scribner's Magazine*, n.v. (1890): 664.

6. "The Ten" was a group of New York and Boston painters who joined in an informal alliance to exhibit together. Their binding tie was a connection with Impressionism, and for some a consequent interest in *Japonisme*. The Tile Club, a New York artists' group, formed in 1877. It included Chase, Winslow Homer, J. Alden Weir, Elihu Vedder, John Twachtman, and Stanford White, who assembled for food and entertainment and the decorating of tiles. They were interested in the decorative arts and in enhancing the prestige of tile painting, and, through their interests in design, in *Japonisme*.

7. Dijkstra, *Idols of Perversity*, 135.

8. Ibid., 143.

9. Virginia M. Allen, *The Femme Fatale: Erotic Icon* (Troy, N.Y.: The Whitston Co., 1983), 3.

10. Debora Silverman, "The 'New Woman,' Feminism, and the Decorative Arts in Fin-de-Siècle France," in *Eroticism and the Body Politic*, ed. Lynn Hunt (Baltimore, Md.: The Johns Hopkins University Press, 1991), 145–147. See also Debora Silverman, *Art Nouveau in Fin-de-Siècle France: Politics, Psychology, and Style* (Berkeley: University of California Press, 1992).

11. According to Leslie Woodcock Tentler in *Wage-Earning Women* (New York: Oxford University Press, 1979), most working-class women also stopped working outside the home after they married. The low wages and limited opportunities for women reinforced the perceived superiority of the stay-at-home life. I am indebted to costume historian Madelyn Shaw for bringing this information to my attention in personal correspondence with Rebecca Stevens in February 1995.

12. Peter Gay, *The Bourgeois Experience: Victoria to Freud*, vol. 1 of *Education of the Senses* (New York: Oxford University Press, 1984).

13. For a discussion of the house as a repressive, controlling space see Mark Wigley, "Untitled: The Housing of Gender," in *Sexuality and Space*, ed. Beatriz Colomina (Princeton, N.J.: Princeton Papers on Architecture, 1992), 327–389.

14. Valerie Steele, *Fashion and Eroticism* (New York: Oxford University Press, 1985), 152.

15. Gertrude Käsebier was a founding member in 1902 of the Photo-Secession group. She was considered a radical, naturalistic photographer because she used natural poses and settings rather than the artificial ones common in the late nineteenth century. Her photographs are soft focused, evocative, and poetic.

16. For this information, I am indebted to Rebecca Stevens, who conducted a telephone interview with Mr. Magee in November 1993.

17. Kathleen Marra Headlee, "The Social Meaning of Clothing," doctoral diss. (Pullman: Washington State University, 1976), 35.

18. One of the best summaries of the Women's Dress Reform Movement in America is Sally Buchanan Kinsey, "A More Reasonable Way to Dress," in *"The Art That Is Life": The Arts and Crafts Movement in America, 1875–1920*, ed. Wendy Kaplan (Boston: Museum of Fine Arts, 1987), 358–369.

19. The best source on the Women's Building is Jeanne Madeline Weimann, *The Fair Women* (Chicago: Academy Chicago, 1981).

20. Frank Lloyd Wright, *An Autobiography* (New York: Hall, Sloan and Pearce, 1943), 15.

21. Ibid., 118.

22. Frank Lloyd Wright, "In the Cause of Architecture," *The Architectural Record* (Mar. 1908): 58.

23. Oscar Wilde, letter to the *Pall Mall Gazette*, October 14, 1884; also published as an essay, "Woman's Dress," in *Miscellanies*, vol. 14 of *The First Collected Edition of the Works of Oscar Wilde, 1908–1922*, ed. Robert Ross (15 vols., repr. London: Methuen & Co., 1969), 49–50; quoted in Wendy Kaplan and Robert Judson Clark, "Reform in Aesthetics: The Search for an American Identity," in *"The Art That Is Life,"* 147.

24. Anne Hollander, *Seeing Through Clothes* (New York: Viking Press, 1978), 336.

25. Ibid., 336–337.

26. Kinsey, "A More Reasonable Way to Dress," 367.

27. "Raising the Standard of Dressmaking," *The Craftsman*, May 12, 1907, 252.

28. Kinsey, "A More Reasonable Way to Dress," 368 n. 18.

29. For an illustration of Traphagen's 1913 evening dress see Lancaster, *The Japanese Influence in America*, 230–233.

30. Rudofsky, *The Kimono Mind*, 42.

31. Joy Melville, *Ellen and Edy* (London and New York: Pandora Press, 1987), 55.

32. Joanna Richardson, *Sarah Bernhardt and Her World* (London: Weidenfeld and Nicolson, 1977), 122.

33. Author's telephone interview with William Emboden in Los Angeles, February 1993. Emboden is connected with the Severin Wundermann Museum in Los Angeles, which is devoted mainly to Sarah Bernhardt and Jean Cocteau. Cocteau, incidentally, had a long interest in Japanese Kabuki costumes. According to Emboden, no total inventories exist of Bernhardt's possessions because she sold many things during her lifetime, and there are no photographs of her in kimonos. There was such a public craze for Bernhardt souvenirs that, even after her death, there were sales of fake Bernhardt memorabilia in the United States.

34. David Dempsey, *The Triumphs and Trials of Lotta Crabtree* (New York: William Morrow, 1968), 10.

35. Lancaster, *Japanese Influence in America*, 258.

36. Hosley, *The Japan Idea*, 175.

37. Vincent asks Theo, "Have you read Mme. Chrysanthème yet?" in two undated letters between August 1888 and May 1889. See *The Complete Letters of Vincent van Gogh*, vol. 3 (London: Thames and Hudson, 1958), 5, 89.

38. Lancaster, *Japanese Influence in America*, 258–259. The first U.S. performance of this opera was in Washington, D.C., in 1906, where it was sung in English. Its first performance in Italian was in 1907 at the Metropolitan Opera in New York (according to John Pennino, assistant archivist at the Metropolitan Opera, in a telephone conversation with Michelle Robinson, curatorial intern at the Spencer Museum of Art, March 23, 1994).

39. Ruth St. Denis was born Ruthie Dennis in 1880. She toured Europe, the United States, and the Orient both as a young dancer and later with her dance company and dancer-husband Ted Shawn. Her interest in Japan and the kimono was part of her wider interest in exotic dances of all types —Egyptian, Indian, and Japa-

nese—and she became famous for performing these in exotic costumes. She knew Mariano Fortuny, Louis Comfort Tiffany, and other important trendsetting designers and artists. St. Denis and Shawn also ran a dance school near Los Angeles, where her pupils included Martha Graham.

40. Information about St. Denis comes from the author's firsthand examination of photographs and her scrapbook–photo albums in the Dance Collection archives of the New York Public Library at Lincoln Center, and from Suzanne Shelton, *Divine Dancer: A Biography of Ruth St. Denis* (New York: Doubleday, 1981).

41. Christena L. Schlundt, *The Professional Appearances of Ruth St. Denis and Ted Shawn* (New York: New York Public Library, 1962), 41 ff.

42. Author interview with B. J. Adams in Washington, D.C., November 13, 1993.

43. I am indebted to Madelyn Shaw for the following note. The absence from the American fashion scene of European style leadership during the long years of World War II encouraged a number of American designers to fill the gap. Many of these designers, among them Carolyn Schnurer and Tina Leser, looked to the traditional textiles and clothing of non-Western cultures for inspiration. *American Fabrics*, a postwar trade journal promoting American designers and manufacturers, often highlighted their work. Specifically, see Cora Carlyle, "Carolyn Schnurer's Flight to Japan," *American Fabrics*, no. 20 (winter 1951/52): 115–122.

44. According to Rebecca Stevens, who spoke with Boyer in fall 1993.

45. This author found indigo-dyed cotton kimonos more interesting and affordable than silk ones when living in Japan in 1964, and had four such kimonos made to wear as dressing gowns when returning to the United States.

46. Fifi White, *Japanese Folk Textiles: An American Collection* (Tokyo: Shikosha, 1987). Also, William Jay Rathbun, ed., *Beyond the Tanabata Bridge: Traditional Japanese Textiles* (London: Thames and Hudson, in association with the Seattle Art Museum, 1993).

47. Schapiro admits that at first she conceived of the kimono as a robe for women—the new woman. Only later did she remember that men also wore kimonos. Norma Broude, "Miriam Schapiro and 'Femmage': Reflections on the Conflict Between Decoration and Abstraction in Twentieth Century Art," *Arts* (Feb. 1980): 83–87.

48. Unfortunately, this highly influential collage/ painting, or "femmage," as Schapiro called these pieces composed of patterned fabric and paint, is no longer in the United States. It was purchased from the Emmerich Gallery by Swiss collector Bruno Bischofberger.

49. According to the artist, the piece was inspired by a 1974 book given to her by Sherry Brody, who collaborated with Schapiro on her *Dollhouse* for the feminist house of installations *Womanhouse,* in Los Angeles in 1971–1972. The book was Seiroku Noma, *Japanese Costume and Textile Arts,* trans. Armins Nikovskis (New York: John Weatherhill, 1974). This information comes from an author interview with Miriam Schapiro in New York, August 1992.

50. Nomura's Hiinagata screens and his *kosode* collection, which now belongs to the Japanese nation, were shown in their entirety for the first time in 1959–1960 at The Metropolitan Museum of Art in New York, and selected pieces were exhibited in Tokyo in 1973, in London in 1980–1981, in New York at the Japan Society in 1984, and at the Los Angeles County Museum in 1992.

51. For example, Christopher Lasch, *The Culture of Narcissism: American Life in an Age of Diminishing Expectations* (New York: W. W. Norton, 1978).

52. The song "I Think I'm Turning Japanese" by the Vapors was on their EMI recording titled *Nuclear Days,* produced in 1980. It reputedly contains veiled references to male masturbation. Once again, Japan is equated in Westerners' minds with "forbidden" sex.

53. Japanese purchases of American real estate and companies receive far more sensational press coverage than the more numerous acquisitions by European nations. Shimomura sees this as evidence that people focus their fears on the people who look the most different from them.

54. Information is based on author interviews with the artist in 1994 and a video produced by the Bernice Steinbaum Gallery in New York; the quotation is from William W. Lew, in *Roger Shimomura: Return of the Yellow Peril,* exh. cat. (Spokane, Wash.: Cheney Cowles Museum, 1993), 3–4 ff.

55. This author remembers a number of art openings and other dressy affairs when the kimono was worn in such a manner in the mid-1980s.

56. The Orizaba Co. imported kimono bales from 1973 to 1988. Ruby Uehara moved from Honolulu to Los Angeles and reopened the company as the Texuba Co. in 1991. She has sold kimonos to people in all fifty states, England, Germany, Canada, and Iran, according to a telephone inquiry by Rebecca Stevens on March 8, 1994.

57. This author participated around 1984 and has three silk bale-kimonos.

58. See Julie Schafler Dale, "The Kimono in the Art-to-Wear Movement," herein, for a complete discussion of the origins and development of the Art-to-Wear Movement in the United States.

59. Thomas Murtha, "The Kimono Is Open," *Datamation* B1 (Nov. 1, 1985): 36 ff.

60. The film *M. Butterfly* (1993), directed by David Gromberg and starring Jeremy Irons and John Lone, was based on the play and screenplay by David Henry Hwang.

43 Katherine Westphal
    Koi, 1985
    Dyed, transfer printed, painted, and pieced paper and Lurex
    Collection the artist

Part Two

The Kimono as an American Art Form

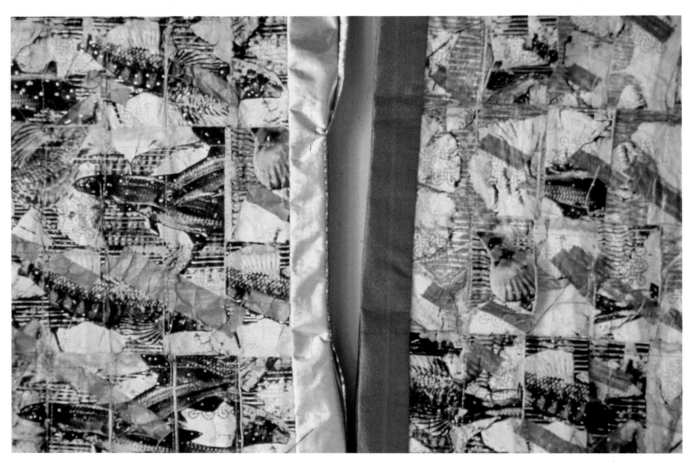

43a Katherine Westphal
    Koi (detail), 1985
    Dyed, transfer printed, painted, and pieced paper and Lurex
    Collection the artist
    (See fig. 43, p. 74.)

ART-TO-WEAR

I think it all began with an apple, many centuries ago.

If you know what wearable art is, you do not need to listen to this. If you do not know what wearable art is, after hearing this you still may not know what wearable art is.

Think of clothing in a new way.

It is not a replacement for the fig leaf.

The decorative can become functional; the functional can become decorative. The shoe is not just to walk in. The hat is not just to keep your head warm or to keep the sun out of your eyes.

Wearable art is not fashion, and it is not necessarily a marketable item.

Wearable Art
  moves through the environment
  interacts with people
  constantly changes

It can express an idea   It can express a mood
  of motion   of sorrow
  of solidity   of joy
  of effervescence   of fear
  of transparency   of hate
  of glitter   of pride
  of crud   of love
  of pattern   of despair
or none of the above.   or none of the above.

It tells us of humanity, who we are, where we are, who we would like to be, our dreams, our fantasies, our realities. It is an adjunct to the person, gentle or flamboyant.

The wearer can become a part of the landscape
  can become a tree
  can become a tall building
  can become a fish in the sea
  can become an oil spill
  can become an ancient princess.

Wearable art can tell a story like a comic strip or like a bas relief on an ancient wall. The story can be: encyclopedic, poetic, narrative, or journalistic, or it can have no story at all. The image, recognizable or not, can wrap around the human form. Discovering its message is like traveling through a wonderful maze of many turns, many vistas. Finding one's way from beginning to end is not important, but to see, to enjoy, to understand
  the play on ideas
  the play on words
  the play on forms
  the play on materials
  the play on play.

It is art moved out of the gallery onto the street. It moves the man or woman into a painting. This painting performance becomes the changing, moving, growing art in the street. The walls of the gallery are replaced by man & woman. They move, they change, the forms change. The performance becomes a spontaneous combination of the colorful, the decorative, the bizarre
  in new situations
  in impossible situations
  in aggressive situations
  in rejected situations.

There is a new audience, an audience exposed to art without going into the citadel of the elite, the gallery or museum. It is for all to enjoy or reject. It is there.

The boundaries are loose but the integrity, the clean discipline of the artist, is solid. The artists break barriers of rigid craft disciplines. They form their own parameters for their work.

—Katherine Westphal

Wearable Art (excerpt of the lecture)
World Crafts Council, Vienna, Austria, 1980

Reprinted with the permission of
Katherine Westphal.

44 Ben Compton
Madame Butterfly, 1977
Stitched, pieced, and appliquéd mixed media
Collection Mrs. Randall Compton

THE
Kimono
IN THE ART-TO-WEAR MOVEMENT
Julie Schafler Dale

Part of making something is that you project an image onto a blank space. But then you also project yourself into that image. When you make something wearable, you not only have the image and are projecting yourself into the image, but you actually take the image and literally drape it around you. For me as an artist that's a third kind of dimension in terms of creating. And I like to think that someone wearing it has the same type of involvement with the work.[1]

—Sharron Hedges, artist

For American artists who approach the human body as a vehicle to animate and display visual imagery, the kimono has proven to be a tremendously versatile and widely appropriate form. Like its use during Japan's Edo period (1600–1868) "when art became fashion,"[2] the kimono has played a critical role in presenting the ideas, feelings, sensibilities, and skills of creators of art-to-wear. In their hands, the kimono has ranged from an easily wearable, gracefully draped garment to a ceremonial, almost ritualistic body covering to a three- dimensional sculptural statement making no more than an allusion to wearability.

Why has the kimono been such a popular form? Why do so many artists, working with such different aesthetic concerns and perceptions, choose this form belonging to, and even symbolizing, a culture that flourishes halfway around the world?

Only by understanding the nature of the Art-to-Wear Movement and the particular concerns of those who gave it life can we begin to understand the multifaceted impact of the kimono on this art form.

The Art-to-Wear Movement Emerges

The Art-to-Wear Movement found its voice and identity in the early 1970s. It was defined by a diverse group of artists whose unorthodox approach to textiles and the body established the idea of clothing as a means of artistic expression. They took for granted their right to question established traditions, break down barriers, challenge perceptions, and chart new territory.

However, these privileges enjoyed by the frontrunners of the movement had been fought for and won by the rebels of the previous decade—an era of reevaluation, confrontation, and change. For the generation that equated freedom of speech with freedom of expression and that believed deeply in the sanctity of the individual, what better canvas than the body and its coverings to express personal identity and ideology?

The youth-led rebellion of the sixties was in many ways a response to the cultural sterility and restrictions of the Eisenhower era during which government, business, and mass communications tightened standards of acceptable practices in education, literature, entertainment, and culture.[3]

Many of the decade's dramas were played out on university campuses, notably the University of California at Berkeley, Columbia University in New York, Kent State in Ohio, Howard University in Washington, D.C., and "Ole Miss" in Mississippi. At these universities and elsewhere, the first wave of "baby boomers," many of whom were well-educated teenagers in an affluent society, sensed the tensions and questioned the contradictions in American life. So unfolded an extraordinary chapter in American history replete with protests against the institutions of education, government, family, and authority in general; new forms of community, music, and personal appearance; new attitudes toward sexuality, spirituality, and the environment; and drug use.[4]

It was a time of confrontation and rebellion whose legacy is written in the populist movements targeting the Vietnam War, civil rights, free speech, ecology, and women's liberation. It was a time of innovation and courage, a time of commitment to ideals, when the individual felt that he or she could make a difference. By challenging the restrictive conditions of the modern world, the counterculture of the sixties sought to redefine the human spirit.[5]

One of the most colorful and visible arenas of rebellion was personal appearance. Alternative dress became a vehicle for political statements and personal expressions and was consciously used to flaunt and accentuate ideological differences. The antiestablishment, antifashion look of the sixties was popularized by huge, youth-attended events such as "Be-ins" and Woodstock; by performers Janis Joplin, Jimi Hendrix, The Grateful Dead, Jefferson Airplane, and others; and by Broadway musicals such as *Hair*. By the end of the sixties, the pop life-style and the cult of alternative dress had spread across the country and infiltrated the mainstream.[6] The concept of alternative dress paved the way for the flower children and hippies whose life-style and philosophy of art and personal adornment had a direct bearing on the Art-to-Wear Movement that emerged in the seventies. Peter Beagle, in *American Denim: A New Folk Art*, says,

> One curious hopeful tendency, persistently surfacing from the looted wreck of the Flower Generation's flimsy dreamboat—and entirely likely to be swamped again by the Death Ship of overpopulation, pollution and famine . . . is the growing need to shape a few things in one's own measure; to leave individual footprints on freeways and clawmarks on the sleek sides of high-rise office buildings, on credit cards, and on newspaper headlines. It is the need to break out of the prison of buying and selling by making something and giving it away; to take no one else's word for what art is, or beauty, or oneself.[7]

The renaissance of traditional crafts in America went hand in hand with the life-styles of those hoping to drop out, start over, and relearn the use of their hands and the attendant self-sufficiency of living off the land. If making one's clothes was not required, certainly decorating them became a growing compulsion. Patched and embroidered, stitched and embellished, the clothes became works in progress and

45   Tim Harding
Swing Dynasty, 1986
Quilted, slashed, and dyed cotton
The Minneapolis Institute of Arts, 87.97

diaries of life rich with autobiographical information and symbols (see figs. 46, 46a). Alexandra Jacopetti writes, "Many of us hungered for a cultural identity strong enough to produce our own versions of native costumes of Afghanistan or Guatemala—for a community life rich enough for us to need our own totems comparable to African or Native American masks and ritual objects."[8]

One of the lasting legacies of these days is the decorated denim phenomenon, brought to the public arena through the American Denim Contest sponsored by Levi Strauss & Co. in 1973.[9] The personal content of these new American folk garments is striking. Many were the by-

products of self-taught craftspeople who instinctively perceived the denim surface as a canvas for personal expression and storytelling. Bearers of information both real and imagined, these denim garments were the patchwork quilts of the sixties. As Judy Manley, who entered the American Denim Contest, said, "My jacket is for a remembering of roots, a chronicle of what has been and who I am. . . . I wear the jacket the way one carries the things of yesterday into the now."[10]

46   K. Lee Manuel
      Geisha Kimono, 1982
      Sewn, painted, and glued mixed media
      Collection the artist

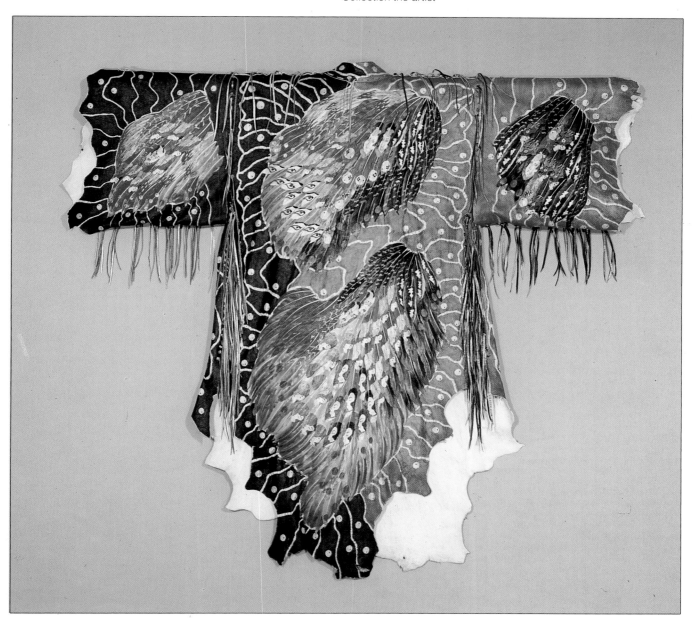

46a   Detail of fig. 46

The Fusion of Art and Everyday Life

Those individuals who consciously chose to explore the idea of clothing as an art form were not necessarily active participants in the political reforms of the sixties, the psychedelia of the counterculture, or the alternative life-style of flower children experimenting with communal living. However, many did come of age during those years and absorbed the spirit of the times.

The idea of using the body as a vehicle to animate and display visual imagery was compatible with a general belief that art should be liberated from the canvas, removed from the wall, extended beyond the museum, and integrated into everyday life.[11] This liberation of art from the con-fines of gallery and museum is documented in the art journals of the day. "Happenings" and "Be-ins" as well as performance, conceptual, on-site, and environmental artworks took place across the country.

The ultimate fusion of art and everyday life, symbolically and literally, came in the wearing of a work of art. Art-to-wear artists, whether schooled or self-taught, applied the principles of color, design, dimension, and composition to the textile and learned to sculpt or paint with fibers and dyes. After exploring color and shape within the flat planes of the textile, they changed its graphic quality by giving it volume and form on the body. In this new and exciting frontier, they dealt with changing interactions and dynamics as volume, imagery, and texture were animated.

47   Diana Aurigemma
       Portable Culture Coat and Carrying Case
        (front view), 1978
       Dyed, appliquéd silk and mixed media
       Collection the artist

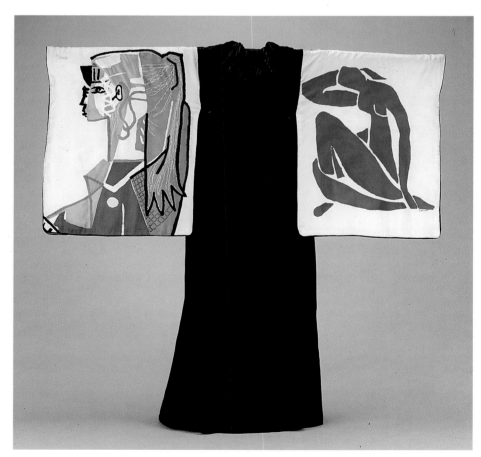

47a   Diana Aurigemma
       Portable Culture Coat and Carrying Case
        (back view), 1978
       Dyed, appliquéd silk and mixed media
       Collection the artist

48   Janet Lipkin
      Mexico at Midday, 1988
      Loom-knitted, ikat- and dip-dyed wool and silk
        with African trade beads
      Collection Sandra Sakata
      Photograph by Bobby Hansson

Some artists were drawn away from the traditional fine arts into the field of wearables by the intimacy of textiles. The seductive, tactile, and direct quality of fiber made for a more personal creative process. Artists also responded to the idea, born in the sixties, of honoring human life by enveloping it in the intimate creation of another's hand. This concept of elevating the quality of everyday life by integrating the fine and decorative arts proved a primary incentive for those who moved toward the creation of a wearable art form. Knitter Janet Lipkin (see fig. 48) sums up this concept: "I try to combine the tribalist with the fine artist—the spiritual with the intellectual. I am married to both these worlds. That's why my work is a garment and not a wall hanging or a painting. It's like what happens to theater when you take away the proscenium arch: the play becomes the audience."[12]

The pieces that emerged from this movement are highly personal in both content and process. They contain messages—autobiographical, political, narrative, or lyrical. Dina Knapp likens a crocheted cape that evolved over eighteen months to "the progression of a chunk of lifetime . . . it glows with human energy because every stitch was touched with meaning."[13] If the pieces do not speak in symbolic or narrative terms, they speak in terms of long hours of hands-on creativity, where the choice of process is an extension of the person. Susan Middleman explains, "The needlework was an outlet that fulfilled a certain compulsiveness in me—a very broad, labor-intensive, very still, never stop 'til finished, never quit aspect of myself. It suited my personality."[14]

The Influence of Non-European Cultures

For many artists, Japan epitomized this integration of the arts with everyday life. More importantly, it symbolized an industrialized country that had retained its appreciation of the handmade object. Japan's influence on decorative and fine arts in America and Europe spurred nothing less than an aesthetic revolution. It began in 1854 when American naval commodore Matthew C. Perry visited Japan, opening it to Americans. The mood of the late nineteenth century, which welcomed the "Japan Craze,"[15] was mirrored in the philosophy that produced the twentieth-century crafts revival, including the Art-to-Wear Movement.

The nineteenth-century Japanophile and mid-twentieth-century craftsperson shared a cultural malaise and disillusionment evidenced in the Victorian aversion to the newly industrialized world and the anti-materialistic, antiestablishment attitudes of the 1960s. One hundred years apart, the Japanophile and contemporary crafts-person were influenced by the concepts that art and craft as well as artist and craftsperson could be one and the same, and that the creative process should be a valued and integral part of daily life. Both groups shared a desire to reform the standards of society and improve the quality of life.[16] Both looked to non-European cultures as examples of more spiritual civilizations that had been spared the destructiveness of industrialization.[17]

Breaking the externally imposed cycle of school and career, young people of the 1960s and 1970s actively sought out these non-European cultures. Driven by the desire to find one's "self" through experience and firsthand knowledge of the world, thousands of young people traveled in search of alternative life-styles. In particular, they were drawn to so-called primitive cultures found in Peru, Mexico, India, Afghanistan, Indonesia, and Africa.[18]

Some traveled under the umbrella of the Peace Corps with the intention of making practical and humanitarian contributions to underdeveloped areas. Others were attracted to what they perceived as cultures unspoiled by Western materialism and industry. Here, they lived cheaply in nonpressured environments, where they participated in local rituals, music, arts, and culture. Returning home, the young travelers brought back experience and knowledge. They also brought back textiles, clothing, and jewelry that quickly became absorbed into their American lives. Alexandra Jacopetti says in *Funk & Flash*, "The United States continues to be the great melting pot. Now we're opening our arms to the spiritual teachings of the world. With the teachings come new images, and icons from Tibet and Nepal are transformed like this. My sixties mind was blown by all the teachings made available. Secret doctrines from all cultures, now easily at hand."[19]

Among the travelers was the new generation of artists and craftspeople eager to explore societies where handwork continued to play an active role. For the textile student anxious to study process and technique, the Far East was particularly significant. Ana Lisa Hedstrom, for example, was first drawn to Japan in 1969 for its ceramics. However, during her subsequent three years of travel throughout Asia, she discovered textiles, which changed the course of her artistic life. She would return often in the years to come as a student, as a scholar, and, finally, as a curator. Marla Weinhoff, who had received a bachelor's degree in anthropology with an emphasis on folk art and folklore, traveled to Japan in 1977 to study *katazome*, or stencil dyeing, as part of her graduate work at U.C. Berkeley, Department of Visual Design. Japanese textile scholar Yoshiko Wada led fourteen textile and art study tours in Japan between 1976 and 1992, offering visits to workshops and craft centers not otherwise accessible to Americans. U.C. Berkeley's Department of Visual Design, chaired by Ed Rossbach, also had a textile/fiber curriculum that sponsored a graduate exchange program with India. The knowledge and experience gained from such travels influenced the Art-to-Wear Movement, and in particular, those artists working in the field of surface design.

At the same time, a plethora of illustrated art books increased Americans' awareness of the art and artifacts of non-European cultures, broadening the definition of art and helping to break down the traditional distinction between the decorative and the fine arts.[20] Max Tilke's *Costume Patterns and Designs;*[21] Dorothy Burnham's catalogue for the Royal Ontario Museum, *Cut My Cote;*[22] and the availability of Folkwear Patterns[23] allowed textile artists to focus on ethnic garments, and this focus influenced the look of art-to-wear in the seventies. A series on textiles from Kodansha International, a publisher of English-language books about Japan, deeply affected American artists' perception of the kimono. Shown flat, the kimono appeared to the Western artist as a two-dimensional canvas rather than a three-dimensional garment. The image stuck, and many who went on to create their own kimonos approached them like the "shaped paintings" found in these and other art books (see fig. 49).

The Kimono as a Timeless Form

To the Westerner, the kimono is perceived as a timeless shape, and, as such, a nonfashion silhouette. Its fundamental, universally applicable form has just one size, one psyche, and one envelope, obliterating even social and sexual differences. The Art-to-Wear Movement has always sought to distance itself from the fashion world and its strong consumer-oriented, nonart connotations. But this has been difficult because the two share some common ground. Both art-to-wear and fashion are vehicles of information, concerned with embellishing the human form, and offer a creative, visual outlet for individual expression. However, fashion, a collaborative effort of the designer, manufacturer, and wearer, is ultimately meant for public consumption, while art-to-wear is a private endeavor — the creation of a single individual concerned with expressing personal ideas, feelings, and aesthetics through composition, color, and texture. The degree of wearability may vary dramatically, from pieces requiring the human body for completion to pieces technically functional but complete visually when mounted on a dowel or form and viewed contemplatively.

Fashion, far more the creative extension of the wearer, offers tools or props that the consumer selects and assembles to make his or her own statement about status, wealth, life-style, or occupation. Art-to-wear reflects the personal and intimate vision of the artist/designer/creator brought to life by a wearer who responds, relates, and chooses to identify him- or herself with the "essence" of the piece. The intimacy between creator, garment, and wearer resulting in the reinforcement of the "self" was recognized in the sixties as an important part of the decorated clothing phenomenon.

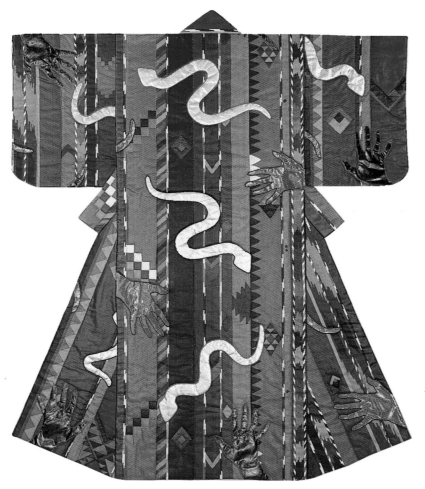

49   Marjorie Claybrook
     Magician's Robe, 1992
     Quilted cotton and lamé
     Collection the artist

Alexandra Jacopetti speaks of this symbolic relationship: "As I worked on the shirt and Roland wears it, he feels the power I invest in the making and he invests further power in the recognition, which further inspires me. An upward spiral."[24]

Artists creating for the body often voice this theme of mutual transformation. Jean Williams Cacicedo, who feels strongly about the functional life of her pieces, speaks about the "spiritual fit" of her garments: "If people can handle and love and cherish my work, they can wear it. I don't design [specifically] for a black man or a blond. If they're compatible with my work, it doesn't matter what they look like. They get possessed. The piece possesses them, and they possess the piece."[25]

Aesthetic Shift

The formative years of art-to-wear were influenced by widespread concern for the environment. This led to a deep respect for natural materials and a renewed interest in the traditional textile techniques of crochet, handweaving, macramé, tie-dye, beading, embroidery, appliqué, quilting, and featherwork. These techniques embodied the textural and organic aesthetic of the 1960s and early 1970s and lent themselves to the simple, easily wearable shapes of ponchos, capes, ruanas, caftans, and halters.[26] By the late seventies, however, the aesthetic pendulum began to swing. Interest in the three-dimensional, textural surface was replaced by interest in a flat, graphic surface, which could accommodate complex patterns and illustrations. This aesthetic shift within the Art-to-Wear Movement accounts for the increased popularity of the kimono form from the late 1970s onward.

The two-dimensional surface of the traditional kimono offered a more appropriate "canvas" than billowing ponchos and capes, while the rectilinear kimono form allowed for graphic, picturelike treatment, accentuating the nonfunctional life of these pieces. The success of the kimono as both a wall-mounted hanging and a functional body covering gave it a unique duality that artists welcomed.

There were other factors contributing to the aesthetic shift in the late 1970s. As artists improved their skills by mastering tools and materials, works that were once the result of what could be accomplished technically were superseded by more tightly controlled and focused works.[27] According to Knapp, "What happens is that in the process of all these years you develop clarity of vision. It's like all the intrusions fall by the wayside, all the things you don't really need. When I see that in other artists' work I sometimes find it disappointing because I want the intricacies to be there. But I also know what happens in growth. You shed and make room for something new and maybe something more pure."[28]

On another level, financial considerations were making new demands on artists, who now had families and added responsibilities. Speed of production became a relevant factor. Compared with the textural, dimensional art-to-wear of the early days of the movement, flat, graphic work was easier to produce, required less time and material, and its end product was easier to wear, easier to incorporate into daily life, and easier to sell.[29] Jo Ann Stabb, artist-designer and teacher, addresses the hazards of the new priorities—and the accompanying technologies—that contributed to the aesthetic shift within the Art-to-Wear Movement:

> The renewal of humanistic values during the 1960s and the resulting renaissance of hand-produced objects have been supplanted by the slick computerized world of the 1980s—an era which values speed, efficiency and infinite replication. Young people interested in making things are drawn to two-dimensional images and sleek surfaces. The photocopy machine and computer now rival drawing, painting and photography as image generators. The availability of nearly instantaneous results threatens to devalue the meaning of time-honored, skills-oriented crafts that are basic to Wearable Art. The highly tactile, coarse hand-wovens and hand-knits produced by the "low technologies" revived in the 1960s are now being replaced by fabrics produced on computerized looms and knitting machines.[30]

50   Nicki Hitz Edson
      Garden Kimono, 1991
      Loom-knitted wool
      Collection Courtney
      MacDonald

51   Linda Mendelson
      *Just Around the Corner There's
      a Rainbow in the Sky,* 1993
      Loom-knitted wool
      Collection Norah Kan Shaykin

Technology Plays a Greater Role

The increased availability of hand-operated knitting looms by the mid-1970s had a dramatic impact on the Art-to-Wear Movement. Many of the artists who had earlier championed the organic aesthetic and expressed themselves through the technique of crochet were now drawn to the hand-operated machines.[31] Janet Lipkin, Marika Contompasis, and Nicki Edson were among those who traded in their crochet hooks for knitting looms.

Others, such as Susanna Lewis and Linda Mendelson, were drawn into the movement by this new technological tool. They faced the challenge of humanizing and dominating the machine and of overriding the "computer" aesthetic in order to make it speak their languages. For example, Nicki Edson designed and knitted strips 40 stitches wide, which she placed side-by-side to create a continuous image. Susanna Lewis employed a similar technique using panels of 120 stitches. These knitted strips, or modules, created within the limitations of the various knitting machines and the artists' experience, lent themselves to the kimono form. The strips formed the basis of construction, while the surface, texture, color, and pattern constituted the focus. For these and other artists grappling with the technical complexities of the loom, the kimono offered a simple, straight-edged pattern that provided a perfect format for their ideas.

The *Trout-Magnolia Kimono* (1977; fig. 52) by Marika Contompasis is an early and historically important example of uniting the kimono form with the knitting loom. While crochet had been about texture and volume, the knitting loom was about surface. Because the machine's gauge produced small increments, it enabled her to create a tapestrylike surface appropriate for drawing and painting images. The kimono, with flat panels and rectilinear modules, naturally lent itself to illustration, while retaining viability and elegance as a garment.

The *Trout-Magnolia Kimono* was conceived as a triptych, with each of the three panels framed in tiny squares. Its beauty lies in its success as both a two-dimensional painting and a three-dimensional body sculpture. The surface plane is broken optically, not literally, by the addition of shadows beneath the floating trout—an effect that creates the surreal illusion of depth. The images wrap gracefully and harmoniously around the torso. The *Trout-Magnolia Kimono* heralds the end of the crochet era and the beginning of the loom-knitting era.

52   Marika Contompasis
      Trout-Magnolia Kimono, 1977
      Loom-knitted wool yarn
      Collection Julie Schafler Dale
      Photograph by Otto Stupakoff

The Birth of the *Shibori* and Surface Design Movements

The birth of the *shibori* movement in America occurred in 1975 at the Fiberworks Center for Textile Arts in Berkeley, California, under the tutelage of Yoshiko Wada and Donna Larsen (see fig. 53). During a six-day workshop devoted exclusively to *shibori*, or Japanese tie-dye, artists studied many kinds of textiles. Subsequently, the kimono, which is often decorated using this dye method, became a focus of investigation.

Shibori embraces a wide variety of resist-dyeing techniques that involve manipulating fabric into bundles by stitching, folding, clamping, pleating, or wrapping. The textured surface of these bundles is then exposed to dyes. These more precise, skilled, and controlled dyeing techniques offered a new aesthetic and fed the '70s' spirit of exploration and discovery.[32] Wada, and co-authors Mary Kellogg Rice and Jane Barton, went on to research this ancient form of resist dyeing

in preparation for their influential book *Shibori: The Inventive Art of Japanese Shaped Resist Dyeing*, published by Kodansha International in 1983. Ana Lisa Hedstrom, a participant in the workshop, went on to teach, explore, and utilize the process, becoming one of the foremost *shibori* dyers in this country (see fig. 54). She focused primarily on *arashi shibori*, which involves wrapping fabric around a tube, securing it with string, and pushing it into folds at one end of the tube.[33] Stimulated by Wada and Hedstrom, the *shibori* movement influenced the entire field of surface design.

By the mid-1970s, it was apparent that those artists concerned with surface embellishment needed an identity independent from artists working with the structural aspects of fiber. Many of these surface design artists were creators of art-to-wear. Spread throughout the country, they lacked opportunities to meet and communicate. Sensing this, two teachers of surface design and weaving, Elsa Sreenivasam at the University of Kansas and Pat Campbell at the Kansas City Art Institute coined the term *surface design* in 1975. They also organized "Communication: In Art, Industry, and Education," the first surface design conference, in April

53   Donna Larsen Endlich
American Noh Robe, 1978
Resist dyeing, *shibori*, and drawing on linen
Collection the artist

1976, at Lawrence, Kansas.[34] At this and subsequent surface design conferences, artists exchanged information on numerous textile-decorating techniques. Particularly influential were techniques used in the patterning of the kimono.

The technique generically known as "tie-dye," which became popular in the United States in the 1960s and 1970s, derived from resist-dyed textiles of India and Africa. It was, and remains, a colorful and idiosyncratic way to embellish mass-produced or handmade clothing. But the more inventive and precise Japanese techniques of *shibori* offered more challenging and sophisticated possibilities.

Pattern-producing dye techniques have been integral to cultures around the world for centuries, and American artists working in the field of surface design have explored many of them. These techniques received accelerated attention with the opening of the 1976 American Craft Museum exhibition "The Dyer's Art: Ikat, Batik, Plangi," which was based on the book of the same title by Jack Lenor Larsen.[35] The exhibition fueled artists' interest in learning the described techniques in their country of origin.

54   Ana Lisa Hedstrom
       Kimono with Pink Grid, 1991
       Resist-dyed and pieced silk
       Collection Ruth and Daniel Rifkin

Consequently, travel to Japan became an integral factor in the growth of the surface design movement in the United States. For example, Ina Kozel went to Japan to study *rōketsuzome*, or wax painting; Marla Weinhoff and John Marshall to study *katazome* (see figs. 57, 58), the use of rice paste squeezed through a stencil; Judith Content, Katherine Westphal, Julia Hill, Susan Kristofferson, and Ana Lisa Hedstrom also traveled to the Far East. They learned that to study surface design in Japan, one studied the kimono. The kimono naturally unites form, function, and technique, which accounts in part for its proliferation in this field. Ina Kozel (see fig. 59) speaks of her experience in Japan in 1976: "I went to Japan to study dyeing and fabric painting, but there, the main vehicle for painting fabric is the kimono. I had to become interested in kimono in order to study painting on fabric. I also saw that the Japanese accepted the kimono as an art form, as a viable means of expression. In fact, they honor the people who make the kimonos."[36]

55   Grace Kraft
      Window Series II, 1980
      Silk-screened silk
      Collection Jesús Bautista Moroles
      Photograph by Gary Leadmon

56   Carter Smith
Fire and Ice, 1991
Shibori on silk
Private collection

57   John Marshall
      *Waves (with Lobster and
      Net),* 1982
      Katazome dyeing on silk
      organza
      Collection Mrs. Lynne Land

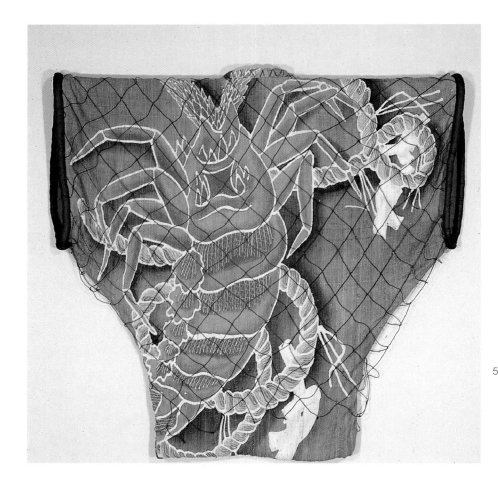

58   John Marshall
      Lobster and Net, 1982
      Tsutsugaki dyeing on silk
      Collection Bettina Schwimmer

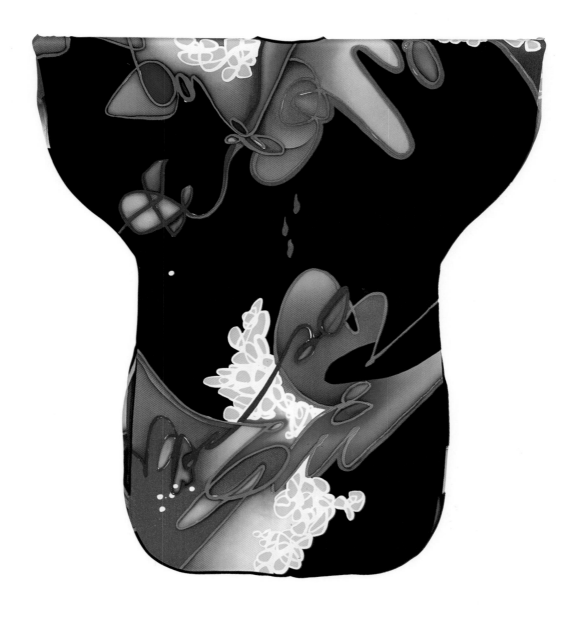

59   Ina Kozel
Bleeding Heart, 1987
Resist dyeing on silk
Collection Sue Peay

The Woven Form

Within the Art-to-Wear Movement, the field of weaving also produced an increasing number of kimonos. The technical limitations of weaving made the construction of garments such as the kimono, consisting of rectilinear, straight-edged modules, both natural and appropriate. In the mid-twentieth century, a general belief prevailed that woven cloth should be presented in a functional, accessible context. The designs for industry of Marianne Strengell, Dorothy Liebes, and Jack Lenor Larsen supported this notion.[37] But in 1972, this idea was challenged by Mildred Constantine and Jack Lenor Larsen in their book *Beyond Craft: The Art Fabric,* which promoted the superiority of cloth without function over its functional counterpart.[38] Despite the controversy, the kimono retained its popularity and acquired an elitist status that made it acceptable even to the nonfunctional weaver of the "art textile." The two-dimensional kimono form allowed clothing designers to be textile designers and textile designers to refer to the human body without making a commitment to functional clothing. Ironically, both the creators of art fabric and art-to-wear sought to validate the textile: the former by making it nonfunctional; the latter by elevating its functional status. The powerful, ritualistic image of the kimono served both these masters.[39]

In the American Art-to-Wear Movement, the kimono as a garment was always incidental to the woven fabric itself. Requiring little or no cutting, tucking, or gathering, it served as a vehicle for showcasing the woven cloth. Its simple form permitted the artist to step back from the construction and become immersed in the creation of the textile. Weavers often refer to the physicality of the process and describe the experience of textiles as being first and foremost sensual, nonanalytical, and tactile. The kimono, respectful of the cloth on both practical and aesthetic levels, has become the classic form of the woven art garment. Veteran weaver Randall Darwall (see fig. 62), who has been a regular participant in the proliferation of craft fairs since the mid-1970s, speaks of the ubiquitous nature of the kimono.[40] "It was just everywhere," Darwall observes, "a real basic format on which you could hang whatever you wanted, like T-shirts."[41]

60   Deborah Valoma
      Following Ariadne's Thread, 1992
      Woven and dip-dyed rayon and cotton
      Collection the artist

61 Diane H. Easton Kent
    Anni Kimono, 1985
    Woven linen
    Collection Christine Carter Lynch

62 Randall Darwall
    Float Weave Kimono, 1979
    Woven and dyed silk
    Collection Pat Garrett

Reasons for the Kimono's Popularity

The reasons why the kimono form lends itself so readily to the creators of art-to-wear hold fairly consistent throughout the various media. Weavers, knitters, quilters, and silk dyers agree on certain universal principles. However, the kimono, as perceived and depicted in the Art-to-Wear Movement, is a Western perception and as such is not grounded in the historically rich and complex kimono lore of Japan. Thus, it is not subject to externally imposed aesthetic restrictions. Even twentieth-century Japanophiles have filtered the kimono through their own eyes to produce work that is interpretive and intensely personal. Indeed, there are as many artists who claim that their decision to work with the kimono form is not influenced by any feelings about Japan as there are artists who attribute their choice to a deep-rooted respect for the Japanese culture. And there are as many artists who have been to Japan as have not. This accounts for the varied and unorthodox look of the kimonos and stamps them with the gutsy individuality that defines art-to-wear in America.

For the Western artist dealing with the human body as a vehicle to display and animate visual imagery, the kimono offers an ideal canvas: a broad, blank, uninterrupted, two-dimensional surface that also functions as a garment. Virtually anything can happen within its silhouette: narrative or abstract, translucent or opaque, rigid or fluid, flat or dimensional, patterned or biomorphic. It lends itself to most fiber techniques, always retaining the suggestion, if not the ease, of wearability.

This canvaslike quality of the kimono has appealed to artists who create work for the body on a number of levels. First, the similarity between the extended rectangle of the kimono and the accepted shape of the traditional fine arts canvas is advantageous. The rectilinear silhouette is easy to assemble on a dowel and mount on a wall much like the traditional Western art canvas. As much as these artists have welcomed the opportunity to break rules, experiment, and broaden perceptions, they have also needed to educate the public about clothing as an art form beyond fashion. The ability to display work within a traditional gallery and museum context has been an important consideration.

Next, the kimono presents cloth in a pure, undistorted way, both on and off the body. In general, the more cutting and shaping involved in the construction of a garment, the more subordinate the fabric becomes to that shape. Because the kimono is constructed from straight-edged rectilinear modules, it requires no cutting; therefore, there is no mutilation and no loss or waste of fabric. The integrity of the cloth is maintained.

Another reason artists choose the kimono form is purely practical. Most people who begin experimenting with clothing as an art form come from art backgrounds or are self-taught. Many have had little or no experience in drafting garment patterns. This makes the simple modular construction of the kimono a natural choice. It also helps that it is an accessible form due to a number of key pattern-oriented publications on the subject. The importance of Max Tilke's *Costume Patterns and Designs* and Dorothy Burnham's *Cut My Cote* has been mentioned. Not only did they draw attention to the existence of ethnic garments, they literally flattened them out, and in the case of Burnham, reduced the garments to their modular components as cut from varying widths of cloth. In 1975, Folkwear Patterns began offering historical and technical information as well as patterns for a number of ethnic garments.[42] The Japanese Kimono, Pattern #113, was issued in 1977, along with other kimono-related garments, such as the *hippari*, and later, the *haori*.[43] In 1977, Folkwear Patterns sponsored "The Art and Romance of Peasant Clothes," a national competition/exhibition for garments made from their patterns. Marika Contompasis's *Trout Magnolia Kimono* was among the winners.[44]

People consider ethnic costumes exotic, sacred, even ritualistic. They reserve them for special occasions and pass them down from generation to generation. Talismans of power, they are often handmade by labor-intensive techniques. The "spirit" of ethnic clothes seemed appropriate to the creators of the Art-to-Wear Movement, who believed

63 Nina Vivian Huryn
50 B00 White, 1984
Stitched, appliquéd, tooled,
  and painted mixed media
Collection Laura Fisher

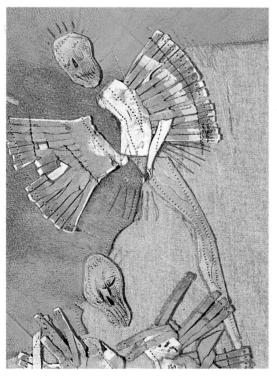

63a Detail of fig. 63

the sentiment of Alexandra Jacopetti that a
garment "carries power, because power has
been invested in it—a circular flow of
energy."[45] Jacopetti continues in her book,
"And here I sit with the experience of
gathering together all these talismans of
people's inner lives, filled with wonder at
their willingness to share these private
messages from within. . . . Timothy Leary
spoke of the revolution of consciousness.
He took to ethnic clothing early—remember
the smiling doctor in the Nehru shirt? All of
those mandalas brought to us by Leary, Carl
Jung, and Inner Space have served as fine
channels to lead us back to ourselves. . . .
Now we make our own."[46]

64   Judith Content
     Sweltering Sky, 1992
     Discharged, dyed, quilted, and appliquéd silk
     Collection the artist

The kimono, which has been worn and collected in America since the nineteenth century, radiates an aura of ceremony and ritual. Its stately, elegant shape, displayed on a stand or hanging on the wall, appears more closely related to a religious vestment than to an everyday Western garment. It lends itself figuratively to larger-than-life treatment. When worn, the kimono holds mystique for Westerners, removing the wearer from the mainstream and suggesting real or imagined power. This power can be spirituality, sensuality, independence, or any number of projected states of being.

That the kimono acts as a symbol or metaphor for the human form is also part of its appeal. It is a visual hieroglyph for the human body, reduced and simplified. The kimono, even in its most basic two-dimensional interpretation, has magnetic appeal and triggers the imagination by suggesting the story of human participation. Artists with varying concerns regarding wearability respond similarly to the kimono's basic structural

65   W. Logan Fry
      Evolutionary Fantasy, 1988
      Direct painting, *ikat*, and resist-dyed silk
      Collection the artist

66 Christine Martens
Vestment II, 1983
Woven and pieced mixed fibers
Collection the artist

66a Detail of fig. 66

reference to the body. For example, Jan Janeiro's series of shadow garments, including the netlike *Skeletal Kimono* (1977; fig. 68), addresses the presence and absence of the human figure, memory, and having been there. The crosslike structure of the kimono form makes allusion to the human figure without being literal. Janeiro speaks of the apex—the place where two centralities meet—as the real "heart" of the piece. Although technically wearable, her gossamer kimono was not made to be worn; yet it addresses the same themes as those concerned with wearability: the human figure, architecture, and the garment. Juanita Girardin (see fig. 67), whose woven kimonos are completely functional, also speaks about the importance of the "heart center"— the trunk of the kimono that generates an aura. She uses embellishment to enhance spirituality, creating "ceremonial" garments to be worn on special occasions.

67   Juanita Girardin
      *The Kimono After
      W. B. Yeats,* 1990
      Woven silk, cotton,
      and rayon
      Collection Robert Ortiz
      Photograph by Erik Borg

The T-shaped skeleton of the kimono became the basis for many garments created by artists within the movement. Indeed, many use the term *kimono* to refer to any simple, T-shaped garment: a square minus two rectangular sections of varying proportions. Dina Knapp's *"See It Like a Native," History Kimono #1* (1982; fig. 69), with its narrow, tubelike sleeves, is an example. Those artists who adapted the modular "T" to improve drape, flexibility, and wearability, likewise feel that their pieces retain the idea or feeling of a kimono at their core. This multireferential thinking accounts for the very broad use of the term *kimono* vis-à-vis garments that do not appear to be kimonos.

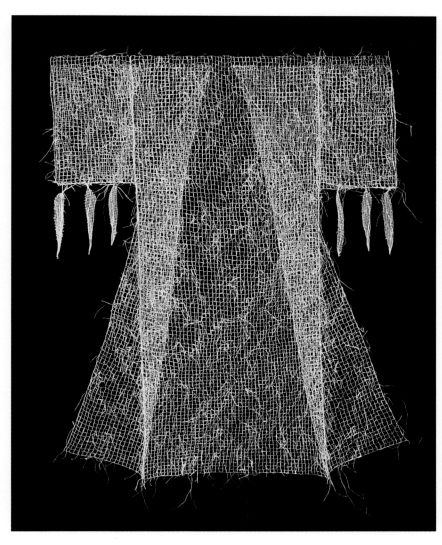

68   Jan Janeiro
      Skeletal Kimono, 1977
      Space-dyed and knotted raffia
      Collection the artist

69   Dina Knapp
"See It Like a Native," History Kimono #1, 1982
Painted, appliquéd, transfer printed, and
   assembled mixed media
Collection the artist

To Jean Williams Cacicedo, the kimono is about simplicity. All her "coats" evolve from two-dimensional drawings of a body with sleeves—the easily recognized T-shaped kimono form (see figs. 70, 70a–d). Yet this traditional shape presented certain problems and restrictions for her when transferred from a two-dimensional paper design to a three-dimensional garment. The pieced and dyed felt she uses is bulky and does not drape properly in the sleeve when cut as a straight-edged module. Because wearability is as important to Cacicedo as visual design, the kimono form needed to be modified. Although the bodies remained tubular, her sleeves were narrowed, or shaped, or in the case of *Global Vision* (1993), tucked at the shoulder to eliminate underarm bulk. Cacicedo, while seeking to retain the experience of ceremony for the modern-day wearer, understands the need for ease of movement and functional freedom as part of this ceremony. This is also true for a number of other artists, including Janet Lipkin and Linda Mendelson, whose loom-knitted garments are derived from the T-shape but adapted for wearability.

Just as the kimono is appealing for its two-dimensional, canvaslike surface, it is also intriguing for its sculptural possibilities. Susan Kristofferson describes the kimono as a two-dimensional plane that can also be a three-dimensional form. Jan Janeiro talks about the structural sense of physical space created by a form that is appropriately a garment. Katherine Westphal (see fig. 43, p. 74) is intrigued by the idea of a moving, changing canvas and by people wearing coverings that look like paintings but have shifting volumes, shapes, and architecture. Yvonne Porcella is interested in the visual flow of imagery, pattern, and color from back to sleeves

to front and from inside to outside. She uses linings to add dimension and to create more patterning and geometry when parts of the outside are seen juxtaposed to these interiors. Risë Nagin and Susan Kristofferson (see fig. 71) explore design possibilities by using layered, translucent fabrics to build a three-dimensional kimono. Although unconcerned about the functional life of their kimonos, both artists found that the construction of a practical garment, with front and back panels, increased the possibilities of layering and the play of transparencies.

69a   Detail of fig. 69

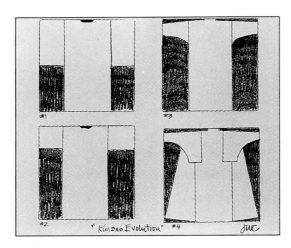

70a   Jean Williams Cacicedo
Sketch #1 for "Global Vision," 1993
Graphite on vellum
Collection the artist
Photograph by David E. Leach

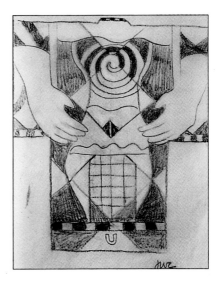

70b   Jean Williams Cacicedo
Sketch #2 for "Global Vision," 1993
Graphite on vellum
Collection the artist
Photograph by David E. Leach

70   Jean Williams Cacicedo
Global Vision, 1993
Felted, woven, and reverse appliquéd wool
Collection Elizabeth Sieradski
Photograph by David E. Leach

70c   Jean Williams Cacicedo
Sketch #3 for "Global Vision," 1993
Graphite on vellum
Collection the artist
Photograph by David E. Leach

70d   Jean Williams Cacicedo
Sketch #4 for "Global Vision," 1993
Graphite on vellum
Collection the artist
Photograph by David E. Leach

Finally, the kimono as a symbol of Japan made it an irresistible choice for certain artists. As a carrier of cultural symbols, the kimono represents an intrigue with the exotic. It speaks of the whole sophisticated aesthetic of Japan as well as the parts of this whole—balance and asymmetry, deceptive simplicity, perfection in form, surface pattern, spatial arrangement, and abstraction of natural forms. But above all, the kimono symbolizes a country that treats its craftspeople as national treasures, and respects the long, labor-intensive process of handwork as a valued part of daily existence. That the kimono is traditionally displayed on a stand and revered as a work of art is an important, positive association for the Western artist.[47]

The Kimono as Cross-Cultural Hybrid

The kimono in the American Art-to-Wear Movement represents the curious marriage of two disparate cultures: one steeped in tradition and dominated by restraint, limitations, and minute refinements of agenda; the other questing, adventuresome, and lacking strong, established traditions. Ironically, the Japanese kimono form was adopted and interpreted by Western artists who were determined to eradicate even the few existing rules. They loved being completely free to explore and create without ties to precedents. Indeed, the entire Art-to-Wear Movement in America sailed forward on the idea that there were no restraints, and its strongest pieces have been born of self-indulgent, energetic, and explosive creativity. The American artist capitalized on the kimono's positive aesthetic references and ignored the traditional kimono rules that exist in Japanese culture.

From this mixing of cultures and ideas spring a group of multifaceted, highly diverse, personal, unexpected, and unorthodox kimonos. They range from those that pay homage to Japan, in aesthetic and technique, to those that use the silhouette only to display the textile in wearable, or three-dimensional form. From this varied group of "individuals" emerge a few broad categories defined by aesthetic, intent, or technique.

71 Susan Kristofferson
Rain(bow) Kimono, 1978 (reconstructed 1994)
Assembled acrylic medium and hand-dyed cotton
Collection the artist

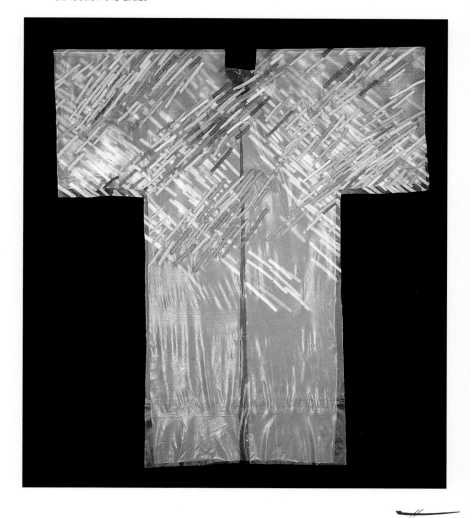

72   Yvonne Porcella
      Pasha on the 10:04, 1984
      Quilted and painted cotton
      Private collection

American Folk Textile Kimonos

Foremost among these are the patchwork quilt kimonos, formed by the marriage of quintessential American folk textile and Japanese costume. Yvonne Porcella, known in Japan as the "kimono quilt lady," has created numerous life-size and larger-than-life patchwork quilt kimonos, including *Pasha on the 10:04* (1984; fig. 72). Although many of her patch patterns are traditionally American—log cabin, nine patch, half-square triangle—and their application to the kimono seemingly incongruous, the kimono quilt is solidly Japanese. The 1979 exhibition "Folk Art & Craft from Japan" at the Asian Art Museum in San Francisco included a *yogi*, a piece described as "bedding in kimono form." This was a traditional, quilted coverlet shaped like a kimono and made for sleeping.[48] Inspired by the exhibition, Porcella developed the kimono/quilt concept, beginning in 1980 with *Bedding in Kimono Form*. She has continued to investigate the kimono format in her art quilts.

A kimono cut from an antique American "crazy quilt" found in the early 1970s in San Francisco represents another twist on this cross-cultural concept (1973–1974; fig. 73). The Art-to-Wear Movement traces its roots to the patched and embroidered clothing of the 1960s. Those original narrative garments and personal talismans included old familiar clothes patched with fabrics of every kind and vintage as well as new clothes invented from pieces of old, such as denims reinforced and resplendent with "power patches" in kaleidoscopic configurations.

Yet patching, the practice of recycling materials—so emblematic of the Yankee pioneer spirit of thrift and survival—is equally part of Japanese heritage.[49] For centuries, the Japanese have recycled cherished materials to give them new and longer life and additional value. Of particular interest is a late-sixteenth-century patchwork robe from Chinese remnants, reproduced on page 9 of the November/December 1992 issue of *Fiberarts*. In every way, this robe and the *Crazy Quilt Kimono* are visual and conceptual cousins.

The stitched and pieced kimonos of Margrit Schmidtke (see fig. 74) can be narrative or abstract, yet both come from a technique that is inspired by her neighbors, the Amish community in Pennsylvania, which has long used the quilt as an expressive vehicle. Through her pieces, Schmidtke speaks of her deep concern for the environment. The kimono silhouette has been selected symbolically, not in reference to Japan, but as a protective mantle; its purpose is to envelope and nurture humankind, the earth, and its fragile and vulnerable environment.

Another interesting hybrid, the *Coverlet Kimono* (1977; fig. 75), loom-knitted by Susanna Lewis, incorporates a traditional American blanket pattern—the Jacquard coverlet—superimposed on a Japanese shape. Lewis's primary message is about keeping warm by literally enveloping oneself in a blanket. However, the purposely irreverent combination of unconventional, nontraditional surface pattern on a traditional Japanese form makes a deeper, more symbolic statement about breaking away. And to Lewis it makes a statement about her perception of the restrictive nature of the kimono vis-à-vis the role of women in Japanese society.

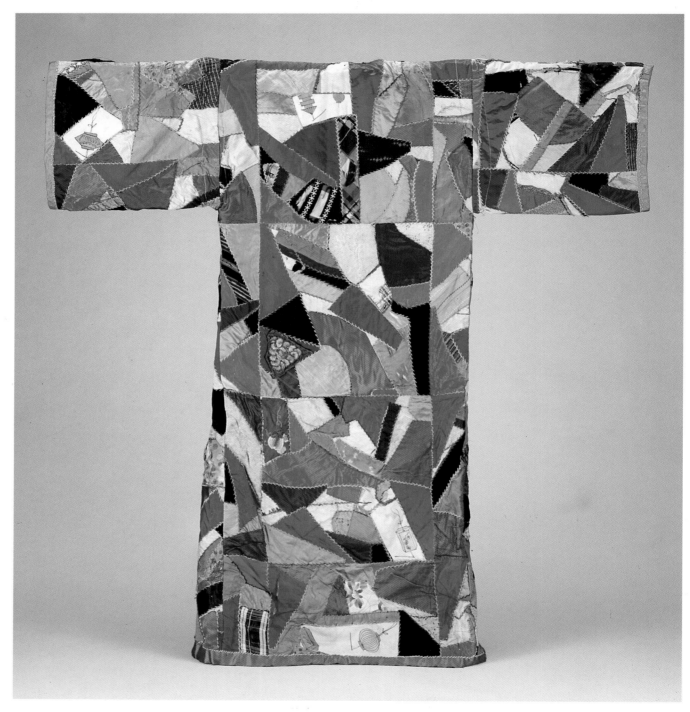

73   Artist unknown
Crazy Quilt Kimono, 1973–1974
Collection Mrs. Norman Schafler

74   Margrit Schmidtke
Will My Garden Grow, Grandma?, 1992
Quilted cotton
Collection the artist

75   Susanna Lewis
Coverlet Kimono, 1977
Loom-knitted wool
Collection John Cianciolo
Photograph by Susanna Lewis

Pop Kimonos

The marriage of a quintessential Western image with an Eastern form has created another striking group of hybrids. Pop kimonos include Janet Lipkin's first loom-knitted garment, a kimono constructed of pieced squares containing the portrait of Mickey Mouse—the archetypal image of her childhood and "a sign of the times"[50]—among solid and variegated colored squares (see fig. 76). The strong, graphic image works perfectly against the two-dimensional knitted surface; the flatness of the cartoon plays off the clean plane of the kimono. The *TV Kimono* (1983; fig. 77) by Marla Weinhoff is another prime example of cross-cultural thinking. Using the Japanese stencil-dyeing technique of *katazome*,[51] Weinhoff created a repeat image of the TV set, an irrefutable symbol of twentieth-century Western culture.

Susan Summa also chose the kimono form to present her pop series *Miss Liberty Takes a Holiday* (see fig. 78). This group of seven loom-knitted kimonos was created for the U.S. Bicentennial Celebration and the Statue of Liberty's 100th anniversary in 1986. "Finally in the midst of all the serious business of 'Save the Statue' and the attendant Centennial publicity," Summa explains, "I decided that the Lady needed to have a little fun—go on vacation—and thus was born the idea of taking her to various ports of call, starting with Miami, continuing to Baltimore, to Texas, and anywhere else my imagination took her. Of course, she had to end up in New York harbor for the big celebration."[52] The simple rectilinear modules required no cutting or shaping, freeing Summa to focus on color and pattern. The straightlaced Miss Liberty is purposely treated in a playful manner as she travels around the world. Although the artist did not intend any cross-cultural reference, one can be inferred.

76   Janet Lipkin
Mickey Mouse Kimono, 1978
Loom-knitted, *ikat*-dyed, and pieced wool
Location unknown
Photograph by Bobby Hansson

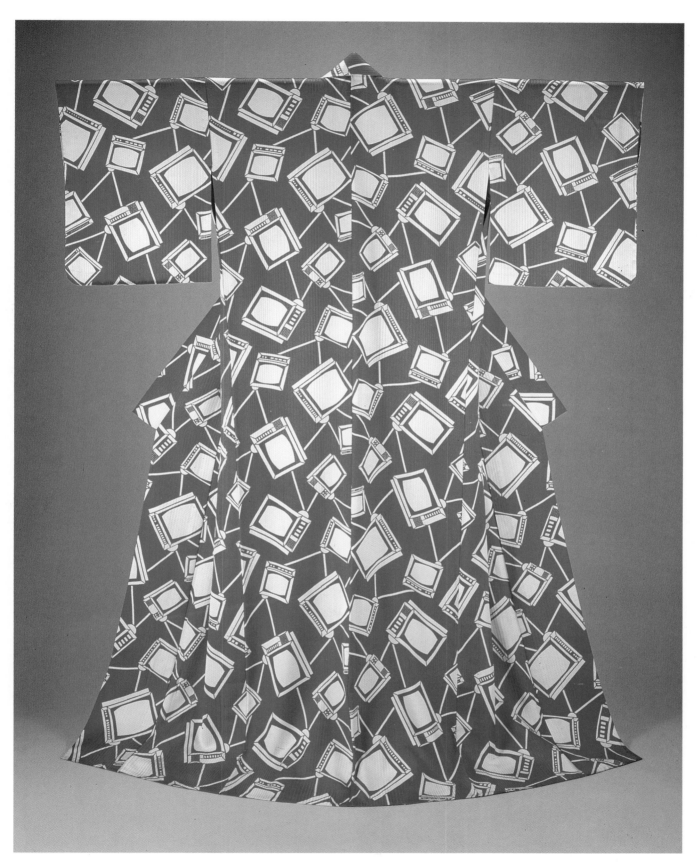

77　Marla Weinhoff
TV Kimono, 1983
Katazome dyeing on silk
Collection the artist

77a   Detail of fig. 77

78   Susan D. Summa
      Liberty Goes Hawaiian, 1986
      Loom-knitted cotton and found objects
      Collection Leslie and Michael Engl

Kimonos Displaying Natural Imagery

Kimonos—painted, woven, stitched, and knitted—also serve as canvases to display varied and personal images of nature. Some are decorative, others are lyrical, and still others carry deep, heartfelt messages. Because the use of the kimono to display nature's world is such a quint-essentially Japanese statement,[53] these pieces seem to pay special homage to their Eastern counterparts. For example, the changing seasons, a recurring theme in Japanese art, is powerfully evoked in a quartet of loom-knitted kimonos by Nicki Edson (1986/88; figs. 79–82). This series shows a single landscape with trees in a stop-frame sequence of spring, summer, fall, and winter. Danielle Ray's *Snow Kimono* (1984; fig. 84) is one of four works also created to illustrate "the harmonies, counterpoints, and changing moods of nature's cycle."[54] Here, the kimono is tapestry woven in monochromatic tones to capture the essence of winter. Its rich

79　Nicki Hitz Edson
Landscape Kimono: Spring, 1986
Loom-knitted, crocheted wool
Collection Christine Carter Lynch
Photograph by Mozelle Tawil

80　Nicki Hitz Edson
Landscape Kimono: Summer, 1986
Loom-knitted, crocheted wool
Collection the artist
Photograph by Mozelle Tawil

surface pattern, continuous image, and lyrical treatment of subject pay gentle homage to its Japanese counterpart.

In significant contrast is Risë Nagin's *Fog Area* (1985; fig. 83), one of six kimonos and two wall hangings in the "Pennsylvania Turnpike" series (1983–1986). These composite images of Western landscapes dealing with our perception of time are a conscious twist on the traditional Japanese landscape kimono. The artist seeks to capture, through the use of translucent fabrics, the quality of light perceived from a moving vehicle, the sensation of objects flying up and disappearing, and the simultaneity of fragmented images. Underlying this personalized, westernized, and abstracted interpretation of landscape is a deep respect for Japanese aesthetics: asymmetry in composition, use of line, contrast of patterned and simple areas, flat motifs floating on fields of pattern, and the "incredible, unabashed beauty that speaks about spiritual things."[55]

82   Nicki Hitz Edson
      Landscape Kimono: Winter, 1988
      Loom-knitted, crocheted wool
      Collection the artist
      Photograph by Bobby Hansson

81   Nicki Hitz Edson
      Landscape Kimono: Fall, 1988
      Loom-knitted, crocheted wool
      Collection Julie Schafler Dale
      Photograph by Bobby Hansson

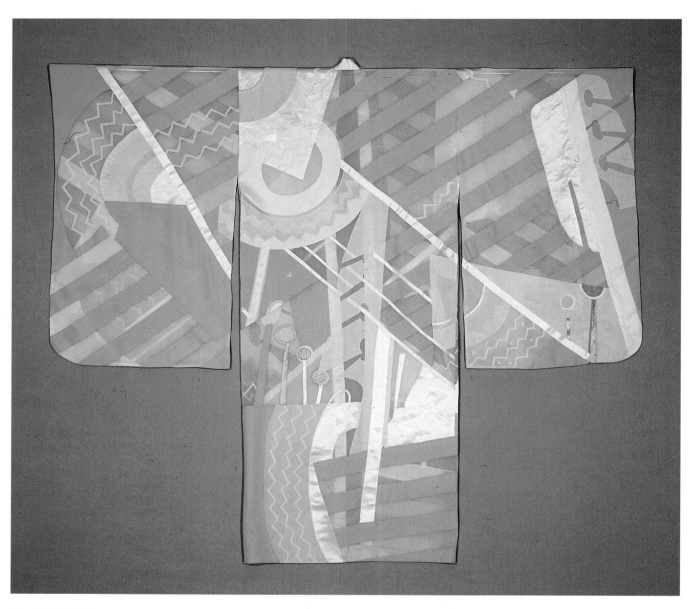

83 Risë Nagin
Fog Area, 1985
Pieced and sewn silk, cotton, and polyester
Collection the artist

84   Danielle Ray
      Snow Kimono, 1984
      Woven wool
      Collection the artist

Performance Kimonos

A particularly intriguing kimono is Susan Nininger's *Going Fishing* (1978; fig. 85), a larger-than-life, idiosyncratic performance piece. Nininger chose the form of a kimono because she felt that the event of fishing was ceremonial and therefore reminiscent of the Japanese tea ceremony, where kimonos are worn.[56] She sensed these events offered parallel experiences in terms of preparation, accoutrements, attitude, and the long hours spent sitting and meditating. This kimono is unrestrained, unorthodox, and full of surprises. It is encrusted with ceramic fish, both heads and tails, which camouflage the fisherman/wearer and act as enticements for other fish. There are fish on the "catcher's mask"/headdress and on the *obi*, and a fishtail pattern is even printed on the velveteen fabric. Knotted bits of stiffer fabric suggest lines and lures. An accompanying cart carries the fishing pole, itself

a ceremonial element. This piece was meant to be worn in performance, so that the different elements of the costume could be revealed to the viewer and wearer through movement.

Nininger points out that the performance costume, in contradistinction to the theatrical costume, carries within itself all of the information necessary to be understood by the viewer; any movement given to it by the wearer will probably derive from, or be inspired by, the piece itself. On the other hand, a theatrical costume is designed only as a visual aid for a specific character whom the actor must, through interpretation, bring to life. The first is an independent, self-sufficient statement; the second, a prop or visual aid.[57] *Going Fishing*, like other majestic and elegant performance kimonos, carries with it a sense of ceremony appropriate to a theatrical presentation and echoes an ancestry rooted in Kabuki theater and *Nō* drama costume.[58]

85 Susan Nininger
Going Fishing, 1978
Sewn and assembled
    mixed media
Collection the artist
Photograph by Roger
    Schreiber

Idiosyncratic Kimonos

Finally, there are individual pieces, which in concept alone derive from an unorthodox union of media and form. The *Priest's Winter Robe* by Susan Dumas, a macramé and quilted kimono, is one such piece. The organic and textural nature of macramé made it a popular craft in the 1970s.[59] Because it, like crochet, could grow in a free-form fashion, it lent itself to the replication of nature's patterns. Within the art-to-wear field, macramé was often combined with natural elements, such as feathers, gems, shells, and beads. It appeared in the form of nonstructural body coverings—halters, neckpieces, collars, and pouches. However, to use macramé in the creation of such a formal, rectilinear shape as a kimono is most unusual. In fact, Dumas explains, she was responding to the rigid nature of her material, jute, by sub-jecting it to the straight lines of the kimono and then consciously softening it with the quilted details. But most impressive is the labor-intensive aspect of this project. Dumas was attracted by the staggering physicality of the process required to create this large, ceremonial piece: the feel of jute running through her fingers during the weeks of cutting cord and wrapping, the daily activities of walking and measuring, the hours spent on each row of macramé.[60] The labor-intensive nature of this piece binds it closely to the spirit of the Art-to-Wear Movement. It also speaks to the Japanese love and respect for long-term projects and processes.

86   Julia Hill
      Birds in the Future, 1977
      Resist-dyed silk
      Collection Jim and Carol Francis

87   Susan Dumas
      Priest's Winter Robe, 1983
      Quilted and knotted cotton and jute
      Collection Mr. and Mrs. Richard Bernstein

A Reflection on the Art-to-Wear Kimono

In reflecting on the diverse kimonos that artists have created since the early 1970s, certain dichotomies come to light. Among these are the contrasting perceptions of the kimono as a fluid sensual form, gracefully draped and comfortably worn, versus a rigid, restrictive garment more structural and architectonic than body oriented, and, therefore, not easily wearable.

Historically, the kimono has been all of these things. It was fluid and sensual in the hedonistic Momoyama period (1568–1600) and into the Edo period, when feminine beauty was mirrored in the lavish and richly patterned kimono, loosely sashed with a slender *obi*. From the eighteenth century onward, the kimono became increasingly formal and restrictive as the *obi* evolved to a stiffer, wider, corsetlike sash, narrowing the silhouette and encasing the body within a tubular form.[61]

It is, therefore, natural and correct that Western artists filtered their perceptions of the kimono through personal experience and vision as well as through the limitations and strengths of the chosen medium. The more wearable, body-conscious pieces, such as those by Kozel, Hedstrom, Hill, Darwall, and Ray, tend to emerge from fields utilizing or creating a more supple, fabric-like surface design and weaving. Those artists working with a heavier, stiffer, more complex cloth that does not easily drape—notably Westphal, Dumas, Martens, Harding, Manuel, and Porcella—focus on the kimono as a T-shaped wall piece, sculpture, or ceremonial garment.

While wearability may not always be a prime concern, reference to the human body remains a constant and central issue. The structural sense of space created by the three-dimensional form intrigues the wide range of artists working within the format of this universal shape. To each, the kimono represents a basic, distilled essence of a garment removed from the demands of fashion. And to each, the simple, elegant line of the silhouette provides a broad canvas on which to express the individuality of the artist's myriad creative gifts.

88   Sharron Hedges
Desert Ikat, 1989
Loom-knitted silk
Collection Sue Hollingsworth

NOTES

1. Sharron Hedges, as quoted by Susan Stowens, "Dina Schwartz & Sharron Hedges," *Currant* (Aug./Sept./Oct. 1976), 47.

2. This phrase was the title of an exhibition and book organized by the Los Angeles County Museum, Dale Gluckman, Sharon Takeda, *When Art Became Fashion: Kosode in Edo Period Japan* (Los Angeles: Los Angeles County Museum, 1992).

3. Michael Schwartz and Neil Ortenberg, editor's preface to *On the Bus*, by Paul Perry (New York: Thundermouth Press, 1990), xx.

4. Ibid.

5. Ibid.

6. Andy Warhol and Pat Hackett, *Popism: The Warhol Sixties* (San Diego, New York, London: Harcourt Brace Jovanovich, 1980), 37.

7. Peter Beagle, *American Denim: A New Folk Art* (New York: Harry N. Abrams, 1975), 8.

8. Alexandra Jacopetti, *Native Funk & Flash: An Emerging Folk Art* (Centerville, Massachusetts: Scrimshaw Press, 1974), 5.

9. Peter Beagle, *American Denim*, front flap. The decorated denim contest sponsored by Levi Strauss & Co. was organized by Richard M. Owens, who conceived the idea for the book. From almost ten thousand entries, seventy-five winning garments were shown at the Museum of Contemporary Crafts in New York, in an exhibition that subsequently traveled to over a dozen museums around the United States and Europe.

10. Ibid., 10. Judy Manley quoted by Beagle.

11. E.g., "Kay Lee [Manuel] didn't want her work to be removed from and out of touch with life and real people. She didn't want it geared for gallery/museum display, but rather 'in homes, on the street, available to and interacting with people.'" In "K. Lee Manuel, Wearable Dreams," *Fiberarts* 3, no. 5 (1976): 12.

12. Janet Lipkin quoted in Doug Bullis, "Janet Lipkin's Clothing," *Ornament* 12, no. 3 (1989): 57.

13. Dina Knapp quoted in Julie Schafler Dale, *Art to Wear* (New York: Abbeville Press, 1986), 23.

14. Ibid., 293.

15. William Hosley, *The Japan Idea: Art and Life in Victorian America* (Hartford, Conn.: Wadsworth Atheneum, 1990), 29.

16. See Nancy Corwin, "The Kimono Mind: *Japonisme* in American Culture," herein, for further discussion of dress reform.

17. Patrick McCaughey, foreword to *The Japan Idea: Art and Life in Victorian America*, by William Hosley, 6.

18. Edward Lucie-Smith, "Craft Today: Historical Roots and Contemporary Perspectives," *Craft Today: Poetry of the Physical*, Paul Smith and Edward Lucie-Smith eds. (New York: American Craft Museum and Weidenfeld & Nicholson, 1986), 35.

19. Jacopetti, *Native Funk & Flash*, 23.

20. Edward Lucie-Smith, *Craft Today: Poetry of the Physical*, 37.

21. Max Tilke, *Costume Patterns and Designs* (London: A. Zwemmer, 1956).

22. Dorothy Burnham, *Cut My Cote* (Toronto: Royal Ontario Museum, MacKinnon-Mancur, 1973).

23. Folkwear Patterns (1975–1987) was founded by Barbara Garvey, Alexandra Jacopetti, and Ann Wainwright in Forestville, California. Their patterns have been reissued by the Taunton Press, Newtown, Connecticut, since 1990.

24. Jacopetti, *Native Funk & Flash*, 13.

25. Jean Williams Cacicedo quoted in Dale, *Art to Wear*, 43.

26. The interest in traditional textile techniques among fiber artists in the 1960s and 1970s owes a great debt to Charles Edmund (Ed) Rossbach, fiber art pioneer and professor of design at the University of California, Berkeley, from 1950 until his retirement in 1979. For a full understanding of his importance to the field see Ann Pollard Rowe and Rebecca A. T. Stevens, eds., *Ed Rossbach: 40 Years of Exploration and Innovation in Fiber Art* (Asheville, North Carolina, and Washington, D.C.: Lark Books and The Textile Museum, 1990).

27. Sharron Hedges, telephone interview with author, March 21, 1994.

28. Dina Knapp quoted in Dale, *Art to Wear*, 31.

29. Linda Mendelson, interview with author, February 21, 1994.

30. Jo Ann C. Stabb, "The Wearable Movement: A Critical Look at the State of the Art," *Surface Design Journal* (fall 1988): 31.

31. Linda Mendelson, interview with author, March 4, 1994. The term *knitting loom* was gradually adopted by those within the Art-to-Wear Movement to differentiate it from the large, commercial machines used by the knitwear industry. The first looms used by the seventies knitters were akin to the traditional Jacquard loom, using hand-punched cards to transmit the information to the knitting mechanism. The next generation of machines, such as the Passap, Superba, and Brother, responded to electronic marks hand-penciled on acetate cards to indicate pattern. Currently, the most sophisticated of the home machines are computer compatible and capable of reading pattern directly from the mechanism. Cross-pollination between the home-knitters and the commercial knitwear industry had both positive and negative impact on the Art-to-Wear Movement. On the one hand, technologies were shared; on the other, the rich aesthetic synonymous with hundreds of hours of labor was easily adapted and displaced by commercial imitations in the marketplace.

32. Ana Lisa Hedstrom, telephone interview with author, March 10, 1994.

33. Ibid.

34. Six hundred people attended this landmark conference; it led to the official founding of

the Surface Design Association in September 1976, in Bloomington, Indiana, at which Elsa Sreenivasam was named the first president. Since that time, the Surface Design Association has sponsored a national conference every second year beginning in 1978 at Purdue University in West Lafayette, Indiana. Its newsletter quickly evolved into the highly respected *Surface Design Journal*. The purpose of the association remains to promote surface design as an art form, to network, teach, and provide technical services pertaining to the how, where, and who of surface design. Elsa Sreenivasam, telephone interview with author, March 8, 1994.

35. Jack Lenor Larsen, *The Dyer's Art: Ikat, Batik, Plangi* (New York, Cincinnati, Toronto, London: Van Nostrand Reinhold, 1976).

36. Ina Kozel quoted in Dale, *Art to Wear*, 261.

37. Marianne Strengell (b. 1909) was a Finnish textile designer-weaver who immigrated to the United States in 1936. She began teaching at the Cranbrook Academy of Art in 1937 and became head of the weaving department in 1942, retiring in 1961. As a teacher and designer for industry she had a far-reaching influence on weaving in the United States.

Dorothy Liebes (1899–1972) was a California designer who opened a hand-weaving studio in San Francisco in 1930 that specialized in custom orders for architects and decorators. She moved her studio to New York in 1952 and eventually turned her talents to industrial work and mass production. She is best remembered for her vibrant color combinations (e.g., red and pink and green and blue) and her use of Lurex and other man-made yarns in combination with natural yarns.

Jack Lenor Larsen (b. 1927) is a writer, artist, and internationally known designer of textiles who in 1952 founded Jack Lenor Larsen Inc., a firm whose name is synonymous with exquisite textiles and rugs for residential and commercial interiors.

38. Mildred Constantine and Jack Lenor Larsen, *Beyond Craft: The Art Fabric* (New York, Cincinnati, Toronto, London: Van Nostrand Reinhold, 1972).

39. Randall Darwall, telephone interview with author, February 24, 1994.

40. The craft fair has played a significant role since the late sixties vis-à-vis the resurgence of the contemporary craft movement in America. These events provided the opportunity for craftspeople to make direct contact with their public as well as their peers. Although once geared toward the exhibition and sale of one-of-a-kind works and a comfortable arena for many major talents in the field, these fairs have become increasingly production oriented. While sustaining the life of handwork in this country, they have diverted many artist-craftspeople from the creation of unique pieces.

41. Randall Darwall, telephone interview with author, April 21, 1993.

42. See note 23 for information on Folkwear Patterns.

43. See Yoshiko Wada, "The History of the Kimono," herein, for discussion of these garment types.

44. Barbara Garvey, telephone interview with author, March 6, 1994. Of the thirty-seven contemporary interpretations of ethnic garments, three were kimonos. These include Marika Contompasis's *Trout-Magnolia Kimono*, Sas Colby's *Kimono Anaïs*, and Penelope Fried's *Silkmoth's Kimono*. Other kimonos included were two traditional Japanese pieces and one by Penelope Kraber that was the exact execution of Folkwear Pattern #113, the Japanese Kimono.

45. Jacopetti, *Native Funk & Flash*, 13.

46. Ibid., 15. See Corwin for a more complete discussion of the kimono in American popular culture.

47. See Corwin for a more complete discussion of the symbolic meanings of the kimono in American art.

48. The *yogi* is a raw cotton stuffed coverlet in kimono form whose use became common in Japan at the beginning of the Edo period (1600–1868). The *yogi* is much wider than a kimono. Michiyo Morioka and William Jay Rathbun, "Tsutsugaki and Katazome," in *Beyond the Tanabata Bridge: Traditional Japanese Textiles*, ed. William Jay Rathburn (London and Seattle: Thames and Hudson, in association with the Seattle Art Museum, 1993), 131.

49. See Wada's explanation in "The History of the Kimono."

50. Ed Rossbach was the first fiber artist to utilize Mickey Mouse as a present-day textile icon. He used the Mickey Mouse image frequently in his fiber art work from 1971 through the early 1980s. He says of the image, "Mickey Mouse amuses me as an image. It seems ridiculous to be laboriously picking-in a Mickey Mouse in figured damask, or to work it in needlepoint lace. In historic textiles it is so acceptable to see saints and classical figures portrayed. I think that I feel as comfortable with Mickey Mouse as those artisans felt with their saints and gods." Ann Pollard Rowe and Rebecca A. T. Stevens, eds., *Ed Rossbach: 40 Years of Exploration and Innovation in Fiber Art* (Asheville, North Carolina, and Washington, D.C.: Lark Books and The Textile Museum, 1990), 134.

51. See Glossary for definition.

52. Susan Summa, "Susan Summa: Miss Liberty Takes a Holiday," Mariposa Gallery, Albuquerque, New Mexico, May 25–June 12, 1986.

53. For a complete explanation of the tradition of illustrating landscapes and objects from nature on Japanese garments see Dale Gluckman and Sharon Takeda, eds., *When Art Became Fashion: Kosode in Edo Period Japan* (Los Angeles: Los Angeles County Museum of Art, 1992), particularly Kirithata Ken's essay "Yuzen Dyeing: A New Pictorialism."

54. Dale, *Art to Wear*, 132.

55. Risë Nagin, telephone interview with author, June 1, 1993.

56. Okakura Kakuzo was the Japanese-born and -educated protégé of Ernest Fenollosa, who was advisor and later curator of the Department of Chinese and Japanese Art at the Museum of Fine Arts, Boston, from 1906 to 1913. According to Okakura the tea ceremony is a development of a Zen ritual. He says "it [tea] is a religion of the art of life. The beverage grew to be an excuse for the worship of purity and refinement, a sacred function at which the host and guest joined to produce for that occasion the utmost beatitude of the mundane." Okakura Kakuzo, *The Book of Tea*, 12th ed. (Rutland, Vt., and Tokyo: Charles E. Tuttle Co., 1964), 33.

57. Susan Nininger, telephone interview with author, June 1, 1993.

58. See Wada, "The History of the Kimono," for discussion of *Nō* robes and Kabuki theater.

59. "Not only did the book [*Macramé: The Art of Creative Knotting* (New York: Van Nostrand Reinhold, 1967)] prolong the life of this ancient craft, but it initiated a surge of interest that gives no sign of abating. On the contrary, the number and types of people who do macramé continue to grow; the technique is being applied to an increasing variety of functional and decorative objects; and the demand for authoritative information on the subject is in evidence everywhere." Virginia I. Harvey, *Color and Design in Macramé* (New York: Van Nostrand Reinhold, 1970), dust jacket.

60. Susan Dumas, telephone interview with author, June 10, 1993.

61. See Wada, "The History of the Kimono," for a fuller explanation.

Interviews

Jane Axtell, August, 20, 1992

Judith Boyd, April 23, 1993

Jean Williams Cacicedo, June 3, 1993

Nancy Chappell, June 1993

Judith Content, July 23, 1992

Marika Contompasis, May 27, 1993

Randall Darwall, April 21, 1993; February 24, 1994

Susan Dumas, June 10, 1993

Nicki Hitz Edson, August 4, 1992

Barbara Garvey, March 3, 1994

Juanita Girardin, April 22, 1993

Tim Harding, August 8, 1992

Sharron Hedges, February 26, 1994

Ana Lisa Hedstrom, April 1, 1992; March 2, 1993; May 5, 1993; March 10, 1994

Julia Hill, July 24, 1992

Nancy Mack Howell, April 25, 1993

Jan Janeiro, June 9, 1993

Susan Kirschner, February 26, 1994

Dina Knapp, September 29, 1993

Ina Kozel, May 5, 1993

Susan Kristofferson, June 9, 1993

Susanna Lewis, May 17, 1993

Janet Lipkin, June 3, 1993

Linda Mendelson, July 30, 1992; July 13, 1993; February 21 and 28, 1994

Risë Nagin, June 1, 1993

Susan Nininger, June 1, 1993

Elinor Pironti, May 6, 1993

Jason Pollen, March 3, 1994

Yvonne Porcella, August 6, 1993

Debra Rapoport, March 8, 1994

Margrit Schmidtke, July 28, 1992

Carter Smith, July 22, 1992

Elsa Sreenivasam, March 8 and 10, 1994

Susan Summa, June 2, 1993

Deborah Valoma, July 20, 1992

Marla Weinhoff, August 6, 1992; March 9, 1994

Katherine Westphal, August 3, 1992

89 *Furisode*, late Edo period, mid-nineteenth century
Embroidery and *yūzen* dyeing on silk
The Textile Museum

Part Three

Toward an American Understanding of the Kimono

90   *Genji monogatari emaki* (Picture scroll of
      the tale of Genji), late Heian period,
      detail of the *Kashiwagi* (Oak tree)
      chapter showing a nobleman and a
      noblewoman
      Tokugawa Art Museum, Nagoya, Japan

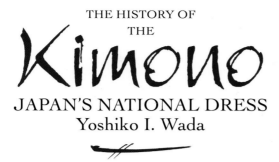

THE HISTORY OF
THE
Kimono
JAPAN'S NATIONAL DRESS
Yoshiko I. Wada

Kimono in Japanese denotes things to wear. *Ki* is derived from the verb *kiru,* to wear, and *mono,* thing(s). *Ki-mono* has been used loosely in Japan since the Meiji period (1868–1912) to refer to anything that clothes a person's body. However, in the Western world the term came to mean the T-shaped outer garment formerly known in Japan as the *kosode*.[1]

First Phase: Ancient Styles of the Garment Before Chinese Influence, Prehistory to the Mid-Sixth Century

Prior to the seventh century and the onset of the Japanese imperial court system, Japan did not have any garment that could be considered the precursor to the kimono style of dress. But it did have two distinctive modes of dress. The first is represented pictorially in extant pottery shards from the first century and in bronze bell plaques from the Yayoi period (200 B.C.–A.D. 250). The second lives on in the *haniwa* figurative tomb sculptures that date back to the late Kofun period (250–552).[2]

The *Wei chih,* or Chinese chronicles of Wei, written between 233 and 297, recounts the history of the Wa people who inhabited the southern Japanese islands. It was probably they who were depicted on both the pottery shards and, later, on the *haniwa* clay burial figures. From sporadic Chinese contacts over many years came descriptions of this indigenous Japanese population—they were a hunting and gathering society that wore tattoos on their faces and pink and scarlet cosmetic paint on their bodies for tribal identification. Unlike the Chinese, who wore caps to cover their heads, these eastern "barbarians," according to the Chinese, were essentially bareheaded, wearing only a cloth band around their heads. The men wore their hair in loops, and both sexes covered their bodies with a poncho-style tunic. This garment, belted at the waist, was made from two lengths of fabric seamed down the front, back, and sides with an opening for the head and arms. It gave the Wa people freedom of movement for activities, such as spinning yarn, milling grain, and hunting.[3]

Excavations of Yayoi burial sites have unearthed fragmentary remnants of woven hemp cloth attached to a dagger in addition to spindle whorls and cocoons from silkworms, which indicate that sericulture and weaving played an active role in these early peoples' lives.[4] Bronze artifacts from that time also show people wearing garments made with rectangular strips of cloth that may have been woven on a type of backstrap loom. The portable loom made use of warp ends attached to a support pole, such as a tree, while the other end was fastened around the weaver's waist. Weft threads were passed over and under the warp threads when the weaver produced tension on the loom by leaning away from the fixed support pole. The width of the weaver's body determined the width of the yardage that was woven; most Yayoi-style textiles were approximately twelve inches wide.

Archeological finds from the late Kofun period include a variety of low-fired clay sculptures in different sizes and motifs.[5] Some of these sculptures depict houses, horses, and weapons that were used during that period. Others show people dressed in ways that indicate their station in life—apparently, rulers and warriors portray the upper class, and shamans, court attendants, and farmers portray the lesser ranks. Many of the aristocratic male and female figurines are shown wearing fitted tops with a right-over-left overlap of the panels in the front (see figs. 91 and 92). Below the top, the elite females wear a long skirt that is pleated or flared, while the upper-class males wear pants. Archeological finds suggest that both males and females, for formal occasions, wore a shorter skirtlike garment, called the *hirami*, over their pants or long skirt.[6] Jewelry, in the form of necklaces and comma-shaped earrings, called *magatama*, was worn by both sexes. The *magatama* stone, together with a sword and metal mirror, symbolize the divinity and authority of the emperor. As with body paints and facial tattoo markings, however, jewelry of all kinds, including earrings, necklaces, and bracelets, became relics of the past by the end of the eighth century.

Second Phase: The Age of Two-Piece Garments Made in the Chinese Style from the Asuka and Nara Periods, Mid-Sixth Century to the End of the Eighth Century

There is evidence that some of the rulers on the Japanese islands made contact with China via the Korean Peninsula as early as the third century. Since neither of the previous garment types—the tunic or the fitted top—had open-necked, lap-over collars and distinct T-shape, they cannot be considered direct antecedents of the kimono; therefore, the historical thread must be traced back to Chinese prototypes. Robes from the Chinese Western Zhou period (1100–771 B.C.) and the Qin dynasty (221–206 B.C.) had rectangular sleeves, attached collars, and a front overlap—qualities imitated in future styles (see fig. 93). As early as the fourth century A.D., a garment much like those worn during the Chinese Han dynasty (206 B.C.–A.D. 220) was noted on images of priestess-queens and tribal chiefs in Japan (see fig. 94). However, it was not until the Sui dynasty (581–618) and the Tang dynasty (618–907) that clothing became part of the Chinese cultural hegemony. And it was this clothing that provided a paradigm for all Far Eastern cultures.

91   *Haniwa* figure showing an elite woman in Kofun-period costume

Great changes transpired during Japan's Asuka period (552–645), which coincided with the reign of Empress Suiko (593–628). As the disparate clans of the land joined together into a single state headed by a powerful central figure, Japan transformed itself into a country much like the one it is today. Japanese scholars began compiling historical texts.[7] The introduction of the Buddhist religion; technological advances in medicine, calendar making, and music; and the adoption of the Chinese political and jurisprudence systems were all part of Japan's transformation. So was the conversion to Chinese dress codes. Needless to say, these times produced a series of social and intellectual shock waves.

Throughout the seventh century there was very little difference between the types of clothing worn by men and women. Regardless of gender, members of the aristocracy wore similar Chinese-style upper body garments and skirts for ceremonial occasions. Additionally, a long skirt, called the *mo,* was worn by Japanese women, while men wore pants, or *hakama,* below their skirtlike apparel.

Gone were the tribal markings and adornments from the earlier period. Being civilized in the eighth century meant being like the Chinese. The kinds of garments worn by women on Japanese tomb murals in the late seventh century were like those that could have been seen in any Chinese palace during that same time period (see fig. 95). Following the relocation of the Japanese imperial court to Nara in 710, many other Chinese-instituted reforms took place, including the adoption of the court dress code, which was sanctioned by the Tang dynasty. Significantly, the Yoro Clothing Code, instituted in 718, stipulated that all robes be overlapped frontally from left to right in typical Chinese fashion. It is this stipulation that provides us with the kimono's earliest ancestry in Japan.[8]

The first evidence of differing styles in upper body garments for men and women appeared late in the Nara period (645–794). While palace robes for men retained their round necks from the Sui dynasty in China, women adopted lap-over necklines worn by Chinese women in the Sui and Tang dynasties. However, the lap-over collar remained a stylistic option for men. As in the Chinese Tang era, Japanese women began to tie their skirts over their upper robes rather than fastening them underneath as they had previously done in Japan.

92   *Haniwa* figure showing an elite man in Kofun-period costume

93   Qin dynasty (221–206 B.C.) male costume
     showing a *tarikubi* lap-over neckline

94   Han dynasty (206 B.C.–A.D. 220) female
     costume showing a *tarikubi* neckline

95   Tang dynasty (618–907) Chinese woman wearing
     a *tarikubi* robe with a short vest and a *mo* skirt

Since late in the Nara period, all kimonolike garments have had lap-over necklines with attached collars that form long lapels bordering the frontal opening. Japanese scholars theorize that this lap-over neck style derived from one of two distinct types of Chinese costumes identified by their collars—the *agekubi,* a high-necked or round collar, and the *tarikubi,* an open-necked or lap-over collar. Horsemen in the north China plains wore pants and a close-fitting tailored jacket with the *agekubi* round collar and straight narrow sleeves. Farming people of southern China wore a wide-sleeved, lap-over robe with sashes and a *tarikubi* collar, a garment like those worn during the Han dynasty. However, most Chinese scholars of historical costumes believe that this theory is an oversimplification because lap-over collars and straight sleeves are also found on figurines and sculptures from the earlier Shang and Zhou dynasties. The royal costume of the Japanese Nara and Heian courts, as distinct from costumes worn by other ranks, was likely a hybrid of two different types of collars worn at the same time. In the tradition of those courts, Crown Prince Naruhito wore a round-necked robe over a lap-over collar in his 1993 wedding (see fig. 96).[9]

Fashionable upper-class women in eighth-century Japan wore robes with *tarikubi* collars under high-waisted skirts. For the next several centuries, gender distinctions in clothing remained constant. Men wore garments in the *agekubi* style, while women wore the *tarikubi* style, which was the precursor to the kimono. The Shōsō-in Treasury at the Tōdaiji temple built in 745 serves as the repository for Emperor Shōmu's valuables and other treasures from the Asuka and Nara periods, including many of the garments. The *agekubi* robes, most of which were worn by palace personnel in a style called the *uenoginu,* differed markedly from the *tarikubi* robes. It is clear that overlapping collars did not

96 Their Imperial Highnesses Crown Prince Naruhito and Crown Princess Masako at their wedding ceremony in Tokyo, 1993
Courtesy The Imperial Household Agency

97 Tang official in literary costume showing an *agekubi* neckline

evolve from the round-collared variants but descended from different branches of the kimono family tree that was rooted in Chinese soil.

Upper-class women of the Nara period also wore a Chinese-style top, called the *kinu*, that tied in the front and had long, straight sleeves. Its under-robe overlapped in a similar manner to the kimono. The tubular sleeves were probably the forerunner to the *ōsode*, the large sleeves of the layered robes worn by Heian ladies. A vestlike sleeveless top, called the *karaginu*, was worn over the *kinu*. It evolved into a short jacketlike robe worn as the outermost layer of the *jūni-hitoe*, or layered robes with large sleeves, reserved for formal occasions in the following four centuries. Men wore an outer garment with a high, round collar that was fastened on the side, concealing a small-sleeved under-robe, the *kosode*, an antecedent of today's kimono.

Third Phase: The Age of *Ōsode* (Large Sleeves) from the Heian Period, Ninth Century Through the Twelfth Century

An imperial edict, passed by Emperor Saga in 818, called for Tang-style formal Chinese attire to be worn at court ceremonies. In 894, due to the waning strength of the Chinese Tang dynasty, the Japanese emperor Uta ended the custom of *kēntoshi*, the sending of emissaries and students to that country. This marked the end of the era during which Japan imported from China information on a wide range of cultural, political, and religious matters, emulating the powerful and influential Tang dynasty in every way. During the ninth century, a Japanese version of female garments emerged from the Chinese-style *kinu* with tubular sleeves and the *karaginu*, robe and jacket, which had been worn over *mo* skirts by elite women (see fig. 98).

98   Heian-period (794–1185) noblewoman in
      karaginu-mo or *jūni-hitoe* attire

cumbersome. This feature, too, became part of the *hitatare* attire in the Kamakura period (1185–1392).

Besides its link to ceremonial occasions, clothing of the elite also began to reflect age and marital status. For instance, married women were required to wear certain colors that differed from the colors worn by young girls. For all elite women, the wearing of the *mo* was still required for formal occasions. During this time, clothing worn by the privileged class at home was less formal and simpler than that worn in public. All clothing distinctions were less apparent in an intimate environment.

99   Heian-period nobleman in *nōshi* attire

While fashions for aristocrats changed dramatically, clothing for the majority underwent little change for almost a thousand years. Men wore a straight-cut, small-sleeved robe—similar to a short version of the present-day kimono—tucked into their trousers in much the same way as the popular *suikan*. Women also wore a small-sleeved, kimonolike garment with a simplified *mo* skirt.[14] The shape of the commoner's garment is linked to the kimono-shaped garment that evolved later, and the nuances of clothing and the fashion statements made by the courtiers during the Heian period are the antecedents of today's unwritten rules for proper kimono attire.

Fourth Phase: Emergence of the *Kosode*—Small Sleeves for Outer Robes from the Kamakura Through the Muromachi Period, End of the Twelfth Century to the Mid-Sixteenth Century

The dynamic and unsettled middle period of Japanese history, from the twelfth to the mid-sixteenth centuries, was marked by fighting among regional clans and their military guards for control of Japan. The *shōen-seido*, a manorial system established in 743 to develop and manage agricultural land and other natural resources, which had been the basis for centralized imperial reign over Japan during the Heian period, began to break down. It became increasingly difficult to collect taxes from faraway *shōen*, or manors. The military class gained prominence and power during this time because their initial role in trying to enforce the flagging feudal system led them to take control of many of the *shōen*. Consequently, the effectiveness of the *shōen* system began to wane as did imperial control, and a powerful military figure, Minamoto no Yoritomo, took control of the country.

Yoritomo established the *bakufu*, a form of military-bureaucratic government, in Kamakura, west of present-day Tokyo, which was considered at that time far away from the imperial capital of Kyoto. In 1192, the emperor, now relegated to nearly figurehead status, appointed Yoritomo as shogun. Yoritomo immediately took over the powers of taxation and began laying the foundation for the *bushi*, the warrior class, to replace the court nobility and control the political and social order.[15] The Kamakura *bakufu* appointed military commissioners, called the *shugo* or *jitō*, to efficiently control the large number of manors scattered around Japan. Eventu-

100   Heian-period lower-class woman wearing *kosode* and *hakama*

140

ally, the more powerful military commissioners formed regional feudal clans, which were headed for centuries by the daimyo, or feudal lords. Despite this new military commissioner system, the introduction of Chinese currency that came into Japan through trade struck the final blow to the *shōen* system by promoting open commerce and freeing the regional manors' dependence on the central government.

These revolutionary changes in control created a sense of social mobility that was reflected in clothing styles. In contrast to what they considered the decadent and extravagant life-style of the Heian courtiers, the *bushi* preferred garments worn by commoners. In this way, they promoted a frugal, practical, and rigorous life-style. These new leaders were influenced by Zen Buddhism, which was more austere and practical than the Buddhism practiced by the nobility. However, as the *bushi* established themselves as rulers, and as the shogun's court became the center of political intrigue as well as intellectual and social intercourse, the warriors themselves developed their own sophisticated styles in dress and the arts.

In the Heian period, the *hitatare* was the formal dress of low-ranking courtiers and commoners; during the Kamakura period, it became the basic garment—with some modification—of the *bushi*.[16] This suit, made from *asa*, ramie or hemp, consisted of a *tarikubi* upper garment with broad sleeves and a loose, pleated pair of pants. Crossed over the chest, the *tarikubi* was fastened with a cord and the top was tucked into the *hakama*. There was no rule about matching the color and design of upper and lower garments, but a matching set was considered more formal than a nonmatching set. The color most fre-

101   Heian-period lower-class man wearing *kosode* and *hakama*

102   *Bushi* man wearing *daimon*, a type of *hitatare*

quently selected was blue with either printed or stenciled patterns in gold or silver, or *shibori* (tie-dye) surface designs. Ankle-length *hakama* were worn for everyday attire and for battle, while long-trailing *naga-hakama,* worn over another pair of pants, were chosen for ceremonies and when an elegant and formal look was desired. When the lap-over neckline became part of men's attire in the Kamakura period, the robes worn by the elite—both men and women—became very much like the present-day kimono. The *hitatare* was worn over a *katabira,* a lap-over, wide-sleeved robe, and a *kosode,* with smaller sleeves and greater fullness in the body than today's kimono, was worn next to the skin.

Cultural sophistication and courtly elegance were considered secondary in the *bushi* society, and women's clothing became far less complex. The long, red *hakama,* the *mo,* the *karaginu,* and the extra layers of robes worn by elite women during the Heian period became a rarity. Instead, *bushi* women wore a long, white *kosode* that reached the floor under a set of robes, which included the solid-colored *hitoe* and the decorated *osode* robe, called the *uchiki* (see fig. 103). It was the *kosode* in white that now finally emerged as the direct predecessor of the modern kimono.

As women's attire became less cumbersome in shape and structure, its surface embellishment became more elaborate. Stimulated by Chinese imports, this new exploration in surface design was accompanied by steady developments in the designs and production of Japanese woven textiles. Along with overturning aristocratic control of the country, the *bushi* elevated textile patterning techniques and designs that were familiar to them as less affluent commoners to the level of accepted style. The common people's dress of the earlier periods was simple and made of natural white material with little decoration. Later, as seen in paintings from the late twelfth century, various *shibori* patterns became evident in their clothing.[17] Historical evidence along with literary references and paintings point to the probability that patterning processes, such as *suri-e,* pigment or dye stenciling, and *katazome,* paste-resist stenciling, were used to decorate men's and women's clothing throughout this middle period of Japanese history.

The Kamakura *bakufu* came under serious challenge in 1321 when Emperor Godaigo (1288–1339) tried to reinstall imperial reign. The *bakufu* sent the army, led by Ahikaga Takauji, to reassert authority in the capital. But contrary to his mission, Takauji overthrew the Kamakura *bakufu* and established a new government in the Muromachi district of Kyoto, and the Muromachi period began. The Ashikaga

103   *Bushi* woman wearing *kosode* under an *uchiki* robe and a *hitoe* robe

shoguns' authority over the daimyo did not equal that of their predecessors, however, and civil wars persisted over the next half century.

By the beginning of the sixteenth century, confusion brought on by the Onin War (1467–1477) resulted in the collapse of central authority. Local lords who had ruled over their individual domains were now joining forces and building armies out of feudal vassals and foot soldiers. The robes of these lords became powerful visual statements for members of the ruling military class. The most notable example was the *dōfuku,* or *dōbuku,* a full- or three-quarter-length cloak originally worn by commoners and military guards for warmth and for travel. During the sixteenth century, this robe became popular among the ruling warrior class, who wore it over many different types of garments, including *hitatare, kosode,* and armor. As a result, there were numerous styles, including sleeved and sleeveless. The *dōbuku* made for horseback riders featured vents in the back, gores on the sides, and broad sleeves. Some had a hole below the left sleeve to allow for a sword to be worn; others featured short collars that were sewn on the diagonal in the manner of the *kosode.*

Undoubtedly, *bushi* rule affected Japanese aesthetics from the late twelfth to the sixteenth century. The simpler life-style promoted by these early frugal warriors led to widespread acceptance among the privileged classes of a clothing style previously worn by commoners. However, different styles of clothing and embellishments began to appear, especially among the growing urban population. And eventually, the *bushi* developed a sophisticated and elaborate clothing aesthetic of their own.

Fifth Phase: Dominance of *Kosode* Among the Ruling Class from the Momoyama to the Early Edo Period, Mid-Sixteenth Century to the Mid-Seventeenth Century

Oda Nobunaga (1534–1582), a military leader who became de facto shogun and captured Kyoto in 1569, began the restoration of centralized rule in the country. Aided by a brilliant general, Toyotomi Hideyoshi (1542–1598), he was able to bring the warring factions of daimyo under his command. As a testament to his power—and to his lavish tastes—Nobunaga erected Azuchi Castle on Lake Biwa, northeast of Kyoto. His choice of glowing colors and rich designs set the fashion for ruling class attire. Even items intended for everyday use gave silent testimony to the ruler's penchant for opulent clothing.

Such extravagant tastes, prevalent during the late Muromachi period and into the Momoyama period, were stimulated by trade with the Chinese Ming dynasty (1368–1644) and with Europeans between 1542 and 1639.[18] This trade primarily benefited the wealthy merchants, the daimyo, and other elite people who had shown an appetite for imports from their close neighbors for almost a thousand years. But trading with Europe led Japan's privileged classes to absorb markedly foreign products and styles. Most noticeable were guns, textile materials, and decorative patterns that were used largely by the military, further enhancing the status of warrior lords. As evidence of the aesthetics and values of this period, *jinbaori,* or battlefield jackets, were made out of imported wool and furs that had never been seen before in Japan. Reminiscent of European coats, some of these jackets were trimmed with imported gold braid, and a few were decorated with an appliquéd European ship design.

Exotic imported fabrics were also used in the accoutrements for the newly popular tea ceremony practiced by the wealthy. The small-sleeved kimono, the *kosode*, which had been worn as an outer garment by military guards and lower-class men and women for hundreds of years, gradually made its way into the everyday wardrobe of all classes. Prior to this time, members of the ruling nobility had worn the *kosode* only as an intimate undergarment or inner robe. The *bushi* men of the late Muromachi period wore *kosode* under their *hitatare* or *kataginu*, depending on the formality of the occasion. With the popularity of the informal sleeveless *kataginu*, the men's *kosode* became more visible and acquired more decoration.

104 *Bushi* man wearing a formal suit called *kamishimo* (*kataginu* and *naga-hakama*)

The men's *kosode* was often decorated by selective warp-resist dyeing, which created dramatic bands of color or a large checkerboard design. These designs, later called *noshime*, became a favorite choice for the crested *kosode* worn by *bushi* under their *kamishimo* during official occasions of the Edo period.[19] The crested kimono robe was decorated across the upper part of the garment with one, three, or five family crests, depending on the degree of formality required. The most formal *noshime kosode* was always five-crested with the design placed in a band around the waist. Therefore, peeking out the sides of the *kamishimo* was a band of decoration, often of plaid, stripes, or *kasuri*, warp-resist—dyed patterns.

Dōbuku robes decorated in the *tsujigahana* style were among the most elegantly wrought textiles fabricated in Kyoto during the Muromachi and Momoyama periods.[20] This pictorial style was made with one or a combination of several of the following surface decoration techniques: *shibori*, *kaki-e*, *suri-haku*, and *nui-haku*. The *shibori*—Japanese version of the tie-dye—used in these textiles were of the *kanoko*, or bound-dots, and *nui-shibori*, or stitch-resist, types. After the thread binding was applied, the fabric was either immersed completely or dipped selectively in dye. *Kaki-e*, or brush painting, often included much shading and feathering to enhance delicate floral patterns or scenery. *Suri-haku*, or gold- or silver-leaf stenciling, and *nui-haku*, a kind of embroidery, were also used. One extant *tsujigahana*-style *dōbuku* with an elegant pine tree design was owned by regent Toyotomi Hideyoshi, who reunited Japan under central rule. Hideyoshi had a vast and exotic wardrobe made from gorgeously patterned Japanese and Chinese silks as well as from imported furs and velvet. Records show that he owned numerous *dōbuku* in the *tsujigahana* style, though only a few such robes have survived.[21]

Under Hideyoshi's rule following the death of Oda Nobunaga in 1582, some of the country's finest castles were erected. Osaka Castle, built in 1583, established Osaka as a symbol of military power in western Japan. By the seventeenth century, Osaka was also an active center of commerce.[22] Momoyama Castle, built in 1596 south of Kyoto in a region called Fushimi, lent its name to the time period extending from Nobunaga's rise to power through the beginning of Tokugawa Ieyasu's rule. Ieyasu, the most powerful of the five daimyo entrusted with the task of protecting the late Hideyoshi's son, had himself, instead of his charge, proclaimed shogun by the emperor in 1603. He established the *bakufu* that same year in Edo, which is present-day Tokyo, and the center of political, social, and commercial activities shifted to eastern Japan. Because the Tokugawa family controlled the country for the next 250 years, the Edo period is also called the Tokugawa period.

Bushi women generally wore a floor-length *kosode*, an inner robe, with another long white *kosode*, called an *aigi*, over it. For formal occasions, a long, highly decorated robe with small sleeves, called an *uchiki* or *uchikake*, was worn over the *aigi* (see fig. 105). This *uchiki* was simpler than the one from the Kamakura period. Eventually, the *uchiki* was reserved for very special occasions or, during the summer, it was tied around the waist with the top part folded down, revealing the white *kosode*.[23] Other inventive ways of wearing a *kosode* and an *uchiki*, the two kimono-type robes, were recorded in many detailed and lively paintings of the sixteenth century. In the early seventeenth century, female entertainers and privileged urbanites often wore a *kosode* without a train or an *uchiki* for most occasions. By belting it around the waist with a plaited cord, called a *nagoya-obi*, they created sweeping movements of bold and gorgeous designs from the shoulders of the robe to the hem. As variations developed in the type, width, length, and knots of *obi*, kimono fashions became more elaborate and flamboyant.

Mostly fragments remain of the *bushi* women's *kosode* and *uchikake*, or outer robes, from this period, but the designs from feminine *tsujigahana* textiles that do exist are unequaled in elegance and subtle beauty. Flowers, such as camellias, wisteria, and hydrangeas were depicted with dew drops and other details. Tiny holes or tears on petals and leaves were delicately filled in by *sumi* ink brush strokes. The unique aesthetics of these textiles depicting the beauty of ephemeral things symbolize the uncertain fate of the *bushi* women in this warrior society.[24]

105 *Bushi* woman wearing an *uchikake* over *aigi* and *kosode* robes

A remarkable kimono-shaped robe developed during this era in the *Nō* theater, which was first patronized by the shogun Ashikaga Yoshimitsu (1358–1408) and later made a key part of male *bushi* cultural activities. *Nō* theater costumes began as real-life clothing worn by people from all walks of fourteenth-century life who formed the basis of *Nō* theater characters. But, like the *bushi* era, which evolved from a relatively simple warrior culture to the lavish reigns of Nobunaga and Hideyoshi, the *Nō* theater displayed increased opulence as it developed during the sixteenth century. The *Nō* costumes, called *Nō-shōzoku*, grew in size, and the silk brocaded robes were woven to create a rich, thick, stiff garment. They projected an exaggerated, angular presence of wealth and power on the stage.[25] During the Edo period, the extravagant *Nō* costumes became treasures of powerful daimyo families—including the Ii, Mōri, Maeda, and Tokugawa families—and a large number of fine examples have been preserved in excellent condition. Many of the costumes, constructed in a basic T

106   *A Picnic Party*, Edo period, seventeenth century,
      Ukiyo-e school
      Color and ink on paper panel
      Freer Gallery of Art, Smithsonian Institution,
      04.56

106a Detail from *A Picnic Party* showing women
      wearing the *kosode* in various styles
      Edo period, early seventeenth century,
      Ukiyo-e school
      Color and ink on paper panel
      Freer Gallery of Art, Smithsonian Institution,
      04.54

shape, resembled oversized *kosode*. Although there were some differences in their proportions, some early examples of *Nō* robes and *kosode* shared the same popular design of the period. When discovered by the West early in the twentieth century,[26] these *Nō* costumes were viewed simply as "kimonos" by the public, and the opulence associated with the kimono in the West largely resulted from this commingling of garment types.

Upper-class interest in lavish decoration and imported elegance culminated in the early seventeenth century into the expanded and high-spirited design styles of elaborate *kosode*. The creators of these *kosode* were patronized by the wealthy women of both the ruling *bushi* class and of the *chōnin*, the urban merchants and artisans.[27] With tight government controls, many aspects of urban and artistic life were forced to become illicit. This created a new sense of aesthetics that was unique to the *chōnin* and contributed to the development of kimono style.

107   *Kosode*, Momoyama period
Embroidery on silk
Kanebo Museum, Osaka
This *kosode* is strikingly similar to the
   one from the Tokyo National Museum
   (fig. 108).

108   *Nō* robe, Momoyama period (1568–1600)
Embroidery (*nuihaku*) on silk with a design of
   flowering plants at the shoulders and hem
   (*katasuso*)
Tokyo National Museum

109 *Nō* robe, Edo period, late eighteenth century
     Karaori (brocade) with *shimekiri* (resist-dyed
        warp) on silk
     The Textile Museum

Sixth Phase: Further Development of *Kosode* in Urban Life, Late Seventeenth Century to Mid-Nineteenth Century (Mid- to Late Edo Period)

Since the unification of Japan in the late sixteenth century, the daimyo concentrated their forces in regional castle towns, contributing to the urbanization of many parts of the country. Expanded interregional trade and the consolidation of military power under various regional daimyo directed by one central government reinforced daimyo's authority over their vassals. This separated the *bushi* from the rest of society, not economically but socially, and strengthened ties within *bushi* society. The government enforced a rigid social order, based on Confucian ideas of hierarchy that made ancestors, elders, and masters revered and loyalty to one's leaders of utmost importance. The *bushi* were placed just below the emperor and the imperial courtiers. They were followed by farmers, who were the poorest, yet constituted the majority of Japan's population and the most necessary to guarantee food production; the artisans came next; and the merchants, considered a necessary evil, were at the bottom of the social ladder. While *bushi* privileges and status stayed intact during this relatively stable period, the role of the *chōnin* expanded. To assert their authority and also to control the country's economy, the *bakufu* passed numerous sumptuary laws intended to restrain the merchants' economic assertiveness and curb extravagances, such as costly dress, among the *chōnin* and professional entertainers. The *bakufu* was also concerned about how this new urban culture influenced the lavish fashions of *bushi* women. Evidence suggests that the urban population was ingenious at circumventing many of the government's prohibitions.[28]

Kyoto, a centuries-old political capital and center of commerce, continued to serve as the hub of aristocratic culture where high-quality crafts were manufactured. Sumptuous silk, for example, was woven in the Nishijin district and embellished by the Kyoto dyers and embroiderers. Osaka grew from a temple town to a seat of military authority, becoming the largest port and center of mercantilism in western Japan. By the mid-eighteenth century, Kyoto and Osaka boasted four hundred thousand inhabitants each, while more than one million people lived in Edo. By 1720, Edo was ranked one of the largest cities in the world.[29]

People were concentrated in those three major urban areas along with a dozen smaller cities across Japan that together formed a network for the vibrant *chōnin* culture. During this time, kimono fashions prompted a multifaceted, fast-paced consumerism that can be likened to the ethos of current Paris and New York. On one hand, a majority of commoners developed their own subtle or understated style of fashion founded on discreet rebellion against the government's class-based restrictions. On the other hand, despite government prohibitions, a small number of disparate groups, including wives of the *bushi* elite, wealthy merchants, and property owners, as well as courtesans in the licensed quarters and Kabuki actors, continued to display the latest and most spectacular fashions.[30]

Due to Osaka's active sea trade and its distance from the *bakufu* in Edo, it was the place where the *chōnin* culture first blossomed. Osaka reached its height of self-indulgence during the Genroku era (1688–1703). The free-spirited nouveaux riches merchants, accumulating wealth through expanded commerce, asserted their power by indulging in a cultural life that paralleled that of the elite. The most visible manifestations of the *chōnin* culture—and what the *bushi* found most objectionable—were Osaka's fashion and theater. For example, extra-long sleeves designed with a machete-shaped curved outer edge, called *sogisode*, meaning "sleeves that kill," appeared at this time. *Kosode* with *sogisode* were often adorned with decorative crests, *date-mon*, and patterned by *suri-haku*. A Kabuki actor specializing in female roles or the son of a wealthy merchant could be seen frequenting the licensed pleasure quarter decked out in such lavish *kosode* and *haori*.[31] Through theatrical works and popular literature, news about clothing styles spread throughout the city and beyond.[32]

The perceived economic overindulgence and cultural assertiveness displayed by people wealthier than, but socially inferior to, the ruling class raised the wrath of stodgy *bakufu* officials.

Despite the strict social codes passed by the *bakufu*, the *chōnin*'s desire to express their own styles and to wear luxurious clothing did not diminish. They created a style of fashion called *iki*, an expression that may be likened to *chic* in French or *cool* in English. This slightly oblique aesthetic style was expressed in the way one carried oneself and in the use of subtle details in materials, patterns, and colors. These subtle details were not specifically controlled by law and therefore allowed individuals to assert their own style in clothing. A savvy merchant who had access to exotic imports might, for instance, use exquisitely printed Indian chintz in silky cotton to make his *juban*, which was worn as an under-kimono beneath a drab, coarse *kosode* in homespun silk or *asa* fiber.[33] These drab, dark *kosode* of *chōnin* men and women were likely patterned with fine stripes in varied subtle hues. A few examples of the enormous number of ingenious variations in these seemingly simple striped designs include *misuji*, or triple stripe, *katsuo-jima*, or bonito fish stripe, and *ryō-komochi*, meaning "accompanied by one child on each side." Government rules limited the extensive use of certain colors and patterning techniques, but the fashion trends being set by Kabuki actors and courtesans and followed by *chōnin* often pushed the limits of those rules. For example, the ladies in the *shitamachi*, the downtown district customarily inhabited by lower-middle-class *chōnin*, might use the expensive color purple seen on a head scarf of a star performer in a Kabuki play in small quantities for their own hair ties or *han-eri*, the decorative band that covered the *juban*'s collars. These *han-eri* were an ideal place to defy government restrictions against the use of showy or colorful cloth for *kosode*; only later in the Edo period did they become an important decorative element in the kimono attire. Then, *chōnin* indulged in wearing bright *han-eri* set off against dark kimonos decorated in subtle stripes or a small printed pattern, called *komon*. While most *chōnin* resisted the sumptuary laws by means of *iki* fashions,

others—the privileged city dwellers and entertainers—were more overtly extravagant and rebellious. These latter two groups became conspicuous consumers of fashion.

The trendsetters and pleasure-seekers of this period were often depicted in wood-block prints called *ukiyo-e*, pictures of the "Floating World." Donald Jenkins in *The Floating World Revisited* defines the philosophical basis for the world represented in these popular Edo prints as the opposite of the prevailing Confucian morality of the time. He calls it a "world that was at once real and imaginary," a place of "pleasure and aspiration" where "the notion of style was preeminent," and the sophisticate, the *tsū*, who carefully acquired his style, was the star of this world.[34] This style often took elaborate and ostentatious forms in contrast to the hidden elegance of *iki* and the monochromatic clothing worn by the majority of the population. Together, these two very different aesthetics—understated chic, or *iki*, and overt extravagance, or *hade*—represented the Edo kimono fashion aesthetic. Yet later in history it was the extravagant *kosode*, not the understated ones, that drew the most attention in the West.[35]

The same structural development of the *kosode* was seen in both *iki* and *hade* styles. In the seventeenth century, women's *kosode* began to show stylistic exaggeration, such as long sleeves and thick padded hems. In addition to the traditional *kosode*, called *tomesode*, which had rounded, short sleeves attached to the bodice completely around the armholes, a new style with long sleeves, called *furisode*, became popular among younger women.[36] Reserved for unmarried women and boys before *genbuku*, the ceremony into adulthood, this style derived from the ornamental *kosode* sleeve worn by younger children in the Kamakura period, which had an extra length, called *furi*, added to lend a certain charm. To counteract the restricted arm movement caused by this extra length, the underarm around the armhole was left unsewn.[37] As the *obi* became wider, the *furisode*'s sleeve grew longer until it finally almost touched the ground during the Hōreki era (1751–1764). This robe was called the *ō-burisode*, big *furisode*; an intermediate length was called the *chū-burisode*.

110 *Chōnin* man wearing a subdued striped *kosode*. A layer of plaid under-*kosode* (*shitagi*) and an elaborate under-kimono (*juban*) peek out as he walks elegantly yet nonchalantly, illustrating the *iki* fashion.

111 Unmarried *chōnin* woman wearing a long-sleeved kimono called a *furisode*

Young women commoners wore the *ō-burisode* for special or formal occasions, while daughters of daimyo and wealthy merchants wore it for everyday use. The traditional *tomesode*-style *kosode* continued to be worn by adults. Later in the Edo period, the custom of leaving underarm openings unsewn became common in all women's clothing to accommodate a wide *obi*. This changed the meaning of *tomesode* to indicate the formal, crested *kosode* patterned with a pictorial design on the lower part of the frontal panels worn by married women.[38]

In addition to the ornamental sleeves, numerous fantastic designs created by new techniques in weaving, embroidery, dyeing, and stenciling began appearing on the *kosode*. Ironically, sumptuary laws actually encouraged inventive dyeing techniques as people sought to create facsimiles of prohibited colors, such as *beni*, safflower red, or *murasaki*, gromwell purple.[39] The *shibori* techniques seen in the *tsujigahana* textiles of the previous period were used but in the more elaborate manner of *hitta-kanoko shibori*. Here, an entire robe was covered with a particular design by pinching minute pieces of the fabric together and tying them with silk floss before dyeing.[40] This labor-intensive technique created one of the most costly designed *kosode* types. Another popular way to embellish Edo *kosode* and *furisode* was the newly developed process of *yūzen* dyeing. Here, rice paste as a resist medium was applied in linear fashion from a tube resembling a modern baker's pastry tube, enabling the artisans to "draw" pictorial motifs that were then filled in by brush painting with dyes in a wide range of colors. The resulting *yūzen* patterns were light in feeling, yet vivid, fluid, and clear, especially when compared with the richly woven or embroidered patterns of the earlier heavy textiles. Contrary to the Heian aesthetics of layering colors on *jūni-hitoe* robes, in this period a singular creative statement—either one large, dynamic design or a minute, overall pattern—was made on the surface of the *kosode*.

In the Edo period, textile arts flourished as a wide range of styles and techniques grew out of the evolving Japanese aesthetic sensibility and artisanship. The fantastic *kosode*, *furisode*, and *Nō* robes from this period gave birth to the kimono we know today in the West. Those first "kimonos" impressed Europeans, who collected and studied them in the late nineteenth and early twentieth centuries. Many Impressionist painters, especially, pored over the *ukiyo-e* prints depicting Edo beauties and Kabuki actors wearing gorgeous "kimonos" in the manner appropriate for the illustrated setting. European fashion designers were also inspired by Japanese garments, in a similar way but to a lesser degree than Japanese of the Meiji period were affected by Western fashion. A reciprocal intercultural inspiration and influence at this time grew into the more recent East-West mixing.[41]

Seventh Phase: The Emergence of *Yōfuku* from the Meiji, Taisho, and Showa Periods, End of the Nineteenth Century to Pre–World War II

It was during the Meiji period (1868–1912) that the Japanese public was first widely exposed to Western influences. At that time, the Japanese government and people were forced to find their place in a global context—an undertaking that had far-reaching effects on the Japanese style of dress and, ultimately, on the significance of the kimono.[42] Americans demanded trading treaties from the Japanese following Commodore Perry's successful negotiations with government officials in 1854. The British, Russians, and French followed suit, and the Japanese policy of isolation of the previous two hundred and fifty years was over.[43] With the admission of foreigners to Japan, there arose concern for the preservation of Japanese national identity. Such sentiment grew when it was revealed that an 1858 treaty with the Americans contained tariff agreements that were disadvantageous to the Japanese.

Expansionist threats from Europe and the United States, coupled with the deterioration of the feudal system, caused the Tokugawa family dominance to crumble under the feet of the advancing imperial army. Some of the daimyo and low-ranking *bushi*, who were dissatisfied with the Tokugawa rule and wanted the country returned to the rule of the emperor, helped propel social and political changes. Japanese imperial power, based on the religious or quasi-mythical belief in a divine lineage, had been respected even by the governing warrior class that turned the emperor into a figurehead. The return of the emperor to real power in 1868 during this wave of Western expansionism played a critical role in consolidating national unity.

Clearly, Japan had encountered a powerful foreign influence before in its relationship with China. This time, however, instead of mostly emulating its strong foreign neighbor, Japan and the new imperial government were cautious of Western advances. The emperor and the Meiji leaders, fearful after China fell prey to the British and French appetite for geographical expansion, concentrated their efforts on the survival of their country. Politicians and educators made every attempt to move Japan out of feudalism. *Bunmei kaika,* meaning "Civilization and enlightenment," was their motto, and catching up with the West—even surpassing Western technological capabilities, while remaining Japanese—was their primary goal. This paradox of maintaining a Japanese cultural identity while undergoing Western-style modernization can be examined through the conflicting ideas about clothes and appearance at this time.

Seeing Western dress as synonymous with modernity compelled many Japanese to cast off their traditional clothes, now perceived as a sign of backwardness. As a result, the neologism *yōfuku,* meaning Western clothing, was created to make a distinction between it and traditional dresswear, *wafuku.* In foreign garb, or *yōfuku,* Meiji politicians at the turn of the century expressed their dominance over the majority of the population who continued to wear clothing of familiar conservative styles and colors. The emperor, on the other hand, seeking to popularize Western clothing, adopted full Western regal dress in his formal ceremonial attire. He criticized the previous court robes, developed during the Heian period, for being of Chinese derivation. This enabled him to justify his conversion to Western clothing since he was not, in effect, casting off pure Japanese robes.

In the mid-1880s a pavilion named Rokumeikan was built in Tokyo to emulate elegant clubs in Paris and London, and government officials and foreign dignitaries mingled there in high Western style. During the so-called Rokumeikan years (1884–1889), the wives of government officials wore only *yōfuku,* which influenced upper-class women and some geisha in Tokyo, Osaka, and Kyoto. Because of the artificial social scene at Rokumeikan and the excessive imitation of all things Western, a movement called "Restore Antiquity" began.[44] The ensuing critique of the 1890s stressed the problems with Japan's blind rejection of its own cultural heritage. Emphasis was placed on women's clothing, and claims were made that Western corsets were endangering women's health. As a result, women reverted to wearing *wafuku,* and the kimono took on a new symbolic resonance, embodying the essence of Japanese tradition—something it would do in Japan and the world for years to come. From this point onward, the kimono became synonymous with Japanese femininity, which ironically supported the Western misconception of the kimono as an exotic feminine garment when in fact it had been worn by both sexes and all classes and ages until the Meiji period.

Nevertheless, by the early twentieth century, Western-style uniforms were adopted by government workers, male students, hospital nurses, and other professionals, as well as by the urban population at large, especially men. Among the more highly educated urban classes during the Taisho period (1912–1926), wearing Western apparel became a sign of Western learning and an expression of modernity. Children, too, were sometimes dressed for special occasions in Western-style clothes, including lace-trimmed or frilly aprons worn over their kimonos. Many men began wearing Western business suits, which after World War II became the unanimous choice among Japanese *salariman* (salary men). The most prestigious, well-tailored suits in the world were made on Saville Row in London, and in Japan, men's suits came to be known as *sebiro,* a Japanese allusion to the name of that famous street.

As with Western clothing, men were the first to adopt Western hairstyles. In record numbers, they cut off their traditional topknots.[45] Women were consistent as well. Most retained the *wafuku* attire, and they modified their elaborate hairdos, only slightly, into a "Gibson Girl" type of bun.[46] This change, though minor, was a significant sign of the times. And it was one of several changes that women in this era made in their behavior and in their style of clothing. Women were seen going out beyond their familiar protected territories, and they wore their kimonos in a way that accommodated their new activities and life-styles. They were far from the cloistered, kimono-clad, erotic objects popular in Western imagination.

112   Meiji girls in formal triple-layer (*mitsu-gasane*)
      kimono with padded hem (*fuki*)

If women were not wearing Western clothing after the "Restore Antiquity" movement, neither were they maintaining the more restrictive kimono of the past. The trailing *kosode* with a wide *obi* knotted in the back or tied in the front was worn by middle- and upper-class married women at home until the Meiji period. By the turn of the century, the *kosode* was worn tucked up below the waist and the *obi* was tied over it, and knotted in the back, allowing freer body movement. With only a few variations in the *obi* and in the overall dimension of the garment, this was the way that working-class women had worn their *kosode* for hundreds of years. Beginning in the early Meiji period, this also became the way that urban, middle-class women dressed themselves in *wafuku*, and this is the same way that women wear kimonos today.

However, there were some differences in the kimonos of the Meiji period from those of the later Taisho and Showa periods, besides the fact that the earlier kimonos had longer sleeves. Meiji kimonos were only roughly divided by the occasions for which they were worn: one for everyday use and another for special events. In the later Taisho and Showa periods, *wafuku* became more specialized in its levels of formality prompted by the new social situations in which women found themselves. For ordinary daily wear, sturdy woven materials of all kinds were popular for kimonos, including silk, cotton, various bast fibers, and newly accessible wool, in dark colors, stripes, and plaids. Special silk wear, reserved for social occasions outside the home, was patterned with *yūzenzome*, *shibori*, *kaki-e*, or enhanced with embroidery. Silk kimonos with family crests were worn on New Year's Day and to wedding ceremonies. They were dark-colored with subtle understated designs even for single young women. The formal Meiji kimono usually came in a set of three kimonos, called *mitsu gasane*, and each had a thick padded hem, called the *fuki*. For most other occasions, middle-class women wore the *kasane*, a set of two kimonos consisting of the *uwagi* or *nagagi*, the outer kimono, and the *shitagi*, the inner kimono.[47] The set could be made in the same, or contrasting, materials and designs. It was worn over the full-length under-kimono, the *juban*, which was also dyed in elegant and sometimes peculiar patterns according to the wearer's taste.[48] Beginning in the late Meiji period, the popularity of *han-eri*, decorative collar bands, increased to the point that, during the Taisho period, not only the colors and the woven texture of the *han-eri* materials but the designs had to be up-to-date.[49]

For Meiji women, peripheral elements of the kimono, including the *han-eri, fuki*, or padded hems, the lining of the robes, and the knot of the *obi* added a degree of individuality to the kimono. The *haori*, a kind of kimono jacket, was reserved for men during the Edo period, but at the turn of the century some women trend-setters began wearing it in public. *Haori* were mainly black-crested or colored in shades of *azuki*, dark red, or *nando*, dark blue, and their longer length balanced the longer sleeves of the Meiji kimonos. In the Taisho period, women's *haori* became very popular and some were decorated with large pictorial designs, called *ebamoyō*. These designs were created by *yūzenzome*, a technique of paste-resist dyeing in multicolors. Also common in the Taisho period, particularly among students and working- and middle-class women, were relatively inexpensive *meisen* textiles, or warp-printed silks, decorated with bold patterns.[50]

All in all, the kimonos—both formal and everyday styles—worn in the Meiji and Taisho periods were relatively loose, flexible garments, rather than the tight and proper outfits they are today. More-over, there was a certain amount of free expression in the way kimonos were worn that made it possible to reflect elite elegance, geisha panache, downtown chic, or middle-class propriety. Many men in the cities, while they went to work in Western clothes, wore *wafuku* for special occasions and at home for relax-ation (see fig. 114). Professional men who still wore traditional attire publicly included Shinto and Buddhist priests, musicians and performers, and practitio-ners of the tea ceremony and other traditional arts.

113   Meiji woman in *wafuku*

114   Meiji man in *wafuku*

Eighth Phase: Remnants of Past Kimono Culture from the Showa and Heisei Periods, Post–World War II Era to the Present

In the twentieth century, Japanese people have steadily assimilated Western culture, first through encouragement by their government, but later, after World War II, on their own. At the same time, the kimono and *obi* together have become the sole representative of native Japanese dress. However, until World War II, most people in rural areas quietly continued to wear the traditional cotton or bast fiber clothing for everyday use. Most of these garments were dyed in indigo. Working-class men and women also wore robes that were a short version of the kimono. Referred to by various regional terms, these robes were tucked into the work pants, *monpe*, or worn over a pair of tight breeches, *momohiki*. Such humble textiles, which had undergone little change for more than a thousand years, were laboriously made, primarily by rural women for themselves and their families. Extant examples of these functional textiles show that they were thoroughly reinforced, recycled, or mended to give the fabrics maximum life. The techniques for doing this included *sashiko*, darning stitches, and *sakiori*, rag weaving with worn cotton fabric strips as weft.[51] Eventually, these traditional work clothes were replaced by mass-produced Western clothes that were cheaper to make, readily available, and considered more up-to-date.[52]

Not long after they were replaced, however, this functional work wear was considered worthy of collecting for its intrinsic beauty. *Mingei*, the folk art movement led by Yanagi Soetsu, who coined the term in the 1920s, contributed to Japanese awareness or rediscovery of these clothes and other items used daily by rural and working urban people.[53] However, folk textiles did not catch on with the majority of the Japanese public before the 1970s, when North Americans and Europeans began raving about the blue and white cotton textiles, such as *kasuri futon* panels, farmers' short jackets, and heavy *sashiko* and *sakiori* coats. These used folk costumes made their way to North America, where they were incorporated, along with a variety of other ethnic garments, into the everyday lives and work of artists, designers, and textile lovers.[54]

115   Child's kimono, late Edo period. The ramie kimono is decorated with *itajime-gasuri*, the ikat weaving technique of resist dyeing the unwoven warp threads by clamping them between boards.
The Textile Museum
Photograph by David Hays, Sotheby's

116 Farmer's coat, Meiji period, late nineteenth
    century
    Rag weave (*sakiori*) with cotton strips as weft
    and hemp as warp
    The Textile Museum
    Photograph by David Hays, Sotheby's

Before World War II, *wafuku*, or traditional attire, was fulfilling increasingly
numerous applications, reflecting the
many social changes affecting women's
activities. This, and an active marketing
strategy, fueled the expansion of the
kimono industry. As more choices became
available to them, Japanese women began
to express their individuality through
clothing. For example, a new type of
semiformal kimono called *hōmongi*, or
"visiting wear," grew out of the need to fill
the gap between everyday and special
attire for urban and upper-class women.
While the *hōmongi* was decorated with
pictorial designs on both upper and lower
panels, the most formal kimonos, the

tomesode or *edozuma* (see note 38), had
pictorial designs only on the lower front
panels. Another new type of *wafuku* was
the summer *haori*, made by various
gauze-type weaves that gave these kimono
jackets cool, airy, and feminine qualities.

These various kimonos and accessories
continued to be worn after World War II
and into the present day. Their popularity
may be due, in part, to the democratization
that occurred in Japan during the Allied
Occupation. Largely due to American
influence, increased numbers of middle-
class women could afford and felt comfortable buying the elite styles of kimonos for
special occasions.

The degrees of formality present in contemporary kimono fashions have their origin in the color-coded robes of the Heian period twelve centuries ago. To see that this code still has relevancy, one has only to examine the fashions associated with a modern Japanese wedding ceremony. Here, fashions clearly indicate gender, age, and family relationships. And now this age-old traditional Japanese clothing system incorporates a certain Western iconography as well.

During the economically stable period of the late 1950s and early 1960s, the people of Japan once again began practicing traditional customs that reflected old values. The marriage ceremony, the most auspicious formal occasion in contemporary Japanese life,[55] and the costumes associated with it became important vehicles to display these values. The nationwide celebration of the current emperor's wedding to Empress Michiko in 1959 helped to stimulate middle-class dreams of a traditional wedding with all its pageantry.

The bride in such a wedding becomes the prominent symbol of Japanese tradition by wearing, during the ceremony, the most elaborate variety of kimono, the *furisode*, sometimes accompanied by the *uchikake*, the Edo-style outer *kosode*. The groom generally wears a Western-style frock coat or tuxedo, although a few wear traditional kimono ensembles with *hakama* and crested black *haori*. The types of kimonos worn by other participants in the wedding are highly significant—the mother, aunt, and married sisters of the bride and groom probably wear *tomesode*, black five-crested kimonos with *susomoyō* designs; single sisters or friends wear *furisode* or *chū-burisode*, floor-length or medium-length swinging-sleeved kimonos; married friends might wear *hōmongi*, the "visiting wear." Increasingly, dressy Western clothes serve as acceptable substitutes for certain kinds of *wafuku*. As the wedding ceremony and reception progress, many brides wear three or four different ensembles: a traditional *furisode-uchikake* set; a typical white Western wedding dress with a veil; possibly a more showy *furisode*; and a Western-style evening gown, perhaps made of bright red lace (see figs. 117, 117a). Today, many young brides

who have never before worn a kimono choose to wear both traditional Japanese and Western ceremonial costumes. This reflects the typical Japanese juxtaposition of the familiar and the unfamiliar, keeping both Japanese tradition and idealized Western femininity intact.

By trying to counteract the decline in the kimono market, kimono industries have affected the role of the kimono in postwar Japan. Targeting primarily young people, they introduced a line of ready-to-wear polyester kimonos that need minimal care; presented a kimono package in coordinated, contemporary hues that eliminated the need of choosing accessories to complete an outfit; and hired Western apparel designers, both Japanese and European, to design kimonos. A successful campaign by a department store in Osaka in 1989 promoted the casual *yukata*, summer cotton kimonos, with a clearly nontraditional merchandising strategy. They marketed the *yukata* to women and men in their mid-teens to early twenties, with Western fashion designer labels and size identifications—for the first time, "S," "M," and "L" were seen on kimonos. Moreover, they displayed them folded or hanging from racks rather than as traditional bolts of kimono fabric, to be sewn later into custom-made garments. (For an account of the traditional kimono shop, see "Changing Attitudes Toward the Kimono: A Personal Reflection," herein, p. 171.) The new marketing strategies present these kimonos almost as an extension of a Western wardrobe, to which Japanese youth are now much attuned. As a result, these *yukata* have become the most trendy garments worn to traditional summer fireworks shows, *hanabi taikai*, which have become popular among stylish youth of the 1990s.[56] However, despite all the efforts of the kimono industry, most young people are *kimono-banare*, meaning they have been weaned away from kimonos and probably will not incorporate traditional attire into their twenty-first- century wardrobes. This could change, however, if cultural activities provide young people with new ways to express themselves through traditional clothing.[57] For example, kimonos could be instituted as special garb for certain school activities.

117 A typical modern wedding in Tokyo, 1993. The
bride is wearing a traditional Japanese robe
(*uchikake*).

117a Later in the ceremony the bride changes into a
Western-style wedding gown.

Another postwar trend by consumers and by the industry is to emphasize the artistic value of handcrafted kimonos. Because women own fewer kimonos and reserve the ones they have for special occasions, there has been an interest in acquiring particularly beautiful kimonos as art pieces for investment as well as for personal pleasure. These collectible kimonos appeal to wealthy, middle-aged or older women, and to celebrities and socialites.

Kimono fashion trends have been set every year by the spring and fall kimono collections of well-established department stores and kimono producers. Interestingly, most of the department stores, including Shirokiya and Matsuzakaya in Tokyo, and Takashimaya and Mistukoshi, which originated in Kyoto, began as either a *gofukuya*, a shop dealing with traditional textiles for kimono wear, or a *furugiya*, a used-kimono shop during the Edo period.[58] In addition to the brand name kimonos from Western fashion collections, there are kimonos signed by individual artists, or *kōgei sakka*, who create works using traditional textile processes. Moriguchi Kakō, an artist known for his dynamic and colorful images of pine trees and plum blossoms, is a master of *makinori yūzen* dyeing, a technique that involves the use of fluid rice paste–resist lines and delicate paste flakes. Shimura Fukumi weaves silk *tsumugi* cloth in variegated hues colored with natural dyes. Her subtle and contemplative striped and plaid-patterned kimonos are reminiscent of the work of American color school painters.

And Taira Toshiko, an expert in the traditional Okinawan *bashōfu*, or banana fiber weaving patterned with ikat, has reestablished this age-old craft as a mainstream textile art.[59] Each of these three kimono artists has been designated a "National Living Treasure" or *jūyō mukei bunka-zai*, "important intangible cultural asset," by the government, which promotes the preservation of traditional arts and industries.

The high technical achievement of these artists' work and their creative expression of ideas serve as inspiration and a sustaining force in the traditional art of kimono making. However, as vital as the kimono garment has been for more than one thousand years, its current viability as an integral part of Japanese clothing is in question. Just as the vicissitudes of history have affected the clothing styles of the rulers and the ruled, they have altered the shapes and patterns of the basic kimono-type garment over time. But what effect will Japan's latest transformation have on the kimono? Will it survive the assimilation of a Western, particularly an American, way of life? If so, in what form and context? And who will wear it? Who will understand and appreciate the subtle colors and signs of kimono codes? It may be that the Japanese kimono will survive as art-to-wear, living through the work of international artists in today's age of global exchange. If that is its fate, the kimono will undoubtedly acquire new meanings and visual codes that reflect the issues and concerns of its twenty-first-century audience.

118   *Yukata* (summer kimono)
      Meiji period, early twentieth century
      Shibori (stitched, clapped, and bound
         resist dyeing) on cotton
      The Textile Museum
      Ruth Fisher Fund

Attitudes

TOWARD THE KIMONO: A PERSONAL REFLECTION
Yoshiko I. Wada

When my two sisters and I were younger, we lived in my maternal grandparents' home in Tokyo. We usually took our baths in the evening so that our bodies were fresh and clean before we retired for the night. During the summer, however, we changed our routine and took a short cold or hot bath before the evening meal. In those summer months, we could hardly wait to finish supper so that we could put on our *yukata* and run outdoors to participate in the folk dance practice sessions for the *Bon Odori* festival. This was held in the small town plaza in front of the train station every August 15 to celebrate the time when our ancestral spirits return to earth.

All three sisters wore fabric with the same design motif because our three *yukata* were made out of two bolts of cloth. We needed Grandmother Tsuru's help to put on our freshly laundered and heavily starched outfits. She separated the sleeves and the bodices in order for us to get into those crisp robes. We each wore a brightly colored, soft silk sash, called a *heko-obi,* which was always decorated with gay *shibori* patterns. As I ran toward the plaza in the warm evening air, I could hear the rustling sound of my long, stiffly starched sleeves swinging through the air beside me.

In the middle of winter, my mother sometimes took us to the public bathhouse in the evening. We regarded it as a special treat because the bath was much larger than the one we had at home, and we could be extravagant in our use of heated water.

Leisurely, we cleaned our bodies, soaking our bones in the hot water. Even though we had to walk home in the cold wintry air, we easily fell asleep because our bodies had been heated so well from the bath. My mother dressed us in thickly padded *tanzen,* which helped retain our body heat. The *tanzen,* made from red wool challis imprinted with orange and yellow roses, were worn over woolen long johns and undershirts. I remember thinking that the flower pattern was odd because it did not seem to be very Japanese.

During the past one hundred tumultuous years, the Japanese people have adopted vastly different approaches to life from those followed in centuries past. Even the clothing has changed; neologisms define and distinguish traditional Japanese attire, *wafuku,* from its Western counterpart, *yōfuku.*

The kind of *wafuku* known in the Western world as the kimono holds a special place in Japanese culture and in Japanese people's lives. It chronicles the history of the time period in which it was worn. Even in the short time span of my personal reflections, there has been a tremendous change in the way that the kimono has been worn and treated in Japanese society.

It was not until recently, when I began to research kimono history for this project, that I realized how different my Japanese upbringing was from that of my fellow artists, with whom I have been associating in the United States since the early 1970s.

I was born during the last year of World War II and brought up with remnants of Old World Japan still flickering through the shadows of confusion and destruction that had been wrought by that long, exhausting war and by Japan's wrenching defeat. In spite of the chaos and the lack of material goods, memories of my childhood are firmly bound by love and the values that were passed on to me by each member of my immediate family. My maternal grandmother, Tsuru, came from a family of kimono makers in Tokyo. (Two branches of Tsuru's family, noted for their expertise in *yūzen* dyeing and embroidery, are still well known for their production of fine kimonos.) Grandmother Tsuru was born in Meiji 14 (1882) and lived until the age of 90. During her long life, she embodied the attitudes and values of the remarkable Meiji period (1868–1912) in Japanese history. A large part of my education, with regard to the kimono culture, came from her and from her only daughter, my mother, Sonoko.

My interest in textiles was also fueled by my paternal grandmother, Motoko, who had twice gone to Europe with my grandfather in the early 1920s when Japan was experiencing an economic boom. They traveled on a luxury liner, and each night they dressed formally for dinner. However, Grandmother Motoko soon grew tired of appearing in the same kimonos. To vary her wardrobe, she substituted an under-kimono, the *juban,* for the outer garments, because as she said, "No Westerner would know the difference." The Western fashions in Europe captivated her, and she learned the art of dressmaking, millinery, macramé, embroidery, and fabric flower making while living in Paris.

Upon returning to Japan, Grandmother Motoko established a Western dressmaking school in Tokyo that operated from the late 1920s until 1955. Although she rarely wore Western-style clothing during the time that I knew her, her decision to establish a business featuring Western fashions rather than Japanese-style clothing shows how much the Paris fashion world influenced her thinking and attitudes toward art. This led her to provide me, from the age of seven, with the opportunity to study French-school painting in artists' studios.

As far back as I can remember, both of my grandmothers wore kimonos most of the time. The only exceptions were during the peak of the hot, humid summer months or when they were engaged in work that might soil their clothes or require freedom of movement.

119   Author's mother, Sonoko, dressed in a kimono with a frilly apron, early 1920s

Archival restoration of photographs by John Friedman.

164

In contrast to my grandmothers, my mother, born in Taisho 9 (1920), breathed the liberated air ushered in by the modern Western culture, and she became accustomed to Western-style clothing while growing up in Tokyo. Consequently, like other boys and girls her age, she grew up with modern ideas woven into age-old customs. Customs surrounding kimonos, for example, were still closely observed while Sonoko was growing up. However, babies and young children wore frilly Western aprons over their traditional kimonos, and most young children wore kimonos and *haori* with shoulder tucks and waist tucks until they were fourteen years old. Because Sonoko was tall for her age, she recalls feeling awkward about having to wear a "child's" kimono when she could have passed for a teenager.

Many young women living in the cities at that time added trendy Western clothing items to their wardrobes. However, with the exception of professionals, such as nurses, who wore specialized attire, most women continued wearing kimonos as a matter of choice. For example, in Figure 120 we see Sonoko and her maid, as they were photographed on hospital grounds in kimonos, while the nurse seen with them, in her white Western nurse's uniform, presents a striking contrast. Those who followed the avant-garde tastes of the time and wore primarily Western attire included celebrities and the wives of prominent doctors, businessmen, and politicians who had visited Europe.

For one of her trips to Europe with my grandfather, my paternal grandmother, Motoko, made for herself a 1920s flapper dress with traditional heavy silk crepe commonly reserved for the formal crested kimono. She had the silk dyed by a *yūzen* dyer, who placed a pine branch design in the lower part of the gown (see fig. 121). This combination was her own response to the *Japonisme* style very popular in Europe at the time. Enlightened intellectuals, some

of whom became political activists for the feminist cause, also followed the trend. These independent-minded women stood somewhat apart from the mainstream of society. Yet, the use of Western-style clothing was encouraged by the new government as it attempted to catch up with the West. This led to an increased awareness, among both working and upper classes, of the expanding rights of women—something that had not been seen before in Japan's patriarchal society.

120   Sonoko and her maid in the early 1920s, both in kimonos. The nurse is wearing a Western nurse's uniform.

During the Taisho period and the early years of the Showa period (1926–1989), the majority of young children—mostly boys like my uncles, seen in the accompanying photograph (fig. 122)—wore *kon gasuri*, or indigo-dyed ikat cotton kimonos, to school. Older children—again, mostly males—who attended urban secondary institutions wore Western-style uniforms. However, female high school and college students wore different uniforms—kimonos and *hakama* (see fig. 123), which were wide skirtlike pleated culottes. The long, red *hakama* had been worn by the imperial court ladies under layers of robes during the Heian period (794–1185), but after that time it was primarily reserved for men. Nevertheless, a widespread resurgence of female students wearing *hakama* occurred during the Meiji period. It was promoted by the women's school established for children of the nobility and the royal family.

At the end of World War I, a wave of economic prosperity in Japan led to greater openness between East and West. The wartime economy fostered technological advances, and the widespread popularity of the new motion picture

121   Flapper dress made by the author's grandmother from silk crepe dyed by a *yūzen* dyer in the traditional pine branch design
Photograph by John Friedman

122 Author's grandmother, Tsuru, wearing the
sokuhatsu hairstyle, and the author's uncles
wearing Western-style school uniforms. The
youngest boy, not yet in school, is dressed in a
kimono.

123 Taisho-period female students in kimonos and
hakama, all wearing the *sokuhatsu* hairstyle

industry increased Japan's fascination with Western modes of dress. At this time, most of my parents' relations lived in Tokyo, where the Great Kanto earthquake and subsequent conflagration struck in 1923, causing major changes. New buildings were constructed with steel, bricks, stones, and concrete rather than wood, which was too easily destroyed. Western styles of construction were introduced and many people who lost their clothes in the earthquake replaced them with *yōfuku* items. These mass-produced, ready-made garments were cheaper than custom-tailored or handmade kimonos. Western-style clothes were also perceived as being more practical than their costly kimono counterparts. Even the traditional underwear, *koshimaki*, which resembled a short sarong, was replaced by what became known as "Western drawers."[1]

When my mother was growing up in Tokyo, the city, still recovering from the earthquake, was the most progressive city in Japan. Equating *yōfuku* with modern attitudes, some private schools required their students to wear uniforms that were modeled after sailor suits or European military dress.

Sonoko had six brothers, five of whom were older than she. Well-educated intellectuals, they viewed themselves as modern, and they took pleasure in wearing European fashions. Moreover, they often spoiled their baby sister. On one occasion, the eldest brother bought Sonoko a green woolen cape embellished with a kangaroo fur collar (see fig. 124). Wearing it made Sonoko feel like a modern and progressive young lady. Capes, worn over Western dresses that were fashionable when my mother was young, were introduced along with large shawls during the Meiji period. They were readily accepted, partly because Japanese women often wore them over kimonos and Western-style dresses for warmth.

My grandfather enjoyed the same sort of Western and Japanese cultural crossover by wearing a *tonbi* coat. This was the Japanese version of the Scottish "Inverness," worn over a man's kimono as an overcoat.[2] The long bodice of this garment had wide, open armholes that enabled the cape to fit over the kimono sleeve. The addition of a kangaroo or mole fur collar gave the cloak extra warmth. Some men continued to wear beautiful, custom-tailored *tonbi* even after Western-style clothing became popular.[3]

124   Sonoko at age nine wearing a green cape with a kangaroo fur collar. Sonoko's artist brother, emulating the French artist look of the 1920s, stands behind her.

When Sonoko reached her late teens, she wanted to wear fashionable Western dresses like some of her friends. Her mother did not always allow it because custom-made Western clothes were very costly, and unlike the kimono, which can be worn for decades and sometimes for generations, *yōfuku* garments tended to go out of style very quickly. Nevertheless, Grandmother Tsuru occasionally indulged her daughter's preference for Western-style outfits. She once bought her a dress with a gray floral pattern from a well-known shop on the Ginza—the only place Sonoko remembers Western underwear being sold. Sonoko recalls her mother saying that a gray dress was *"jimi,"* meaning that its color was too subdued for a young girl to wear. To brighten up the dress, Tsuru added embroidery, repeating the floral motifs with colored threads. This made the dress more like a *furisode*, the type of kimono garment appropriate for a young unmarried woman to wear and which was often decorated with embroidery.

Although Sonoko was very taken by Western clothing in her teens, by the time of her marriage in 1941 she, like most young women of that time, did not think of wearing anything but *wafuku* for her wedding (see fig. 125). Female family members and friends also wore formal *tomesode* for the ceremony. Sonoko was dressed in the traditional *furisode* without the *uchikake*, which has become part of postwar wedding regalia. My father, Shusuke, wore a Western morning coat with tails, as did most of the other men in the wedding party. (For a description of a contemporary Japanese wedding similar to the weddings of my two sisters in the 1960s and 1970s, see "The History of the Kimono," herein, p. 158.)

125   Author's parents' wedding party in 1941. Bride is dressed in a wedding *furisode* without the *uchikake*. Groom is in a Western wedding coat with tails.

Being close to both grandmothers, I was brought up with traditional Japanese values as well as the newly introduced Western ones—European concepts first, followed by the more predominant American ones. This hybrid of Eastern and Western traditions was characteristic of the Showa period. For me, this time of diversity is full of vivid memories of both my grandmothers.

At the peak of her career in the 1930s, Grandmother Motoko was among those trendsetters who introduced European fashion elements to Japan. However, she had been raised in a strict, upper-middle-class Japanese environment, and as the only daughter of a well-to-do businessman, she retained her Japanese cultural values. She studied traditional Japanese dance and practiced the time-honored tea ceremony, art forms in which the kimono played an important role. She also loved the Kabuki theater and had a front-row season ticket, which I was often invited to share with her. It was tight and somewhat uncomfortable for both of us to sit through an entire show in one seat, but I enjoyed the colorful costumes and the visually exciting drama so much that I went along willingly. The costumes, worn by actors who played both female and male roles, have traditionally influenced the style of the kimono among the *chōnin*, or commoners, since the Edo period (1600–1868). In fact, Westerners typically gained knowledge of the Japanese kimono by looking at woodblock prints featuring performance artists from the Kabuki stage and courtesans from the licensed "pleasure quarters."

Grandmother Motoko was sixty-nine when she passed away in 1958. By that time, Western-style dresses had become fashionable, and techniques to make them were popular in my homeland. Many young women, preparing for their upcoming roles as housewives and mothers, attended *hanayome gakko,* or bride-training schools, where these dressmaking skills were taught.

During the late 1950s and 1960s, the kimono held a symbolic place in the minds of young, upper- and middle-class girls because it connected the past and Japan's cultural traditions to their current lives. It also helped retain a sense of classical values because the kimono had been an important part of the traditional dowry system. For me, the kimono was also the repository of my personal family history. My mother once told stories about trading her beautiful kimonos—many of which were made by relatives—for food. In those war-torn times, farmers were willing to trade food for used kimonos from the city dwellers. Immediately after the war, when material for making kimonos was scarce in Japan, many merchandise dealers solicited the sale of kimonos from upper- and middle-class housewives in the cities who were in need of postwar currency and goods. They then engaged in black-market transactions with the farmers and the nouveaux riches entrepreneurs of postwar society.

In spite of these hardships, my mother saved several special kimono wardrobe items, including her formal *tomesode,* a multicolored *fukuro-obi* that was brocaded with silver and gold threads, and a gorgeous purple *haori* with a family crest. All of these were worn on festive special occasions. She also kept her black kimono and *obi* for funeral wear, as there were quite a few funerals during those hard times. My parents' generation does not like to talk about the tremendous hardships they suffered during and after the war, but I believe that my mother felt the pain of losing her kimonos very deeply.

During the first two decades of postwar economic recovery in Japan, it was necessary for most of Japan's citizens to be frugal, so people returned to their traditional ways in their everyday life. For example, I recall seeing my aunt using the *hari-ita,* a six-foot-long narrow board, to block-dry kimono cloth after it was taken apart and washed, as well as *shinshi,* bamboo stick stretchers with needles on both ends, to stretch the laundered kimono cloth widthwise for drying. Before the advent of ready-made wash-and-wear fabrics, such as polyester, the kimono had to be taken apart each time it was washed, then resewn before the garment could be worn again. That made it possible for this perpetually recyclable fabric to be readjusted to fit the new wearer or remade into some other textile article. My mother also brought a *hari-ita* and the *shinshi,* standard items in a young bride's trousseau, to her first home as a married woman. Revival of tradition was important for women like my mother. And despite the rigors of daily life and a not-so-ample family purse, she still managed to have Western-style clothes made and to accumulate a trousseau of kimonos for each of her three daughters.

During this time, good-quality Western clothes were still custom-made, and my mother and I enjoyed selecting fabrics for various items, such as overcoats, suits, and dresses. In a similar way, we selected materials for different types of traditional kimonos. My mother had a couple of favorite *gofuku-ya,* or kimono shops, that she patronized in downtown Kobe. Each had a front window where an eye-catching kimono and compatible *obi* were prominently displayed in various colors, textures, and motifs. The motifs reflected seasonal signs, such as Hina dolls for the early March Hina Festival, or an ocean wave pattern that offered a cooling respite for the eyes during the hot summer days.

Inside the shop, there was a traditional platform area where cloth was reviewed. Many fourteen-inch-wide bolts of fabric lined the walls in display cases, while others were piled atop woven reed mats, called *tatami,* on the floor. At our request, the shopkeeper rolled out fabrics of different colors and designs, much as a magician would pull colored handkerchiefs and flowers from a hat.

In addition to making selections from the shops, my mother bought kimono items from an elderly kimono merchant from Kyoto who visited our home every few months. He wrapped his merchandise in a big *furoshiki,* a large, square cotton cloth, which he carried as a bundle on his back when he made his rounds from one town to the next. When he untied his *furoshiki* bundle—always an exciting moment— exquisite colors and textures spilled onto the floor in wonderful combinations. One or more of his kimono items always seemed just right for a female member of my family. He knew our ages, our tastes, our budget,

and any important occasion that might be coming up. He also had an overall knowledge of our individual kimono wardrobes. All of that was taken into account, together with the traditional seasonal calendar of events, when he selected items to carry with him. His remarkably astute selections often amazed me.

The kimono wardrobe that my mother selected for me included a formal *tomesode,* a black, five-crested kimono with dramatic pictorial designs. Following in importance were a *haori,* or short coat, which also had *mon,* or family crests, on it; a *fukuro-obi,* a special *obi* brocaded on one side with a flat twill pattern on the other side; an *ama-gotō,* which served as a kimono overcoat on rainy days; and several kimonos that were embellished with traditional handcraft processes, including *yūzenzome, rōketsuzome, katazome,* and *kaki-e,* as well as direct painting and various weaving techniques. It was also necessary to have a few *hitoe,* unlined summer kimonos, and several *naga-juban,* under-kimonos, in three different weights: silk for most seasons and occasions; patterned gauze linen for the summer; and casual *mo-su-rin,* wool challis, with its rather garish designs that had become popular winter wear.

My wardrobe also included numerous accessory items, such as the *obi-age,* a silk scarf decorated with *kanoko shibori,* which covered the surface of the fabric with minute dots that stood out like tiny white points of light against a dyed background. This type of scarf was used to cover the little pillowlike bun holding the *obi* knot in the back and was tied in the front above the *obi* as a decorative element. The *obi-jime,* a silk cord that held the *obi* knot in place, accentuated the *obi*'s front.

Proper footwear completed the trousseau. *Zori,* padded platform-style sandals or thongs made from patterned or solid-colored leather or brocaded fabric, were worn with most types of kimonos. I also had two pairs of *geta,* wooden platform thongs, or clogs. One pair was made of natural paulownia wood and worn with a country-style cotton or ramie kimono, and the other pair, made of black lacquered wood, was worn with a summer *yukata,* an unlined cotton kimono, often used as after-bath wear. These kimono ensembles and accessories had been fully assembled for me by my mother by the time I got married in 1967.

Now times have changed. My two nieces, born in the 1970s, own only a few basic kimono ensembles, including a *furisode,* a *hōmongi,* a *yukata,* and the necessary accessories—a very scant wardrobe when compared with their mothers' and mine. However, I know that my nieces will receive most of their mothers' kimonos when they marry, since many of the items will then be considered too bright in color for their middle-aged mothers to wear.

When I was growing up, the formal kimono was worn on special occasions, while Western-style clothing was popular for everyday wear. In the comfort of their homes, many people preferred to relax in *tanzen, yukata,* and other traditional attire. Contrary to the way *yukata* are incorporated into contemporary Japanese life, my mother told me that neither her father nor her brothers wore *yukata* during the summer. Instead, they wore *shiro-gasuri,* or white ikat summer kimonos. The male members of my mother's middle-class, intellectual family did not wear the kind of dress that was popular among local residents in the *shitamachi,* the downtown area.[4] I recall my own father wearing white *kasuri* summer kimonos, garments that were labor-intensive to make and, hence, not as casual as *yukata.* In other seasons, the *tanzen* was worn. It is a heavier garment made of silk or wool with padding usually added for extra warmth.

Although *yukata* and *tanzen* are rarely worn at home, variations of these garments have become standard amenities at traditional Japanese hotels and inns over the past three decades. In fact, the *yukata* now serves as both a housecoat and sleepwear, *nemaki,* for hotel guests. These simplified versions of the kimono closely resemble the American definition of the kimono (a dressing gown) in usage and construction. Recently, there has been a revival of the *yukata* in Japan, especially among the younger generation. As a result, *yukata* designs have become increasingly colorful

and modern, reflecting the Western fashion trends that appeal to contemporary Japanese youth. This phenomenon brings the cultural influences full circle.

An amusing trend related to me by my niece involves young women wearing *hakama* over kimonos for their college graduation ceremonies in Japan (see fig. 126). This trend—termed *re-to-ro,* meaning nostalgia, or to bring back old styles—refers to the Meiji and early Taisho periods, when these students' grandmothers wore *hakama,* sometimes with lace-up boots. Some young women in the 1990s also wear these old-style lace-up boots. However, they seem simply to be making a trendy fashion statement without the substance of their grandmothers' fashion commentary on women's position and role in Japanese society.

Since I have been in the United States, I have encountered students from Japan dressed in *yukata* at cultural events or some other international gathering. This seemed odd to me because dressing in a *yukata,* a casual summer kimono, would be inappropriate on such occasions in Japan. Nevertheless, I was sympathetic to the predicament of these young women. Probably unfamiliar with semiformal kimonos, they did not know how to dress themselves in a traditional manner with layered accoutrements. Most likely, they did not know how to make a big knot on their backs with the stiff *obi.* Besides, there's another problem—it would be too bulky and cumbersome to carry a complete ensemble of kimono attire from Japan for such infrequent occasions.

This lack of knowledge among young Japanese women concerning kimonos and how to wear them triggered a proliferation of a type of learning institution known as *kitsuke kyōshitsu,* which offers instruction to women on how to dress in traditional kimono attire and on different styles of kimonos and on what occasions to wear them. Students who advance to the highest levels in these institutions often secure jobs as professional dressers at beauty salons, where they ensure that all of the members of a wedding party (or other formal event) are properly attired.

Being of the postwar generation, I took a course at a *kitsuke kyōshitsu* on one of my long visits back to Japan in 1981. This course offered modern adaptions of traditional kimono dressing techniques such as velcro attachments and metal clips with elastic belts to hold the slippery layers of the kimono in place. Even after receiving a certificate of completion of the basic kimono dressing course, I still need nearly two hours to put on my formal kimono outfit.

This phenomenon indicates that clothing skills, once considered common knowledge and an essential part of everyday life in Japan, have become obsolete, and that young women now need lessons in these lost arts. One reason for this may be the cultural gap that occurred during the Showa period. The mothers of these young people grew up in wartime Japan, when material goods were scarce. And at the height of the war, the wearing of kimonos was discouraged because they hampered women's abilities to fight and flee easily, and because the silk kimonos' large sleeves appeared frivolous and incongruous in wartime Japan. The government and other citizen organizations solicited dress designers, including my grandmother Motoko, to come up with a new type of national costume, called *kokuminfuku*. Instead of promoting

126   University students wearing kimonos and *hakama* on their graduation day in Tokyo, 1994. Some are wearing Western lace-up boots and others are wearing traditional *zori*.
Photograph by Mihoko Kajikawa

practical Western clothing, because Japan was at war with a number of Western powers, the designers turned to traditional Japanese clothes for inspiration. Some early models of *kokuminfuku* had a kimonolike short top with narrower sleeves that looked like farmers' work clothes, and a pleated skirt resembling a short version of *hakama*. At the peak of the war, women became accustomed to wearing another type of *kokuminfuku*, which included *monpe*, farmers' work pants gathered at the ankles, and a blouse, or short version of the kimono worn on the upper part of the body.

Furthermore, when the Japanese experienced the economic boom of the 1970s, many young women began living away from home, resulting in their breaking away from traditional family-oriented upbringing and education. At the same time, for many college students and white-collar workers in big cities, foreign travel to Europe and North America became a fad, and clothes, purses, shoes, jewelry, and even perfume with foreign designers' labels became incomparable status symbols. Most young Japanese women at that time, and to this day, would not think of spending discretionary income on traditional kimonos, which they consider outmoded.

These are some of the dilemmas that younger Japanese women face with regard to incorporating the national costume into their current life-styles. Nonetheless, news of the recent revival of *yukata* in Japan indicates interest among today's youth in traditional events, such as the summer festivals, where those garments have always played a vital role.

As you can see from the changes in traditional values experienced by four generations of women in my family, the kimono is losing ground in Japan. This is due to many cultural and socioeconomic changes in postwar Japan, not the least of which is the widespread adoption of Western-style clothing. But patterns in clothing, like other patterns in life, influence each other as they evolve. And this interconnectedness offers a sense of enrichment and fullness even in times of change.

Needless to say, the kimono's use and meaning in Japan is quite different from its use and meaning in America. When I made the decision to marry and start a new life in the United States, my mother helped me compile all of the household and wardrobe items considered essential. Included among the many traditional clothing items was a black *shibori furisode*, a formal kimono with long flowing sleeves that is reserved exclusively for unmarried girls. Her justification for putting the *furisode* in my trousseau was that I—having just turned twenty—was still so young, and she thought the austere black-and-white color combination would be subdued enough for a married woman. She also believed that Americans would be unaware of the kimono code requiring wives to wear short-sleeved garments with quiet designs. She reasoned that if invited to a festive or formal occasion, I would have something to wear that would be considered a gorgeous evening gown by American standards. Although I do not remember wearing that *furisode* to compete with American formal dresswear, I did wear it—while still in my twenties—to two family weddings, one in the United States and one in Japan.

After the death of Grandmother Tsuru, an uncle who had inherited the family home cleaned and purged the house in a way that only Japanese people of his generation could have understood. The emperor, who had been thought of as a god, was likened after the war to an evil criminal by the U.S. occupation forces, and many people, including my uncle, had to question their time-honored values. As a result, Uncle Musashi burned the huge family Buddhist altarpiece and replaced it with a much smaller one because it took up less space in the home.

My uncle also intended to burn two boxes that my grandmother had filled with kimono scraps and old rags. Fortunately, my mother rescued those precious fragments, knowing that I would cherish those pieces of cloth as Grandmother Tsuru had. Reliquaries of a sort, those boxes contained various silks from kimonos, *haori*, and *juban*. Only a few remnants remained from her *obi*, however, as those were made

127 Repaired piece of silk kimono fabric from the
     author's grandmother's scrap box, early
     twentieth century
     Photograph by John Friedman

127a Reverse side of repaired fabric in fig. 127,
      showing patching with various colored
      silk scraps
      Photograph by John Friedman

127b Detail of fig. 127a
      Photograph by John Friedman

128   Fashion by Fifi White designed for Asiatica.
      Fabrics are recycled from used kimonos.

129   Jacket by Janet Kaneko Loo
      made with various shirred
      fabrics, including old kimonos

from heavier woven materials that were rarely cut. There was also a bolt of light-weight, red silk fabric for making a *juban*. Stitches running lengthwise through the entire bolt strengthened the frail cloth. The remnants kept by Tsuru must have come from her personal kimono collection and from garments made for other members of her family. My mother recognized a few of the patterns. Many of the fabric pieces were extensively, yet exquisitely, repaired, and it was moving to see them come to life when taken out of the boxes. For me, it was like looking at a visual prayer.

More than ten years ago, I gave one of the precious repaired silk remnants to artist Sheila Hicks after she had completed a textile project based on the extensive mending work done by nuns from a particular convent in France. She loved it! The piece spoke to her in a silent language that she readily understood, having worked with similar fragments and reconstructed bits of cloth. She found the nuns' mending and repairing work a life-sustaining, feminine activity with spiritual qualities. This was reminiscent of the way I felt about my grandmother's mended scraps of cloth.

I later saw this reverence for cloth and fiber in the work produced by artists who were part of the contemporary Art-to-Wear Movement in America, my adopted homeland. Some of these artists capitalized on the modular construction and exquisite materials of kimonos by simply taking apart new or used kimonos and recycling the fabric, creating a unique Western-style garment. Other kimonos, discarded by the Japanese, were imported to North America and simply used as dressing gowns. And still others have been collected and preserved as souvenirs for posterity by lovers of textile art.

An elegant fashion company known as Asiatica recycles old and imperfect kimonos and uses them as raw materials for the creation of new and beautiful dress wear (see fig. 128). Once the kimonos are taken apart and laundered, designer Fifi White sorts the fabrics according to color and texture. Then, she refashions these fabrics into elegant Western-style garments and accessories that appeal to those who

appreciate unusual or exquisite fabrics featuring unique styling, fine tailoring, and excellent traditional Japanese craftsmanship. White, who has a background in weaving, has stated in an article in *ELLE Decor* magazine: "We don't cut up things that shouldn't be cut up: Rather, we rescue them. I think of it as resurrection—a reincarnation."[5]

The artist Janet Kaneko Loo also works with rectangular modules retrieved from recycled cast-off kimonos (see fig. 129). Her process is akin to that of the deconstruction process sanctioned by recent work in the fine arts field. After the kimono has been disassembled into various panels, Kaneko creates new modular compositions by using a wide variety of fabrics and setting off individual kimono segments in a dramatic way. Then, she deconstructs the pieced fabric a second time using a shirring, or plissé, technique that blurs the pre-existing patterns on the surface of the garment. The result: opulent art-to-wear clothing in a variety of rich textures.

The practice of recycling is very much a part of the Japanese kimono culture. Often the kimonos of my female relatives have been redyed, once or twice during the lifetime of the owners and sometimes after their deaths. Changing colors and designs makes the garments more appropriate for the wearers as they reach different stages in their lives. At other times, kimonos of various family members were restyled to keep them current. Some of the better kimonos were redyed if they had lost their magnificent original colors or were badly stained.

Kimonos and *haori* were also redyed and refashioned into children's kimonos, *futon* covers, and *juban*. Although it has been common to recycle clothing within a family, most Japanese prefer not to buy or wear used kimonos with another person's karma attached to them. For example, most urban Japanese would not think of wearing workmen's clothes, especially used ones! However, since the 1970s I have often seen used traditional farmers' work clothes, made of blue and white *kasuri* cotton, brought to the United States by people who found them fashionable,

130 Early Showa-period folk *kasuri* jacket
Collection Yoshiko I. Wada
Photograph by Bobby Hansson

beautiful, and inexpensive. Farmers' jackets were given several different names in the United States, including *hippari*, *uwappari*, *happi* coats, or kimono jackets. Patterns for making these jackets were included in the ethnic series of Folkwear Patterns that became commercially available in 1977.[6]

Like other precious traditional costumes, kimonos were reused in appropriate ways whenever possible. It was this sense of preciousness for kimonos, specifically, coupled with the high regard I held for textiles in general, that I—and many other Japanese people—brought to the shores of America. Reverence for cloth and the wealth of traditions that cloth represents resonates within myself and my fellow American fiber artists. In response to Americans' growing eagerness to learn about Asian textiles, I began researching and teaching *kasuri*, *shibori*, and other textile traditions in the mid-1970s. This, along with making art, resulted in my co-authoring a monograph called *Ikat: An Introduction* as well as a definitive book on a wide range of tie-dye processes, *Shibori: The Inventive Art of Japanese Shaped Resist Dyeing.*[7] American artists began to add Japanese textile features to their own art-making vocabularies and to employ those traditional processes in the creation of new and exciting artworks. As they continue adding new variations to Japan's time-honored themes, these Western artists will further enrich the fiber idioms of both countries.

Over the years, the experience of working with American students has made me realize the impact of Japanese textiles on my creative process, and enhanced my desire to preserve the cultural heritage of my native homeland. My own attitudes toward textiles are embodied in the kimono. My understanding of the cross-cultural nature of our modern world increased after teaching generations of young Americans the intricacies of Eastern *kasuri* and *shibori* fiber techniques and traditions, in the same way that their European ancestors handed down their knowledge of Western-style dressmaking techniques to Japanese people of my grandmother Motoko's generation. With the passage of time, each group will continue to borrow ethnic knowledge, reinterpret it, making it their own for a brief period of time, and pass it back across the cultural waters dividing East and West. Such alterations and additives will continue the never-ending cycle of cross-cultural influences.

I am proud to say that many of my American students have become noteworthy fabricators of art-to-wear textiles, drawing a major part of their creative sustenance from the kimono tradition and the rich cultural heritage to which I am heir by having grown up in Japan.

As I stand on the Western shores of America and look out across San Francisco Bay to my Eastern homeland so many thousands of miles away, I am aware that a new age is dawning—one that will embrace the conjoining of the East and West as the cultural waves engendered by the Pacific Rim gain added momentum. And if we, as artists, can reach out and enjoy a cup of coffee together in your milieu and a cup of tea in mine, while sharing stories about the garments we wear and the time-honored traditions they represent to each of us, we will continue to grow in cultural richness, and meld our clothing styles to reflect the new world in which our children will grow up.

NOTES

**The History of the Kimono—
Japan's National Dress**

1. See Tanno Iku, ed., *Sōgō fukushoku jiten* (Encyclopedia of costumes) (Tokyo: Yuzankaku, 1980), 111, for a detailed discussion of the terminology for Japan's national costume.

2. Izutsu Gafu, *Nihon josei fukushokushi* (History of Japanese women's costume) (Kyoto: Korinsha, 1987), 165; and Richard Pearson, ed., *Ancient Japan* (Washington, D.C.: Smithsonian Institution, 1992), 16.

3. Tsunoda Ryosaku and L. Carrington Goodrich, *Japan in the Chinese Dynastic Histories: Later Han through Ming Dynasties* (South Pasadena, Calif.: P. D. and Ione Perkins, 1951), 8–16.

4. Pearson, *Ancient Japan*, 135.

5. Ibid., 203.

6. *Nihon shoki* (The chronicle of Japan), published in 720, mentions that Empress Suiko passed an edict in 605 to formalize the use of *hirami* in the court. Tanno, *Sōgō fukushoku jiten*, 339.

7. Pearson, *Ancient Japan*, 259–260.

8. Izutsu, *Nihon josei fukushokushi*, 31. See discussion of the Yoro Clothing Code, the *Yoro ritsuryō*, 31.

9. The historical study of Chinese and Korean costume in relationship to Japanese costume, and the effect that foreign influence had on the development of the Japanese kimono, is a rich and complicated subject needing further exploration. See Xun Zhou and Chunming Gao ed., *5000 Years of Chinese Costumes*, The Chinese Costume Research Group of the Shanghai School of Traditional Operas (San Francisco: China Books and Periodicals, Inc., 1987).

10. Later in the Heian period, sumptuary statutes limited the basic set to five; hence the late Heian outfit was sometimes referred to as *itsutsuginu*, meaning "five robes." Tanno, *Sōgō fukushoku jiten*, 19.

11. Liza Dalby, "The Cultured Nature of Heian Colors," in *Kimono: Fashioning Culture* (New Haven, Conn.: Yale University Press, 1993), 217–269. For more discussion of Heian court life, see also William H. McCullough, *A Tale of Flowering Fortunes: Annals of Japanese Aristocratic Life in the Heian Period*, trans. Helen Craig (Stanford, Calif.: Stanford University Press, 1980).

12. Those codes were *Taihō ritsuryō*, completed in 701 (Taiho 1); and *Yorō risturyō*, completed in 718 (Yoro 2). Shimizu Yoshiko and Yoshioka Tsuneo, "Genji Monogatari no iro" (Colors from the tale of Genji), *Bessatsu Taiyō* (Special edition of the *Taiyō* magazine), no. 60 (winter 1987): 3–31.

13. Murasaki Shikibu, *The Tale of Genji*, trans. and abr. Edward G. Seidensticker (New York: Vintage Books, 1985), 94. See also Shimizu Yoshiko's comments about this chapter, "Hana no En" (Festival of the cherry blossoms), in Shimizu and Yoshioka, "Genji Monogatari no iro," 6–7.

14. Izutsu, *Nihon josei fukushokushi*, 54–56.

15. The official title was "Seii tai shōgun," which was an appointment made by the emperor to designate the general in charge of guarding and controlling northeastern Japan. Customarily the Genji (Minamoto) clan was given the title, followed by the Ashikaga clan, and eventually the Tokugawa clan in the Edo period. Takayanagi Koju and Takeuchi Tadazo, eds., *Nihonshi jiten* (Encyclopedia of Japanese history) (Tokyo: Kadokawa Shoten, 1979), 527.

16. This men's outfit had a variety of styles; for example, *daimon*, which was patterned with large family crests and embellished with decorative cords at the bottom of the sleeves, along the front shoulder seams, and on the neck bands, or *suō*, which was a simplified version of *daimon* and was distinctive for its sturdy leather ties attached to the garment's neck band. Tanno, *Sōgō fukushoku jiten*, 334.

17. See the *emakimono*, picture scrolls, such as the "Legends of Shigisan Temple," and "fan sutra" paintings of Shitenno-ji from the late twelfth century for a depiction of commoners' lives, in Yoshiko Wada, Mary Kellogg Rice, and Jane Barton, *Shibori: The Inventive Art of Japanese Shaped Resist Dyeing* (Tokyo: Kodansha International Ltd., 1983), 16–18. The technique of *suri-e*, stenciling pigment or dyes through patterns, was mentioned in *Kojiki*, the chronicle of Japanese mythical and imperial history completed in 712, and *Man'yoshu*, an eighth-century anthology of Japanese poems. Sophisticated and beautiful extant examples from the late sixteenth and early seventeenth centuries of *katazome*, paste-resist stencil dyeing on cloth and leather, were identified as coming from a section of armor and a jacket worn under the armor belonging to the *bushi*. For additional information, see Maeda Ujo, "Nihon Kodai no Ai" (Indigo of ancient Japan), *Sen Shoku to Seikasu*, no. 10 (fall 1975): 75, and Kamiya Eiko, *Katazome* (Kyoto: Unsundo, 1976), 8.

18. See note 42 for the reaction to this period of trade with European countries.

19. These designs were originally called *koshi-gawari*, meaning changing around the hip, and *dan katami-gawari*, meaning changing in blocks on the half of the bodice, thus creating the huge checkerboard pattern. There is an extant example of this type of *kosode* given by Hideyoshi to be put on a *shinto* figure on one of the floats called "Ashikariyama" in the Gion Festival in Kyoto. The *noshime* design was established for the robes of the *bushi* character in *Nō* theater around this time and can still be seen in contemporary *Nō* performances. Yoshioka Sachio, "Kinu gasuri no bi: Noshime shōzoku ni Tsuite" (The beauty of silk ikat: Regarding noshime costumes), in *Noshime:*

Stripes, Lattice, and Ikat in Edo Period (Kyoto: Kyoto Shoin, 1986), 179.

20. Extant *tsujigahana* textiles are dated from a brief period between the Muromachi and the Momoyama periods, approximately one hundred years, although the term may not have applied to this entire group of textiles in this time period. Ito Toshiko, *Tsujigahana: The Flower of Japanese Textile Art*, trans. Monica Bethe (Tokyo: Kodansha International Ltd., 1983), 15.

21. Toyotomi Hideyoshi was known to be generous to those who served him well, often rewarding them with his personal articles, including his *dōbuku*. However, after the fall of the Toyotomi clan, many of his former retainers joined Ieyasu and must have discarded anything that might have raised the new master's suspicion against their loyalty. Ito, *Tsujigahana: The Flower of Japanese Textile Art*, 78.

22. Hideyoshi was given the surname Toyotomi and the title of *dajo daijin*, or prime minister, by the emperor in 1586, which practically put him in a position equivalent to shogun status. In 1573, the previous shogun, Ashikaga Yoshiaki, was forcibly removed from the position by Oda Nobunaga. Takayanagi Koju and Takeuchi Tadazo, eds., *Nihonshi jiten* (Encyclopedia of Japanese history) (Tokyo: Kadokawa Shoten, 1979), 527.

23. See the portrait (1589) of Lady Asai Nagamasa, sister of Oda Nobunaga, wearing the *uchikake* in this manner called *koshimaki*, from the collection of the Jimyoin Temple in Wakayama. Izutsu, *Nihon josei fukushokushi*, 81.

24. For an example of a tragic story involving the death of one *bushi* lord that affected the fate of all of the women in his household, see Ito, *Tsujigahana: The Flower of Japanese Textile Art*, 110. Toyotomi Hidetsugu, Hideyoshi's adopted son and heir, was forced to die by Hideyoshi's order in 1595, after the birth of Hideyoshi's own son. Hidetsugu's wife, his concubines, and his children were then put to death in Kyoto, and their remains were unceremoniously deposited in a river.

25. The *Nō* drama developed out of folk performances of wandering acting guilds known as *sarugaku* players. Four of these guilds attached to the Nara temple of Kofukuji are the forerunners of the modern *Nō* schools of Kanze, Hōshō, Kongō, and Komparu. See Monica Bethe, "Nō Costumes from Conception to Use," in *Pattern and Poetry: Nō Robes from the Lucy Truman Aldrich Collection at the Museum of Art, Rhode Island School of Design*, exh. cat., ed. Susan Anderson Hay (Providence, R.I.: Rhode Island School of Design, 1992), 36.

26. For a story about an American who collected *Nō* robes in the 1920s, see Susan Anderson Hay, "Providence, Paris, Kyoto, Peking: Lucy Truman Aldrich and Her Collections," and Nagasaki Iwao, "A History of Nō Costume," trans. and adapt. Monica Bethe, in *Pattern and Poetry*, ed. Hay, 10–27. For an expanded

discussion of the Western collection of oriental textiles, see Corwin, herein, 23–44.

27. The *chōnin* comprised two classes of the Tokugawa class system of *Shi no ko sho* (*bushi*, farmer, artisan, and merchant). The imperial family and the nobility, as well as the outcasts, existed outside of this system. Within the *chōnin* there were four categories: landlords, landowners, tenant shopkeepers, and artisans who rented from the propertied *chōnin*. Significantly, only the *chōnin* property owners had a voice in city politics. Takayanagi, *Nihonshi jiten*, 635.

28. Donald Shively, "Sumptuary Regulation and Status in Early Togugawa Japan," *Harvard Journal of Asiatic Studies* 25 (1965): 123–164.

29. Out of more than one million residents in the capital city of Edo, the center of the *bakufu* government, 50 percent of the population consisted of the shogun and his immediate retainers and the families of the approximately 260 daimyo, as well as their vassals, attendants, and service personnel. As a result of the alternate attendance system, *sankin kōtai*, which meant that each daimyo had to reside every other year in Edo, interregional trade increased and the Edo economy was boosted by the daimyo expenditures necessary to maintain the extra household in the capital. Edo consequently emerged as a center of consumption. Most of the regional personnel who accompanied their masters were without families, and thus they were active patrons of the theaters and the courtesans' quarters. William Hause, "A New Society: Japan Under Tokugawa Rule," in *When Art Became Fashion: Kosode in Edo-Period Japan*, exh. cat., eds. Dale Gluckman and Sharon Takeda (Los Angeles: Los Angeles County Museum, 1992), 49. See also 47–51 for more discussion of Edo life.

30. The Kabuki theater originated from *kabuki odori*, a kind of dance performed in Kyoto in the early Edo period by the dancer named Okuni of the Izumo region. Courtesans in Edo and Osaka, as well as in Kyoto, began copying her style of dance and performed it in groups. In 1629 the *bakufu* prohibited these performances. As a result, all women performers were replaced by adolescent male dancers, but this too was prohibited in 1652. Eventually adult men were allowed to perform, and this type of theater, which included voice and musical instrument accompaniment to dance and acting, became very popular among the *chōnin*. Takayanagi, *Nihonshi jiten*, 209.

31. See the painting by Nishikawa Terunobu (fl. 1716–1735) showing one such Kabuki actor specializing in a female role (*onnagata*) in a fashionable *kosode* in Gluckman and Takeda, "Introduction," in *When Art Became Fashion*, 31.

32. The *chōnin* cultural life included literary works like the popular seventeen-syllable poetry called *haikai*, and picture books, or *ukiyo-sōshi*, as well as theatrical productions by the

Kabuki theater, and by the puppet theater called *Ningyo joruri*. Well-known Osaka literati such as Matsuo Basho, the traveling *haiku* poet; Ihara Saikaku, author of several adventure stories of amorous men and women; and Chikamatsu Monzaemon, considered to be Japan's equivalent to William Shakespeare, produced a large number of works at this time that became classics. Takayanagi, *Nihonshi jiten*, 326.

33. *Asa* or other bast fibers, made from the inner bark of various plants, were the main source of material for the majority of people's clothing from the time of the prehistoric Wa people. Fine silk was reserved for the ruling classes and the privileged. Cotton production began in the late fifteenth century, but at that time production was limited to warmer regions. Cotton became prevalent among the *chōnin* by the eighteenth century, yet it remained a luxury for the rural population of the regions that were not suited for its cultivation. See Sadako Fukui, *Zusetsu Nihon no kasuri bunkashi* (Illustrated history of Japanese ikat) (Kyoto: Kyoto Shonin, 1974), 2–5. See also the Seventh Phase, herein, 152–155, for a discussion of *sakiori* and *sashiko* techniques for ingenious uses of cotton in folk dress.

34. Donald Jenkins, *The Floating World Revisited*, exh. cat. (Portland: Portland Art Museum, 1993), 15–16. The term *tsū* originated in the "pleasure quarters" of the Edo period. It probably came from the term indicating a "commuter," or regular, patron who was popular for his savvy, elegant style, and generosity.

35. This kind of Edo *kosode* is epitomized by the exquisite pieces shown in the exhibition "When Art Became Fashion" in Los Angeles in 1992–1993. This extraordinary show was organized by Dale Carolyn Gluckman and Sharon Sadako Takeda at the Los Angeles County Museum. The accompanying catalogue, *When Art Became Fashion: Kosode in Edo-Period Japan*, is the most comprehensive discussion of the elaborate *kosode* from the Edo period.

36. The length of the sleeve is determined by the part that hangs down on the side when the kimono is worn; the width of the sleeve is the measurement from the shoulder seam to the wrist opening and is relatively consistent because the sleeve is made with one kimono cloth width, which is around fourteen inches. The width of a Japanese kimono sleeve is what is normally considered the *length* of a sleeve in a Western garment.

37. This opening under the arm was termed *yatsukuchi*. Tanno, *Sōgō fukushoku jiten*, 354.

38. This Edo-period–style decoration on *tomesode* became known as *Edo-zuma*, or Edo-style frontal panels; hence the term also indicated the *kosode* of this type and was used interchangeably with the term *tomesode*.

39. For an in-depth discussion of dye colors, especially red, in the Edo period, see Monica Bethe, "Reflection on *Beni*: Red as a Key to Edo Period Fashion," in *When Art Became Fashion*, 133–153.

40. The design was called *jiochi*, meaning "omitting ground," to create a positive design by selectively not tying the kanoko dots. Wada, Rice, and Barton, *Shibori*, 59.

41. See Corwin, "The Kimono Mind: *Japonisme* in American Culture," herein, for more extensive coverage of the American response to the Japanese styles and fashion at the turn of the last century, as well as my discussion of the more recent phenomenon of the West responding to the East in "Changing Attitudes Toward the Kimono: A Personal Reflection," herein.

42. In the period from 1542 to 1639, Portuguese, Spanish, and Dutch traders had entered Japan in small numbers, and the shogunate ruling powers, seeing a threat in the Jesuit and Franciscan missionaries accompanying the Portuguese and the Spanish, had them expelled from the country. The Protestant Dutch were, however, allowed to be the sole foreign trading agent and permitted to occupy Deshima, a small man-made island off the port of Nagasaki on the southern island of Kyushu, from 1639 until late in the Edo period in 1844. Julia Meech-Pekarik, *The World of the Meiji Print: Impressions of a New Civilization* (New York: John Weatherhill, 1986), 3–4.

43. James Fallows, "When East Met West: Perry's Mission Accomplished," *Smithsonian* 25, no. 4 (July 1994): 21, 22–30.

44. Meech-Pekarik, *The World of the Meiji Print: Impressions of a New Civilization, 144–157*, and Dalby, *Kimono: Fashioning Culture*, 80–83, 86, for a discussion of the Rokumeikan era and the reaction to it.

45. In a dramatic gesture, Emperor Meiji cut his topknot in 1872. Meech-Pekarik, *The World of the Meiji Print*, 102.

46. Women began adopting a hairstyle similar to the Victorian women's bun, called *sokuhatsu*. For more about these hairstyles see Tanno, *Sōgō fukushoku jiten*, 253; and Dalby, *Kimono: Fashioning Culture*, 74–75.

47. Motoyoshi Shunzaburo, *Gendai kimono yogo jiten* (Dictionary of modern kimono terminology) (Tokyo: Fujin Gahosha, 1976), 84.

48. This garment is an excellent example of the Japanese preference for patterning inner garments, not meant for public display; the bold and showy patterns on the linings of the *haori* short kimono jackets, or on the *shitagi*, are also clear-cut examples of this paradoxical design approach. Refer back to the Sixth Phase, on *iki*.

49. A case in point was the 1917 mid-air somersault demonstrated by an American flier, one Smith, which amazed the Tokyo residents. The next day the Mitsukoshi department store in Tokyo introduced the *han-eri* decorated with tiny somersaulting planes and they sold out immediately. Manji Kato, "Taisho no han-eri"

(The *han-eri* of the Taisho period), in Kondo, *Taisho no kimono* (The kimono of the Taisho period) (Tokyo: Minzoku-isho Bunka Fukyu Kyokai, 1981), 45–49.

50. Motoyoshi, *Gendai kimono yogo jiten*, 199–200; and Kondo, *Taisho no kimono*, 24.

51. For additional regional terms and more information about *sakiori* and other recycling traditions in Japanese rural clothing, see Toshida Shin-ichiro and Dai Williams, *Riches from Rags: Sakiori & Other Recycling Traditions in Japanese Rural Clothing*, exh. cat. (San Francisco: San Francisco Craft and Folk Art Museum, 1994).

52. See my "Changing Attitudes Toward the Kimono," herein, for some of the work wear that was brought into mainstream Japanese life during World War II.

53. Victor and Takako Hauge, *Folk Tradition in Japanese Art* (New York: John Weatherhill, 1978), 14.

54. Japanese recycling techniques for folk wear have been adapted by contemporary Americans such as weaver and creator of wearable art Trudie Roberts, or have been used as inspiration for new artistic creations such as those of Tim Harding discussed in Julie Schafler Dale, "The Kimono in the Art-to-Wear Movement," herein.

55. The wedding industry, which orchestrates the wedding ceremony and all the fanfare connected to it in a kind of package deal—including the reception meal, the beauticians, the honeymoon, and the *hikidemono*, wedding favors for the guests—became a huge business in postwar, newly affluent Japan, and this kind of wedding became a virtual necessity for all middle-class Japanese.

56. See Kitamura Fumiko, "Gyaru-tachi no Yukata Senpū" (The Yukata sensation among young women), *Senshoku to Seikatsu: Textiles in Living*, no. 160 (July 1994): 39–41.

57. For further discussion of the state of the kimono industry in Japan and its marketing strategy to appeal to contemporary youth, see Betsy Sterling Benjamin, "Reinventing a Tradition: The Kimono Adapts to the Nineties," *Japan Scope* 3, no. 2 (summer 1994): 36–37.

58. *The Takashimaya Hyakugoju-nen shi* (150 years of the history of the Takashimaya Department Stores) (Tokyo: The Takashimaya Department Stores, 1955).

59. Such artists promoted by the kimono industry may be, like these three, members of well-established exhibition associations such as Nitten or Dento Kogei Ten.

Changing Attitudes Toward the Kimono: A Personal Reflection

1. A department store fire in 1913 that resulted in the deaths of women who refused to jump from the burning building because of their need to protect their maidenly modesty (they were not wearing underpants) contributed to the increased wearing of "Western drawers." See Tanno, ed., *Sōgō fukushoku jiten*, 196.

2. They were sometimes called *tonbi*, black hawk, because the black-caped garment resembled the form of that predatory bird, whereas at other times these coats were simply referred to as *"in-baa-nesu,"* the Japanese corruption of "Inverness." Another Japanese term for these coats was *nijū mawashi*, or double layered. See Tanno, *Sōgō fukushoku jiten*, 304.

3. When the *tonbi* were no longer in fashion and had been discarded by almost everyone, foreigners began foraging for them in the flea markets in the big cities in Japan. Finding the old-fashioned overcoats to be attractive, they then imported them to the United States to be worn as unisex coats, especially during the 1970s. This is an example of East and West cross-cultural activities that have affected world fashion.

4. See Dalby, *Kimono: Fashioning Culture*, 93–94.

5. Peggy Landers Rao, "East Meets Midwest: Everything's Up-to-Date in Kansas City," *ELLE Decor* (June/July 1991): 156.

6. At that time, I assisted the people who produced Folkwear Patterns in drafting the pattern pieces and calculating the yardage requirements that were needed to make the kimono, Pattern #113, and the *hippari*, Pattern #112.

7. Yoshiko Wada, *Ikat: An Introduction* (Berkeley: Kasuri Dyeworks, 1975); and Yoshiko Wada, Mary Rice, and Jane Barton, *Shibori*.

Bibliography

Allen, Virginia M. *The Femme Fatale: Erotic Icon.* Troy, N.Y.: The Whitston Co., 1983.

Baarsen, R. J., et al. *Japanese Influence on Dutch Art: Imitation and Inspiration from 1650 to the Present.* Exhibition catalogue. Amsterdam: Rijksmuseum, 1991.

Beagle, Peter. *American Denim: A New Folk Art.* New York: Harry N. Abrams, Inc., 1975.

Beall, Karen F. "Swatches—The Odyssey of Japanese Cloth: A Study in Recycling." *Fiberarts* (Nov./Dec. 1992): 9–10.

Benjamin, Betsy Sterling. "Reinventing a Tradition: The Kimono Adapts to the Nineties." *Japan Scope* 3, no. 2 (summer 1994): 33–37.

Boodro, Michael. "Art and Fashion: A Fine Romance." *Art News* (Sept. 1990): 120–127.

Broude, Norma. "Miriam Schapiro and 'Femmage': Reflections on the Conflict Between Decoration and Abstraction in Twentieth Century Art." *Arts* (Feb. 1980): 83–87.

Brown, Jane Converse. *The Japanese Taste: Its Role in the Mission of the American Home and in the Family's Presentation of Itself to the Public as Expressed in Published Sources—1876–1916.* Ann Arbor: UMI Press, 1987.

Brzostoski, John. "The Nō Robe as Perfection." *Craft Horizons* 37, no. 4 (Aug. 1977): 22–27.

Bullis, Douglas. "An Eloquent Array: Ana Lisa Hedstrom." *Ornament* 16, no. 4 (1993): 41–79.

———. "Janet Lipkin's Clothing." *Ornament* 12, no. 3 (1989): 53–57.

———. "Transforming the Kimono." *Ornament* 12, no. 4 (1989): 22–87.

Burke, Mary. "History of the Collection." In *A Selection of Japanese Art from the Mary and Jackson Burke Collection.* Exhibition catalogue. The Tokyo National Museum; exhibition organized by the Tokyo National Museum, the *Tokyo Shinbun*, and the *Chunichi Shinbun*, May 21–June 30, 1985.

Burnham, Dorothy. *Cut My Cote.* Exhibition catalogue. Toronto: Royal Ontario Museum, MacKinnon-Mancur, 1973.

Clifford, James. "On Collecting Art and Culture." In *The Predicament of Culture: Twentieth Century Ethnography, Literature, and Art.* Cambridge, Mass.: Harvard University Press, 1988.

Constantine, Mildred, and Jack Lenor Larsen. *Beyond Craft: The Art Fabric.* New York, Toronto, Cincinnati, London, Melbourne: Van Nostrand Reinhold Company, 1972.

Dalby, Liza Crihfield. *Geisha.* New York: Random House, Vintage Press, 1985.

———. *Kimono: Fashioning Culture.* New Haven, Conn.: Yale University Press, 1993.

Dale, Julie Schafler. *Art to Wear.* New York: Abbeville Press, Publishers, 1986.

Dempsey, David. *The Triumphs and Trials of Lotta Crabtree.* New York: William Morrow and Co., 1968.

Dijkstra, Bram. *Idols of Perversity: Fantasies of Feminine Evil in Fin-de-Siècle Culture.* New York and Oxford: Oxford University Press, 1986.

Edel, Chantal. *Once Upon a Time: Visions of Old Japan. Photographs by Felice Beato and Baron Raimund von Stillfried. And the Words of Pierre Loti.* Translated by Linda Coverdale (originally published in France under the title *Mukashi, Mukashi, 1863–1883*). New York: Friendly Press Inc., 1986.

Fallows, James. "When East Met West: Perry's Mission Accomplished." *Smithsonian* 25, no. 4 (July 1994): 20–30.

Fiberarts Design Book, II. Ashville, N.C.: Lark Books, 1983.

Fiberarts Design Book, III. Edited by Kate Matthews. Ashville, N.C.: Lark Books, 1987.

Fiberarts Design Book, IV. Edited by Nancy Orban. Ashville, N.C.: Lark Books, 1991.

Fiberarts Design Books. Ashville, N.C.: Fiberarts Magazine, 1980.

Fukui Sadako. *Zusetsu Nihon no kasuri bunkashi* (Illustrated history of Japanese ikat). Kyoto: Kyoto Shoin, 1974.

Gay, Peter. *The Bourgeois Experience: Victoria to Freud.* Vol. 1 of *Education of the Senses.* New York: Oxford University Press, 1984.

Gilbert, Jeffrey. "The Origins of Photography in Japan." Vol. 1 of *Nihon shashin zenshu* (The complete history of Japanese photography). Tokyo: Shogakukan, 1985.

Gluckman, Dale Carolyn, and Sharon Sadako Takeda, eds. *When Art Became Fashion: Kosode in Edo Period Japan.* Exhibition catalogue. Los Angeles: Los Angeles County Museum of Art, 1992.

Goebel, Erica. "The Clothing of Ina Kozel." *Ornament* 12, no. 1 (1988): 55–80.

Goines, David Lance. *The Free Speech Movement: Coming of Age in the 1960s.* Berkeley: Ten Speed Press, 1993.

Goldberg, JoAnn. "With a Wizard's Hand: Linda Mendelson." *Ornament* 11, no. 2 (1987): 43–47.

Grilli, Elise. "Okakura Kakuzo, a Biographical Sketch." In *The Book of Tea,* edited by Okakura Kakuzo. Rutland, Vt.: Charles E. Tuttle Co., 1956.

Hanmaker, Barbara. "K. Lee Manuel's Splendid Ceremonial Raiments." *Ornament* 12, no. 4 (1989): 41–83.

Harrington, Elaine. "Frank Lloyd Wright and the Art of Japan." *Wright Angles: Newsletter of the Frank Lloyd Wright Home and Studio Foundation* IVL (Mar. 1992).

Hauge, Victor, and Takako Hauge. *Folk Tradition in Japanese Art.* New York: John Weatherhill, Inc., 1978.

Hay, Susan Anderson, ed. *Patterns and Poetry: Nō Robes from the Lucy Truman Aldrich Collection at the Museum of Art, Rhode Island School of Design.* Exhibition catalogue, with an essay by Nagasaki Iwao and Monica Bethe. Providence: Rhode Island School of Design, 1992.

———, ed. "Providence, Paris, Kyoto, Peking: Lucy Truman Aldrich and Her Collections." In *Patterns and Poetry: Nō Robes from the Lucy Truman Aldrich Collection at the Museum of Art, Rhode Island School of Design.* Providence, R.I.: 1992.

Headlee, Kathleen Marra. "The Social Meaning of Clothing." Ph.D diss., Washington State University, Pullman, 1976.

Hearn, Lafcadio. *Glimpses of Unfamiliar Japan.* 1894. Reprint, Tokyo: Charles Tuttle Co., Inc., 1976.

Hollander, Anne. *Seeing Through Clothes.* New York: Viking Press, 1978.

Hosley, William. *The Japan Idea: Art and Life in Victorian America.* Exhibition catalogue. Hartford, Conn.: The Wadsworth Atheneum, 1990.

Ito Toshiko. *Tsujigahana: The Flower of Japanese Textile Art.* Translated by Monica Bethe. Tokyo: Kodansha International Ltd., 1981.

Izutsu Gafu. *Nihon josei fukushokushi* (History of Japanese women's costumes). Kyoto: Korinsha, 1987.

Jacopetti, Alexandra. *Native Funk & Flash: An Emerging Folk Art.* Centerville, Mass.: Scrimshaw Press, 1974.

Japanese Kimono, The, Pattern #113. Forestville, Calif.: Folkwear Patterns, 1977.

Jenkins, Donald. *The Floating World Revisited.* Exhibition catalogue. Portland, Oregon: Portland Art Museum, 1993.

Kamiya Eiko. *Katazome* (Stencil dyeing). Kyoto: Unsodo, 1976.

Kaplan, Wendy, and Robert Judson Clark, eds. *"The Art That Is Life": The Arts and Crafts Movement in America, 1875–1920.* Exhibition catalogue. Boston: Museum of Fine Arts, 1987.

Kinsey, Sally Buchanan. "A More Reasonable Way to Dress." In Wendy Kaplan and Robert Judson Clark, eds., *"The Art That Is Life": The Arts and Crafts Movement in America, 1875–1920.* Boston: Museum of Fine Arts, 1987.

Kirihata Ken. *Beauty of Textile Arts in Kyoto: 16th through 19th Centuries*. Exhibition catalogue. Kyoto: The Kyoto National Museum, 1975.

Kitamura Fumiko. "Gyaru-tachi no yukata senpu" (The Yukata sensation among young women). *Senshoku to Seikatsu: Textile in Living*, no. 160 (July 1994): 39–41.

Klinkow, Margaret. *The Wright Family in the House Beautiful*. Text of a slide lecture, Frank Lloyd Wright Home and Studio Foundation, Oak Park, Ill., 1991.

Kondo Tomie. *Taisho no kimono* (The kimono of the Taisho period). Tokyo: Minzoku-isho Bunka Fukyu Kyokai, 1981.

Lachowsky, Michele. *Fashion and Art: From the 50's to the Present Day*. Exhibition catalogue. Brussels: Les Expositions du Palais des Beaux Arts, 1994.

La Farge, John. *Bric-a-Brac: An Artist's Letters from Japan*. N.p., 1897.

Lancaster, Clay. *The Japanese Influence in America*. New York: Walton H. Rawls, 1963.

Larsen, Jack Lenor, with Alfred Buhler, Bronwem, and Garrett Solyom. *The Dyer's Art: Ikat, Batik, Plangi*. New York, Cincinnati, Toronto, London: Van Nostrand Reinhold Company, 1973.

Lasch, Christopher. *The Culture of Narcissism: American Life in an Age of Diminishing Expectations*. New York: W. W. Norton Co., 1978.

Lehmann, Jean-Pierre. *The Image of Japan: From Feudal Isolation to World Power, 1850–1905*. London: George Allen and Unwin, 1978.

Lew, William W. *Roger Shimomura: Return of the Yellow Peril*. Exhibition catalogue. Spokane, Wash.: Cheney Cowles Museum, 1993.

Lucie-Smith, Edward. "Historical Roots and Contemporary Perspectives." *Craft Today: Poetry of the Physical*. New York: American Craft Museum and Weidenfeld & Nicholson, 1986.

Lusk, Jennie. "Kimono East/Kimono West." *Fiberarts* (Sept./Oct. 1980): 71.

Maeda Ujo. "Nihon kodai no ai" (Indigo of ancient Japan). *Senshoku to Seikatsu: Textile in Living*, no. 10 (fall 1975): 72–75. Kyoto: Senshoku to Seikatsu sha, 1975.

Marshall, John. *Make Your Own Japanese Clothes*. Tokyo and New York: Kodansha International, 1988.

————. "The Classic Kimono: Style from East Inspires Designs in the West." *Threads* (Dec. 1990/Jan. 1991): 39–43.

Meech, Julia, and Gabriel Weisberg. *Japonisme Comes to America*. New York: Peter Lang, 1991.

Meech-Pekarik, Julia. *The World of the Meiji Print: Impressions of a New Civilization*. New York: John Weatherhill, Inc., 1986.

Melville, Joy. *Ellen and Edy*. London and New York: Pandora Press, 1987.

Milinaire, Caterine, and Carol Troy. *Cheap Chic*. New York: Harmony Books, 1975.

Motoyoshi Shunzaburo. *Gendai kimono yogo jiten* (Dictionary of modern kimono terminology). Tokyo: Fujin Gahosha, 1976.

Nishimura Hyobu, Jean Mailey, and Joseph S. Hayes, Jr. *Tagasode: Whose Sleeves . . . : Kimono from the Kanebo Collection*. Exhibition catalogue. New York: Japan Society, Inc., 1976.

Noma, Seiroki. *Japanese Costume and Textile Arts*, vol. 16. Translated by Armins Nikovskis. New York: John Weatherhill/Tokyo: Heibonsha, 1974.

Oak Leaves (newspaper, Oak Park, Ill.), March 24, 1906.

O'Toole, Patricia. *The Five of Hearts: An Intimate Portrait of Henry Adams and His Friends, 1880–1918*. New York: Clarkson Potter, 1990.

Paul, Margot. "A Creative Connoisseur: Nomura Shojiro." In *Kosode: 16th–19th Century Textiles from the Nomura Collection*. Exhibition catalogue. New York: Japan Society and Kodansha International, 1984.

Pearson, Richard, ed. Ancient Japan. Washington, D.C.: Smithsonian Institution, 1992.

Perry, Paul. *On the Bus*. New York: Thunder's Mouth Press, 1990.

Pisano, Ronald, and Alicia Grant Longwell. *Photographs from the William Merritt Chase Archives at the Parrish Art Museum*. Southampton, N.Y.: The Parrish Art Museum, 1992.

Porges, Maria. "Coat Tales." *American Craft* (Oct./Nov. 1989): 46–51.

"Raising the Standard of Dressmaking." *The Craftsman*, May 12, 1907.

Rathbun, William Jay, ed. *Beyond the Tanabata Bridge: Traditional Japanese Textiles*. Exhibition catalogue. London: Thames and Hudson, in association with the Seattle Art Museum, 1993.

Richardson, Joanna. *Sarah Bernhardt and Her World*. London: Weidenfeld and Nicolson, 1977.

Robins, Corrine. *The Pluralist Era: American Art, 1968–1981*. New York: Harper & Row, 1984.

Rudofsky, Bernard. *The Kimono Mind: An Informal Guide to Japan and the Japanese*. Garden City, N.Y.: Doubleday, 1965.

Russell, Nancy Ukai. "Kosode Dress in Edo Japan." *Ornament* 16, no. 2 (1992).

Said, Edward. *Orientalism*. New York: Vintage Books, 1978.

Schlundt, Christena L. *The Professional Appearances of Ruth St. Denis and Ted Shawn: A Chronology and Index of Dances, 1906–1932*. New York: New York Public Library, 1962.

Shelton, Suzanne. *Divine Dancer: A Biography of Ruth St. Denis*. New York: Doubleday, 1981.

Shimizu Yoshiko and Yoshioka Tsuneo. "Genji monogatari no iro" (Colors from the tale of Genji). *Bessatsu Taiyō* (Special edition of the *Taiyō* magazine), no. 60 (winter 1987). Tokyo: Heibonsha, 1988.

Shively, Donald. "Sumptuary Regulation and Status in Early Tokugawa Japan." *Harvard Journal of Asiatic Studies* 25 (1965): 123–165.

Silverman, Debora. *Art Nouveau in Fin-de-Siècle France: Politics, Psychology, and Style*. Berkeley: University of California Press, 1992.

———. "The 'New Woman,' Feminism, and the Decorative Arts in Fin-de-Siècle France." In *Eroticism and the Body Politic*. Edited by Lynn Hunt. Baltimore: Johns Hopkins University Press, 1991.

Smith, Richard Gordon. *Travels in the Lands of the Gods (1898–1907)*. Diary. Edited by Victoria Manthorpe. New York: Prentice-Hall, 1986.

Stabb, Jo Ann C. "The Wearable Movement: A Critical Look at the State of the Art." *Surface Design Journal* (fall 1988): 29–31.

Steele, Valerie. *Fashion and Eroticism*. New York: Oxford University Press, 1985.

Stewart, Susan. *On Longing: Narratives of the Miniature, the Gigantic, the Souvenir, and the Collection*. Baltimore: Johns Hopkins University Press, 1984.

Stinchecum, Amanda Myer. *Kosode: Sixteenth–Nineteenth Century Textiles from the Nomura Collection*. Exhibition catalogue. New York: Japan Society and Kodansha International, 1984.

Stowens, Susan. "Dina Schwartz & Sharron Hedges." *Currant* (Aug./Sept./Oct. 1976): 47–49.

Summa, Susan. *Susan Summa: Miss Liberty Takes a Holiday*. Exhibition catalogue. Albuquerque: Mariposa Gallery, 1986.

Takashimaya Hyakugojunen-shi (150 Years of the history of the Takashimaya department stores). Tokyo: Takashimaya Department Stores, 1955.

Takayanagi Koju and Takeuchi Tadazo, eds. *Nihonshi jiten* (Encyclopedia of Japanese history). Tokyo: Kadokawa Shoten, 1979.

Tanno Kaoru, ed. *Sōgō fukushoku jiten* (Encyclopedia of costumes). Tokyo: Yuzankaku, 1980.

Tilke, Max. *Costume Patterns and Designs*. London: A. Zwemmer, 1956.

Tomita Jun and Tomita Noriko. *Japanese Ikat Weaving: The Techniques of Kasuri*. London: Routledge & Kegan Paul, 1982.

Tsunoda Ryosaku and L. Carrington Goodrich. *Japan in the Chinese Dynastic Histories: Later Han through Ming Dynasties*. South Pasadena, Calif.: P. D. and Ione Perkins, 1951.

Twombly, Robert C. *Frank Lloyd Wright: His Life and His Architecture*. New York: John Wiley and Sons, 1979.

Wada, Yoshiko, Mary Kellogg Rice, and Jane Barton. *Shibori: The Inventive Art of Japanese Shaped Resist Dyeing*. Tokyo: Kodansha International Ltd., 1983.

Warhol, Andy, and Pat Hackett. *Popism: The Warhol Sixties*. San Diego, New York, London: Harcourt Brace Jovanovich, 1980.

Watanabe, Toshio. *High Victorian Japonisme*. New York: Peter Lang, 1991.

Weimann, Jeanne Madeline. *The Fair Women*. Chicago: Academy Chicago, 1981.

White, Fifi. *Japanese Folk Textiles: An American Collection*. Tokyo: Shikosha, 1987.

Wigley, Mark. "Untitled: The Housing of Gender." In *Sexuality and Space*. Edited by Beatriz Colomina. Princeton, N.J.: Princeton Papers on Architecture, 1992.

Wilde, Oscar. Letter to the "Pall Mall Gazette," October 14, 1884. Published as an essay, "Woman's Dress," in *Miscellanies*. Vol. 14 of *The First Collected Edition of the Works of Oscar Wilde, 1908–1922*. 15 vols. Edited by Robert Ross. Reprint, London: Methuen & Co., 1969.

Wolfe, Tom. *The Electric Kool-Aid Acid Test*. New York: Farrar, Straus, Giroux, 1968.

Wright, Frank Lloyd. *An Autobiography*. New York: Hall, Sloan and Pierce, 1943.

————. "In the Cause of Architecture." *The Architectural Record* (Mar. 1908).

Xun Zhou and Chunming Gao, *5000 Years of Chinese Costumes*. Edited by The Chinese Costumes Research Group of the Shanghai School of Traditional Operas. San Francisco, Calif.: China Books and Periodicals, Inc., 1987.

Yamanaka Norio. *The Book of Kimono: The Complete Guide to Style and Wear*. Tokyo: Kodansha International Ltd., 1982.

Yoshida Shin-ichiro and Dai Williams. *Riches from Rags: Sakiori & Other Recycling Traditions in Japanese Rural Clothing*. Exhibition catalogue. San Francisco: San Francisco Craft and Folk Art Museum, 1994.

Yoshioka Sachio. "Kinu gasuri no bi: Noshime shozoku ni tsuite" (The beauty of silk ikat: Regarding noshime costumes). In *Noshime: Stripes, Lattice, and Ikat in Edo Period*. Kyoto: Kyoto Shoin, 1986.

Appendix One

GLOSSARY OF TERMS

A

age Tucks at the waist that are put into childrens' kimonos and *haori*.

agekubi A high-necked or round-collared garment derived from a Chinese garment.

aigi A kimonolike robe worn under *uchikake* by *bushi* women during the Edo period (1600–1868).

ama-gōto A kimono type of overcoat worn on rainy days or at any other time as an outer garment meant to protect a good kimono.

asa A general term for a variety of bast fibers, used specifically to denote hemp (*Cannabis sativa*), but also for ramie (*Boehmeria nivea*), jute, flax, and other fibers.

awase A garment of double thickness. This term often refers to a lined garment.

B

bakufu A form of military-bureaucratic government in feudal Japan, headed by a shogun, a military dictator whose rule became hereditary. The *bakufu* was founded in Kamakura in 1185, later moved to Kyoto, and then to Edo (Tokyo) in 1603, before being overthrown in 1867.

bushi A member of the warrior class that rose to power at the end of the Heian period (794–1185), forming the *bakufu* government under the shogun.

C

chōnin Townspeople who comprised two classes, the artisans and merchants, during the seventeenth to the nineteenth centuries.

chū-burisode *Furisode* with intermediate-length sleeves.

chūsen A kind of dyeing process where paste mixed with dye is applied to fabric through a stencil.

D

daimon A warrior's robe with large crest designs worn during the Muromachi period (1392–1568).

daimyo A territorial baron of the *bushi* class in Japan's feudal era (1100–1868) wielding much power in the *bakufu* government.

date-mon A decorative crest.

dōbuku A medium-length outer cloak worn by the warrior class during the Muromachi period (1392–1568).

E

eba-moyō Large pictorial designs continuing across the various panels of the garment, achieved by transferring the design from the pre-basted material to the final garment.

edozuma Edo-style pictorial decoration on the lower portion of the frontal panels of a kimono.

e-gasuri Pictorial ikat weaving. The Japanese process involves creating figurative images on the weft by binding yarns to form resist patterns prior to weaving the fabric.

e-moyō Pictorial design, as opposed to geometric or abstract patterns.

eri A collar or neckband that is attached to the top of a kimono, where slits in the fabric have been made to form the neckline.

F

fuki The edging of a special lining at the hemline and sleeve edges of a kimono that is similar to Western-style piping. It is hemmed in such a way as to reveal a faint border of complementary or harmonious color. It is a vestigial reminder of the *jūni-hitoe* worn by ladies of the Heian court (794–1185).

fukuro-obi A double-sided tubular woven sash, brocaded on one side and having a flat twill pattern on the reverse side.

furisode A kimono with long swinging sleeves that nearly touch the ground, worn by young unmarried women from the middle Edo period (1688–1789) to the present day. Because this type of sleeve was showy, it was considered to be inappropriate attire for a married woman.

furoshiki A large square cloth that is used to wrap and carry a bundle.

furugiya A used-kimono shop.

futon Thick bedding stuffed with cotton batting. The term refers both to the bottom mattresslike mat that is placed on the floor for use as a bed in Japan and to the quiltlike coverlet on top.

G

geisha A Japanese woman who is trained from an early age in singing, dancing, and the art of conversation to serve as a hired companion to men.

geta A type of footwear worn in Japan consisting of a raised wooden sole that is fastened to the foot by a thong that goes between the first and second toes.

gofukuya A shop where kimono cloth, kimonos, and their accoutrements are sold.

guta resist A commercial brand name for a modern French resist medium that is used for painting on silk, and is similar to the resist paste used in *yūzenzome*.

H

hakama Full-cut trousers or culottes worn by both men and women over a kimono. Style of wear has varied greatly from when they were first worn in the Kofun period (250–552) until today.

han-eri A decorative neckband that covers the *juban*'s collar.

haniwa Figurative tomb sculptures made of clay dating back to the Kofun period (250–552).

haori A short, kimono-style jacket with gussets on the sides, worn over the kimono. The front is left open rather than overlapped and is tied with silk cords.

happi (Used interchangeably with *hanten*.) A short, smocklike coat originally worn in the Edo period (1600–1868) by workers on *bushi* estates, marked with the crest of the particular *bushi* family employer. This term currently refers to short jackets decorated with logos of all kinds.

hari-ita A board, six feet long and slightly wider than fourteen inches, that is used for blocking and drying a kimono that has been disassembled and temporarily restitched to reform an original bolt of fabric when the garment requires laundering.

heko-obi A brightly colored soft silk sash that was worn by children over kimonos and *yukata*.

hippari A colloquial term for a functional short kimono jacket often worn with *monpe* pants or over a kimono like a smock.

hirami Short skirtlike garment worn by men and women over pants or a long skirt, respectively, in the seventh and eighth centuries.

hitatare A three-quarter-length outer garment that evolved from the *suikan*, worn by men during the Kamakura period (1185–1392). It is distinguished from the *suikan* by its overlapping neckband; it was worn tucked into pants and was usually made of matching fabric.

hitoe or **hitoe-mono** Similar to the older term *katabira*, meaning any unlined robe. In modern kimono terms it is an unlined summer kimono made out of cotton or silk.

hitta-kanoko A type of *shibori* design created entirely by white dotlike points that are created by pinching minute pieces of the fabric and tying them with silk floss before dyeing.

hōmongi A semiformal kimono that is worn to socialize outside of the home. This category of kimono became established in the late Meiji period (late nineteenth and early twentieth centuries).

I

ikat Malay term accepted worldwide for the process called *kasuri* in Japanese.

iki An expression of style involving subtle details of material, patterns, or color developed during the Edo period (1600–1868) among the *chōnin*.

itajime-gasuri An ikat weaving technique where unwoven warp threads are clamped between boards before they are submerged in a dye vat. The design emerges when the patterned threads are woven into a cloth.

J

jimi Refers to subdued or somber colors, used in conjunction with small or subtle pattern motifs, often worn by older women.

jinbaori A battlefield jacket worn by high-ranking warriors from the late fourteenth century to the nineteenth century.

juban An undergarment whose construction varies; it can be long, short, or sleeveless. The most familiar form of the *juban* in contemporary Japan is similar to that of the kimono, and called *naga-juban*, a full-length under-kimono. Traditionally, the patterns and colors are bold, but newer versions tend to be in pale colors. The word is believed to be derived from the Portuguese *gibao*, a short, sleeveless garment.

jūni-hitoe Attire of the Heian period (794–1185) worn by ladies of the court. Literally, this term, which came into existence in the Edo period (1600–1868), means "twelve unlined robes." Each robe is dyed a different shade or color, and all of them are worn together in a way `that is calculated to show individual layers in subtle color combinations at the neck, sleeve, and hem edges. *Kariginu-mo* and *nyōbō-shōzuku* were the terms used in the Heian period.

K

Kabuki A form of Japanese theater based on popular themes that began in the seventeenth century. All of the male and female roles are performed by men, and the drama is enhanced by dance and song.

kaki-e Hand-painting on fabric, usually with *sumi* ink. The best-known example is the use of *kaki-e* in *tsujigahana* textiles.

kamishimo A sleeveless upper garment, used for ceremonial attire, worn by the *bushi* during the Edo period (1600–1868).

kanoko shibori A method of resist tie-dyeing where small increments of fabric are bound or wrapped tightly before the cloth is immersed in dye. When the binding threads are removed, a white spot with a tiny raised dot of color at the center is formed. It is a decorative technique that can be used to fill space, create linear patterns, or add texture to the cloth itself.

karaginu Literally, "Chinese costume or vest," which was the antecedent of the Japanese short jacketlike robe worn on the outermost layer of the *jūni-hitoe*.

karaginu-mo Multiple layers of broad-sleeved garments completed by a short jacketlike robe (*karaginu*) and a decorative remnant of the Chinese skirt (*mo*) that was worn for very formal occasions during the Heian period (794–1185). Popularly known as *jūni-hitoe*.

karaori The name of the brocaded weave (*ori*) that was introduced into Japan from China (*Kara*) in the fourteenth century. Also a stiff *kosode* type of robe made of brocaded fabric worn in the *Nō* theater. It is often decorated with feminine patterns that include fans, fences, flowers, baskets, and shells.

kariginu A term that literally means "hunting robe"; it refers to the attire worn by men of noble rank during the Heian period (794–1185). Originally used for traveling, hunting, and other sports, the casual top worn over trousers was later used for everday wear.

kasane Literally, "layering." The term is usually applied to robes.

kasane no irome Heian (794–1185) aristocratic aesthetics based on color combinations commonly applied to layered robes.

kasuri The Japanese term for ikat, which is a process of patterning cloth by binding yarns before they are woven in order to prevent certain areas from receiving the dye. It involves preliminary calculations to determine where the reserved areas of yarn will appear in the final woven piece.

kata age Shoulder tucks put into childrens' kimonos and *haori*.

katabira Originally, it was an unlined robe. Later, the term specifically referred to an unlined summer garment usually made from *asa* or sometimes from summer silk (silk that still retains gum, so that the texture is crisp).

kataginu A sleeveless vest, sometimes crossed at the chest, worn by men from the late Kamakura period to the end of the Edo period. It was worn with pants over a kimono.

kata-ura A special type of fabric used for lining the inside of the torso part of a *haori* jacket.

katazome Paste-resist stencil dyeing. Rice paste is applied through a special paper stencil to keep selected areas from taking dye. It is often dip-dyed, but sometimes dye is applied by brush.

kimono sakka Contemporary artists who design and produce one-of-a-kind kimonos.

kinu Historically a term broadly used for clothing of any kind, not to be confused with its contemporary homonym meaning "silk." In the third to fifth centuries it meant an upper garment for either men or women. This term is combined with descriptive prefixes (and *k* becomes *g*) in *uenoginu* (*ueno* = outer), and *karaginu* (*kara* = Chinese or imported).

kise An approximately two-millimeter overlap of fabric that is folded over the seam and pressed into place on the outside of a kimono in order to conceal the stitching that holds the seams together.

kogei sakka Contemporary artists working with traditional craft media as distinguished from anonymous artisans and craftspeople.

kogin A variant form of *sashiko* quilting on cotton getting its name from the short jacket worn by farmers called *koginu*. White thread is stitched onto an indigo-dyed fabric following the direction of the weft threads. Used for the formation of densely patterned geometric designs, this kind of decorative stitching, originally used on work clothes, is now used for surface decoration.

kokuminfuku During World War II the term was created for garments that were designed to be practical for work wear and wartime functioning. These garments, which were considered to be patriotic, allowed for easy movement and were a mixture of Western and Eastern styles.

kon gasuri An indigo-dyed *kasuri* cloth or garment that was popular among the rural population as well as among students and children in the urban areas during the Taisho and early Showa periods (1912–1940).

koromo The ancient word for robe that is found in early history texts such as the *Nihon-shoki*, written in A.D. 720.

koromo-gae A seasonal ritual that involves putting away one set of kimonos and bringing out an alternate set for the other half of the year. Since the reign of Emperor Godaigo (1318–1339), this custom has been observed twice a year in the beginning of summer and at the beginning of the fall season.

koshimaki A summer style of draping the outer robe around the waist that revealed an under *kosode* robe. This style began during the Muromachi period (1392–1568) among the *bushi* women and continued through the Edo period (1600–1868). The outer robe was worn off the shoulders and was then wrapped around the waistline and tied in place with a sash. In contemporary Japanese the term refers to a rectangular cloth worn as traditional underwear for women, similar to a Western slip.

kosode A word that literally means "small sleeves." Originally, the *kosode* was an undergarment during the Heian period (794–1185) with smaller sleeves and sleeve openings than the outer robes (such as the *jūni-hitoe*). Later, it developed into an outer garment, and then evolved into the modern kimono.

makinori yūzen A combination of the *yūzen* process and the use of fine paste flakes (*makinori*) as a resist medium that creates a very delicate mottled effect.

mingei A term coined by Yanagi Sōetsu in the 1920s: *min* from *minshū* (ordinary people) and *gei* from *kōgei* (skilled craft), which referred to "folk crafts." In 1925 Yanagi and his friends, potters Hamada Shōji and Kawai Kanjirō, initiated the *mingei* movement, which involved the collection of old folk crafts in addition to the promotion of a contemporary aesthetic ethic that equated function with beauty and beauty with labor and collective effort.

mitsu-gasane Formal set of three robes worn by women in the late eighteenth century and the nineteenth century.

mo A pleated apronlike skirt first appearing in fourth- and fifth-century clay figurines, called *haniwa*. At the beginning of the Nara period (645–794), aristocratic women wore a trailing *mo* over a long, wide-sleeved robe. A vestigial remnant of that *mo* skirt was worn by female court attendants who were on official duty at the imperial palace during the Heian period (794–1185). At that time, the *mo* was frequently embellished by ink paintings (*kaki-e*) of landscapes or other scenes.

mon Family crest or logo, which when used on a kimono indicates formal wear.

monpe Work pants, gathered at the ankles, that were worn by women in Japan during World War II.

mo-su-rin or **moslin** A soft, lightweight wool challis fabric that is usually printed with a design, popular for winter wear.

N

naga-hakama A term that refers to *hakama,* or divided skirtlike pants, when they are longer than ankle length so that they trail behind the wearer.

nagagi A full-length outer kimono.

naga-juban An ankle-length under-kimono.

nagoya-obi From the late sixteenth century to the middle of the seventeenth century, a narrow *obi,* made of twisted silken cords, popularly worn by men and women. The contemporary term refers to an informal lightweight *obi* that is partly sewn up.

nemaki Refers to all kinds of sleepwear including a robe similar to the *yukata.*

Nō robe A *kosode*-style garment that is worn in conjunction with *Nō* theatrical performances. *Nō* drama, which was supported by the shoguns, evolved from an agricultural festival dance to a very highly refined form of dramatic art during the Muromachi period (1392–1568).

nōshi The simpler form of the *sokutai,* worn without a train over pants called *sashinuki.*

nuihaku A method of decoration involving a combination of embroidery and the application of metallic leaf. Also the name of a *Nō* robe decorated with this type of embellishment, used as an inner robe in women's roles.

nui-shibori A patterning method in which stitching is applied on the fabric and the thread is then pulled tightly and bound. Sometimes designs are outlined with stitching and capped to reserve this shaped area.

O

obi A sash worn with the kimono. A woman's *obi* is wide and is tied in a large knot or bow. A man's *obi* is narrow and is worn around the hips.

obi-age In present-day usage, it is a decorative silk scarf worn with an *obi* to cover a small padded pillow to hold the *obi* knot. *Obi-age* came into fashion during the Meiji period (1868–1912), and during the Taisho period (1912–1926), *shibori* became the most popular means of decorating these scarves.

obi-jime A silk cord, worn with a kimono, that helps to hold the *obi* knot in place.

ō-burisode *Furisode* with extra-wide sleeves that almost reach the ground, the most formal kimono for an unmarried woman.

o-haki-mono (haki-mono) Refers to shoes: *geta*s and *zori*s.

Okinawan robe A wide-sleeved, loosely worn robe, used by the Okinawan people, or Ryukyu islanders, as they were previously called. Although it is similar to the kimono in that it has overlapping front panels, it is not worn with an *obi,* and the bodice and sleeve proportions are different from those of a kimono.

okumi Two half-width panels of cloth that are sewn onto the front panels of a kimono to create overlap extensions.

ōsode A robe with broad open sleeves with wrist openings that extend the full width of the sleeve, worn by noblewomen during the Heian period (794–1185) in multicolored layers.

R

rōketsuzome Wax-resist dyeing (batik). This method of dyeing was revived in the early Taisho period (1912–1926) by Tsuruichi Tsurumaki, a textile artist and scholar.

S

sakiori The process of weaving a heavy cloth using strips cut from worn kimonos that are recycled as wefts. Also the name for the textile made in this way.

sakura gasane Heian (794–1185) aristocratic aesthetic involving layered colors, specifically, translucent white silk placed over red silk to create an elusive pink, termed "cherry blossom," worn by young women and young male courtiers.

sashiko A quilting technique where one or more layers of cotton or ramie cloth are stitched together with a running or darning stitch that was initially used to extend the life of indigo-dyed work clothes worn by families of farmers and fishermen. The extra layers of cloth also gave the garment some added insulation. Also articles made in this manner.

shibira datsumono A simplified pleated apronlike skirt worn by women who were servants or commoners during the Heian period (794–1185). It was an abbreviated form of the *mo* worn by female courtiers.

shibori This term refers to a resist-dyeing technique and the fabric that is produced by this process. Cloth may be folded, stitched, bound, or sheathed in numerous combinations in such a way as to protect parts of the fabric from dye penetration when it is submerged in a vat of dye.

shimekiri A technical term used to indicate the binding of warp threads in order to create a variegated background. It was used in *Nō* robes in conjunction with a brocaded type of fabric. This process is similar to warp ikat, *tate-gasuri.*

shinshi Flexible split bamboo sticks with pins embedded in each end, used to stretch fabric widthwise while it is being dried or dyed.

shitagi Kimonolike robe worn between the *uwagi,* the outer robe, and the *juban,* the under-robe, by women and men during the eighteenth and nineteenth centuries.

shinto An ancient animist native Japanese religion, modified by influences from Confucianism and Buddhism, and later taking on the worship of heroes or mythical figures.

sode Sleeve(s). Garments with varying sleeve styles are identified in terms of their sleeve type as in *kosode, ōsode,* and *furisode.*

sokutai Formal attire of the Heian (794–1185) nobleman, consisting of a hugely exaggerated outer robe, the *uenoginu,* with its long train, a set of white outer and red inner pants, *hakama,* and several layers of kimonolike robes.

suikan A simplified and more practical version of the *kariginu,* the *suikan* became popular among the commoners in the mid-Heian period. Later in that period courtiers and warriors wore this robe as casual wear.

sumi A type of ink that is used in a Japanese style of writing and painting made when black sticks of carbon mixed with glue are ground on the inkstone with water.

suō An unlined stencil-dyed matched suit made of hemp or ramie that was worn by commoners and low-ranking warriors around the mid-Muromachi era (1450–1500). In the Edo period (1600–1868) it became acceptable as semiformal wear for *bushi* men.

surihaku A patterning technique in which adhesive is applied with a stencil design and gold or silver leaf is placed over the area.

susomoyō Pictorial design appearing only on the lower panels of the kimono.

tan A standard measurement for a bolt of kimono cloth that is sufficient to make one kimono, about fourteen inches wide and twelve yards long.

tan-mono A bolt of kimono fabric measured in the standard *tan* unit. Kimono yardage in traditional shops is sold by the bolt only.

tanzen A kimono-style robe made out of silk or wool that is sometimes padded for extra warmth and worn at home during the winter months.

tarikubi The open-necked or lap-over collar on an ancient Chinese robe-style garment worn during the Han dynasty (202 B.C.–A.D. 220) that may have been a source for the lap-over neckline of the Japanese kimono.

tate-gasuri Warp ikat weaving. *Tate* literally means "vertical," and *gasuri* is *kasuri* or ikat.

tomesode The most formal type of kimono worn by married women. It is usually black and has five crests in addition to auspicious pictorial designs that are dyed and embroidered onto the lower part of the garment.

tonbi A man's cloak with a cape that has a long bodice and large armholes for kimono sleeves to pass through. The term means "black hawk," because the black-caped coat reminded the onlooker of that predatory bird. The *tonbi* coat has sometimes been known as *in-ba-nesu,* a Japanese corruption of the Scottish word *Inverness,* denoting a Western garment called an Inverness cape.

tsujigahana The name given to a group of textiles that became fashionable during the latter part of the fifteenth and early sixteenth centuries. It mainly refers to silk garments (*kosode* and *dōbuku*), which are known from the literature and surviving examples. Stitched *shibori* of both small and large areas, as well as *surihaku, nuihaku,* and *kaki-e* are used to achieve the typical embellishment style associated with *tsujigahana.*

tsumugi A kind of silk cloth woven with silk yarns hand spun in order of quality from silk wadding to double cocoons to cocoon waste. This cloth has a textured body that can be nubby in the least-fine quality of this silk.

uchigi See **uchiki**.

uchikake This outer robe of the *kosode* style became part of the upper-class *bushi* women's formal attire during the Muromachi period (1392–1568). In the Edo period (1600–1868), it was worn by both *bushi* women and women of the *chōnin* class for formal or ceremonial occasions. At the present time, it is worn only for traditional weddings; thus, it is sometimes translated as "wedding robe."

uchiki A single- or multilayered large-sleeved outer robe, worn by court ladies of the Heian period (794–1185).

uenoginu or **hō** An *agekubi* type of outer robe with or without a long, trailing back worn over one or two layers of broad pants as an imperial palace uniform during the late Nara and Heian periods (710–1185).

ukiyo-e Woodblock prints of everyday life during the Edo period (1600–1868), reflecting the culture of the townspeople.

uwagi An upper garment worn by women during the Heian era (794–1185), it was often embellished with a brocaded pattern.

uwappari Colloquial term for a short kimono jacket or top, interchangeably used with the term *hippari*.

wafuku A term created in the late nineteenth century to refer to Japanese-style clothing, to differentiate it from the new Western styles entering Japan.

yōfuku A term created at the end of the nineteenth century to refer to newly introduced Western-style attire, to distinguish it from traditional Japanese clothing (*wafuku*).

yukata An unlined cotton kimono-style garment usually worn after the bath or for summer casual wear, it is traditionally embellished by paste-resist stencil dyeing, or *shibori*, and indigo dye. The term is derived from *yu-katabira*, a single-layered informal robe that was worn after bathing during the Edo period (1600–1868).

yumaki An apronlike skirt, worn by women during the Heian period (794–1185), that was an abbreviated form of the Chinese *mo*. Unlike the *shibira-datsumono*, which it resembles, the *yumaki* has no pleats.

yūzen or **yūzenzome** A method of polychrome fabric decoration using paste as the resist medium. The paste is applied with a cone-shaped applicator delineating the delicate design area, and dyes are then applied with small brushes. It began and became highly popular in the Edo period (1600–1868) and is still widely practiced today.

zōri A type of footwear that consists of a flat, often padded sole held onto the foot by a thong slipped between the first and second toes, and that is dressier than the *geta*.

Appendix Two

ART HISTORICAL PERIODS IN JAPAN

Yayoi period	200 B.C.–A.D. 250
Kofun period	250–552
Asuka period	552–645
Nara period	645–794
Heian period	794–1185
Kamakura period	1185–1392
Muromachi period	1392–1568
Momoyama period	1568–1600
Edo period	1600–1868
Meiji period	1868–1912
Taisho period	1912–1926
Showa period	1926–1989
Heisei period	1989–present

SOURCE: Compiled from the historical tables in Andrew Nathaniel Nelson, *The Modern Reader's Japanese-English Character Dictionary* (Rutland, Vt., and Tokyo: Charles E. Tuttle Co., 1962), 1016–1017. Please note that there exists only limited agreement on the designation of the names and dates and that this list describes primarily art, rather than political, periods.

Index